DATE DUE

DEMCO 38-296

The Book of
Mosts

Also by H. Aaron Cohl

Are We Scaring Ourselves to Death?

The Book of
Mosts

H. Aaron Cohl

St. Martin's Press
New York

A THOMAS DUNNE BOOK.
An imprint of St. Martin's Press.

Library of Congress Cataloging-in-Publication Data

Cohl, H. Aaron.
    The book of mosts / H. Aaron Cohl. —1st ed.
        p.   cm.
    ISBN 0–312–15482–8
    1. Curiosities and wonders.   I. Title.
    AG243.C586   1997
    031.02—dc21   97–6274

First edition: October 1997

10 9 8 7 6 5 4 3 2 1

For Christine

And a heartfelt thank-you to Dan Doyle for his timely and imaginative research, and to all at Affinity Communications Corporation for their unending creativity

Contents

Introduction

I LOVE FACTS. Not the dry, educational trivia I memorized in grade school, but the outrageous and outlandish excesses that draw millions to their TV sets and magazine racks every day. I'm not interested in the mediocre; it's the most brilliant, the most flamboyant, the most unbelievable facts that set my pulse racing.

That was the inspiration for *The Book of Mosts*. I hope to take you through the worlds of Food and Drink, Pets, Crime, Natural Disasters, and Movies and TV. There are twenty-two chapters, each filled with more facts and more fun than the last. It is, dear reader, the most I could do for you!

I hope you'll enjoy *The Book of Mosts* as much as I enjoyed writing it.

Mosts
from the World of
Geography

FOUR AND ONE-HALF billion years ago, the planet Earth began to form. Since then it has been a bit on the busy side, building mountains, rivers, and seas while also sustaining life-forms. It's the **most** amazing of all the known planets and it should become even more so when you consider the following **mosts.**

But I'll Get a Nosebleed Up There!

THINKING of climbing a mountain but you're not sure which one? Well, if you want a true challenge, how about attacking the highest above sea level? Of course, the higher the mountain, the more likely the nosebleed. Which mountains are the **most** feet above sea level?

	Mountain	Mountain Chain	Location	Height (ft)
1.	Mt. Everest	Himalayas	Nepal-Tibet border	29,028
2.	K-2	Himalayas	Kashmir	28,250
3.	Mt. Kanchenjunga	Himalayas	Nepal-India border	28,208
4.	Mt. Lhotse I (Everest)	Himalayas	Nepal-Tibet border	27,923
5.	Mt. Makalu I	Himalayas	Nepal-Tibet border	27,824
6.	Mt. Lhotse II (Everest)	Himalayas	Nepal-Tibet border	27,560
7.	Mt. Dhaulagiri	Himalayas	Nepal	26,810
8.	Mt. Manaslu I	Himalayas	Nepal	26,760
9.	Mt. Cho Oyu	Himalayas	Nepal-Tibet border	26,750
10.	Mt. Nanga Parbat	Himalayas	Kashmir	26,660

The above should also answer any question you may have about which mountain chain has the **most** vertical feet.

SOURCE: The National Geographic Society

I

Nosebleeds Closer to Home

WE'VE seen which mountains are the tallest in the world, but now let's take a look a little closer to home. Following is a list of the mountains with the **most** vertical feet in the United States, Canada, and Mexico.

	Mountain	Location	Height (ft)
1.	McKinley	Alaska	20,320
2.	Logan	Yukon	19,850
3.	Citlaltépetl (Orizaba)	Mexico	18,700
4.	St. Elias	Alaska-Yukon border	18,008
5.	Popocatépetl	Mexico	17,930
6.	Foraker	Alaska	17,400
7.	Iztaccíhuatl	Mexico	17,343
8.	Lucania	Yukon	17,147
9.	King	Yukon	16,971
10.	Steele	Yukon	16,664
11.	Bona	Alaska	16,550
12.	Blackburn	Alaska	16,390
13.	Kennedy	Alaska	16,286
14.	Sanford	Alaska	16,237
15.	Vancouver	Alaska-Yukon border	15,979
16.	South Buttress	Alaska	15,885
	Wood	Yukon	15,885
18.	Churchill	Alaska	15,638
19.	Fairweather	Alaska-Yukon border	15,300
20.	Zinantecati (Toluca)	Mexico	15,016

The tallest mountain in the "Lower 48" is Mt. Whitney in California. At 14,494 feet, it would place number 29 in the above list.

SOURCE: The National Geographic Society

Nosebleeds in South America

THE Andes. The name calls up images of soaring condors and thick-wooled alpacas. Many of the peaks of the Andes stand in excess of 20,000 feet, making it the world's second-highest mountain chain, after the Himalayas. See what summits have the **most** elevation and in which country they are located.

	Mountain	Location	Height (ft)
1.	Aconcagua	Argentina	22,834
2.	Ojos del Salado	Argentina-Chile border	22,572
3.	Bonete	Argentina	22,546
4.	Tupungato	Argentina-Chile border	22,310
5.	Pissis	Argentina	22,241
6.	Mercedario	Argentina	22,211
7.	Huascarán	Peru	22,205
8.	Llullaillaco	Argentina-Chile border	22,057
9.	El Libertador	Argentina	22,047
	Cachí	Argentina	22,047

SOURCE: The National Geographic Society

Nosebleeds in the Land of Legend

EVERYONE's heard of the foreboding Mt. Kilimanjaro, possibly because it is one of the most majestic mountains in the world or perhaps because it is so steeped in legend and myth. In either case, consider the size of Africa's **most** dominating mountains, forming a wonderful contrast to its deserts and plains and tropical and sub-tropical shores.

	Mountain	Location	Height (ft)
1.	Kilimanjaro	Tanzania	19,340
2.	Kenya	Kenya	17,058
3.	Margherita	Uganda-Zaire border	16,763
4.	Ras Dashan	Ethiopia	15,158
5.	Meru	Tanzania	14,979
6.	Karisimbi	Zaire-Rwanda border	14,787
7.	Elgon	Kenya-Uganda border	14,178
8.	Batu	Ethiopia	14,131
9.	Guna	Ethiopia	13,881
10.	Gughe	Ethiopia	13,780

If the list continued, Morocco's **most** elevated peak, Mt. Toubkal (13,661 feet), would occupy the eleventh position.

SOURCE: The National Geographic Society

Nosebleeds in Europe

SOME of us may think of the Alps as a place of skiing and international jet-setting. And with good reason: some of the world's most fashionable ski resorts are located in the mountain chain that contains **most** of Europe's great mountains. See what peaks you recognize from books and movies and otherwise. Some are famous, others are not, but all are among the **most** grand.

	Mountain	Location	Height (ft)
1.	Mont Blanc	France-Italy border	15,771
2.	Monte Rosa	Switzerland	15,203
3.	Dom	Switzerland	14,911
4.	Liskamm	Italy-Switzerland border	14,852
5.	Weisshom	Switzerland	14,780
6.	Taschhorn	Switzerland	14,733
7.	Matterhorn	Italy-Switzerland border	14,690
8.	Dent Blanche	Switzerland	14,293
9.	Nadelhorn	Switzerland	14,196
10.	Grand Combin	Switzerland	14,154

Please note that in the truest terms, the European continent includes the Caucasus chain of mountains that run through Russia. The highest peak, Mt. Elbrus (18,510 feet), exceeds any peak in the Alps, but as the popular perception of Europe is that it is the landmass south and west of the old Soviet border, only those peaks perceived as "European" (the Alps) are included. The Pyrenees, predominantly in Spain, are not included, as they do not meet **most** requirements in terms of height.

SOURCE: The National Geographic Society

Hot Rocks! Run *from* the Hills!

CONSIDER this, the world's **most** daunting volcano, Mt. Llullaillaco in Chile, is 1,780 feet higher than North America's greatest mountain, Mt. McKinley. The point is that volcanoes are often enormous structures classifiable as mountains themselves. Read on to see which volcanoes have the **most** height and where **most** volcanoes are found.

	Volcano	Latest Eruption	Location	Height (ft)
1.	Llullaillaco	1877	Chile	22,110
2.	Guallatiri	1960	Chile	19,882
3.	Lááscar	1995	Chile	19,652
4.	Cotopaxi	1940	Equador	19,347
5.	El Misti	1870(?)	Peru	19,101
6.	Tupungatito	1986	Chile	18,504
7.	Orizaba	1687	Mexico	18,405
8.	Popocatépetl	1995	Mexico	17,930
9.	Ruiz	1991	Colombia	17,716
10.	Sangay	1993	Ecuador	17,159
11.	Guagua Pichincha	1993	Ecuador	15,696
12.	Purace	1977	Colombia	15,601
13.	Kliuchevskoi	1995	Russia	15,584
14.	Rainier	1894(?)	Washington	14,410
15.	Wrangell	1907(?)	Alaska	14,163
16.	Shasta	1786	California	14,162
17.	Colima	1994	Mexico	14,003
18.	Galeras	1993	Colombia	13,996
19.	Mauna Loa	1984	Hawaii	13,680
20.	Cameroon	1982	Cameroon	13,354

Notice anything worrisome in the above table? Did it catch your attention that **most** of our largest volcanoes are still active today? As the title says, run *from* the hills!

SOURCE: *Volcanoes of the World,* Geoscience Press; Global Volcanism Network, Smithsonian Institution; as of June 1995

Ring of Fire

YES, it is a song that June Carter wrote for her husband Johnny Cash, but it also refers to a zone running along the west coasts of North and South America and the east coasts of Asia, Japan, New Guinea, and New Zealand, creating a kind of fiery ring around the Pacific Ocean. **Most** of the world's volcanoes—approximately 75 percent—fall within the boundaries of this ring. Other volcanoes can be found in the Mediterranean region and in Iceland.

The Most High Among the Most

Now that we've looked at a number of mountains and volcanoes around the world, let's look at which peaks rise the **most** on each continent.

	Continent	Highest Point	Location	Height (ft)
1.	Asia	Mt. Everest	Nepal-Tibet border	29,028
2.	South America	Mt. Aconcagua	Argentina	22,834
3.	North America	Mt. McKinley	Alaska	20,320
4.	Africa	Kilimanjaro	Tanzania	19,340
5.	Europe	Mt. Elbrus	Russia	18,510
6.	Antarctica	Vinson Massif	Antarctica	16,864
7.	Australia	Mt. Kosciusko	New South Wales	7,310

SOURCE: The National Geographic Society

You'll Need Oxygen Down There Too!

WE'VE looked up, so let's now look down—at where **most** of the world's greatest depths occur. If you're thinking under the ocean, you're right. Particularly in areas known as trenches; black, endless drops that fall farther than the highest mountains rise. Now let's take a peek at what trenches plunge the **most** in each ocean and where they're located.

	Name of Area	Body of Water	Nearest Land	Depth (ft)
1.	Mariana Trench	Pacific	Guam-Philippines	35,840
2.	Puerto Rico Trench	Atlantic	Puerto Rico–Virgin Islands	28,232
3.	Java Trench	Indian	Java, Indonesia	23,376
4.	Eurasia Basin	Arctic	Norway	17,881
5.	Ionian Basin	Mediterranean Sea	Greece	16,896

The above account only for the deepest spot in each ocean. If depth were the sole classification, the Pacific would contain the **most,** with eight spots deeper than the Puerto Rico Trench.

SOURCE: Defense Mapping Agency, Hydrographic/Topographic Center, U.S. Department of Defense

No Land in Sight

FIRST there is the Pacific, then the Atlantic, but what oceans, seas, and gulfs follow in terms of the **most** area of the globe covered by them? We'll answer that for you.

	Body of Water	Area (sq mi)	Average Depth (ft)
1.	Pacific Ocean	64,186,300	12,925
2.	Atlantic Ocean	33,420,000	11,730
3.	Indian Ocean	28,350,500	12,598
4.	Arctic Ocean	5,105,700	3,407
5.	South China Sea	1,148,500	4,802
6.	Caribbean Sea	971,400	8,448
7.	Mediterranean Sea	969,100	4,926
8.	Bering Sea	873,000	4,893
9.	Gulf of Mexico	582,100	5,297
10.	Sea of Okhotsk	537,500	3,192
11.	Sea of Japan	391,100	5,468
12.	Hudson Bay	281,900	305
13.	East China Sea	256,600	620
14.	Andaman Sea	218,100	3,667
15.	Black Sea	196,100	3,906
16.	Red Sea	174,900	1,764
17.	North Sea	164,900	308
18.	Baltic Sea	147,500	180
19.	Yellow Sea	113,500	121
20.	Persian Gulf	88,800	328
21.	Gulf of California	59,100	2,375

SOURCE: Defense Mapping Agency, Hydrographic/Topographic Center, U.S. Department of Defense

The Most Space

THE world has approximately 58,433,000 square miles of land. What are the biggest regions in the world covering the **most** area?

	Region	Area (sq mi)	Percent of Total Land Area
1.	Africa	11,707,000	20.0
2.	Asia	10,644,000	18.2
3.	North America	9,360,000	16.0
4.	Former U.S.S.R.	8,647,000	14.8
5.	South America	6,883,000	11.8

Region	Area (sq mi)	Percent of Total Land Area
6. Antarctica	6,000,000	10.3
7. Oceania	3,284,000	5.6
8. Europe	1,905,000	3.3

In the above table, Asia includes the Philippines, Indonesia, and European and Asiatic Turkey; North America includes Hawaii, Central America, and the islands of the Caribbean; the former U.S.S.R. includes both European and Asian countries once in its possession; Oceania includes Australia, New Zealand, Melanesia, Micronesia, and Polynesia; and Europe includes Iceland.

SOURCE: U.S. Bureau of the Census, International Data Base

Islands

MENTION "island" and immediately we think of something tropical and warm, a gentle sea, sun-drenched land, rustling palms, tanning oil, and getting away from it all. . . .

Are you still there, or have you already embarked on your vacation? Tempting, isn't it? The truth is, not all islands are tropical, some are downright frigid. And a number of them are large enough to be near continental in size. In fact, the larger ones contain some of the **most** industrial countries on earth. Some islands even contain more than one country.

Following are the largest islands determined by the **most** area they cover.

	Island	Owner	Ocean	Area (sq mi)
1.	Greenland	Denmark	Arctic	840,000
2.	New Guinea	Papua New Guinea, Indonesia	Pacific	306,000
3.	Borneo	Malaysia, Brunei, Indonesia	Pacific	280,100
4.	Madagascar	Madagascar	Indian	226,658
5.	Baffin	Canada	Arctic	195,928
6.	Sumatra	Indonesia	Pacific	165,000
7.	Honshu	Japan	Pacific	87,805
8.	Great Britain	United Kingdom	Atlantic	84,200
9.	Victoria	Canada	Arctic	83,897
10.	Ellesmere	Canada	Arctic	75,767

SOURCE: National Atlas Information Services

The Most Ocean-Front Property

LOOKING for ocean-front property? Then look in the following states where there is the **most** of it.

	State	Body of Water	Coastal Miles
1.	Alaska	Pacific and Arctic	6,640
2.	Florida	Atlantic and Gulf of Mexico	1,350
3.	California	Pacific	840
4.	Hawaii	Pacific	750
5.	Louisiana	Gulf of Mexico	397
6.	Texas	Gulf of Mexico	367
7.	North Carolina	Atlantic	301
8.	Oregon	Pacific	296
9.	Maine	Atlantic	228
10.	Massachusetts	Atlantic	192
11.	South Carolina	Atlantic	187
12.	Washington	Pacific	157
13.	New Jersey	Atlantic	130
14.	New York	Atlantic	127
15.	Virginia	Atlantic	112
16.	Georgia	Atlantic	100
17.	Alabama	Gulf of Mexico	53
18.	Mississippi	Gulf of Mexico	44
19.	Rhode Island	Atlantic	40
20.	Maryland	Atlantic	31

The U.S. has a total of 12,383 coastal miles.

The remaining two coastlines in Delaware and New Hampshire have 28 and 13 miles of ocean-front property, respectively.

In referring to "ocean front," the table does not account for coastline that is technically part of a bay, estuary, or other body of water largely surrounded by land. Thus, none of Connecticut's shoreline qualifies as "ocean-front," as all of it is on Long Island Sound. The same is true for Rhode Island, Maryland, and other states that would seem to have among the **most** ocean-front miles.

SOURCE: Department of Commerce, National Oceanic and Atmospheric Administration, National Ocean Service

Biggest Lakes

A lake is a body of water surrounded by land. But some are of such size that if you were on a boat in the middle, you'd never know land existed. Discover which lakes cover the **most** area by reading on.

	Lake	Continent	Area (sq mi)	Length (mi)	Max. Depth (ft)
1.	Caspian Sea	Asia-Europe	143,244	760	3,363
2.	Superior	No. America	31,700	350	1,330
3.	Victoria	Africa	26,828	250	270
4.	Aral Sea	Asia	24,904	280	220
5.	Huron	No. America	23,000	206	750
6.	Michigan	No. America	22,300	307	923
7.	Tanganyika	Africa	12,700	420	4,823
8.	Baikal	Asia	12,162	395	5,315
9.	Great Bear	No. America	12,096	192	1,463
10.	Nyasa (Malawi)	Africa	11,150	360	2,280
11.	Great Slave	No. America	11,031	298	2,015
12.	Erie	No. America	9,910	241	210
13.	Winnipeg	No. America	9,417	266	60
14.	Ontario	No. America	7,340	193	802
15.	Balkhash	Asia	7,115	376	85
16.	Ladoga	Europe	6,835	124	738
17.	Chad	Africa	6,300	175	23
18.	Maracaibo	So. America	5,217	133	115
19.	Onega	Europe	3,710	145	328
20.	Eyre	Australia	3,600	90	4

SOURCE: Geological Survey, U.S. Department of the Interior

Rivers Flowing the Most Miles

SOME rivers just don't know when to stop. Consider the following that rage and meander along the **most** miles.

	River	Length (mi)	Location of Source	Outflow
1.	Nile	4,145	Lake Victoria	Mediterranean Sea
2.	Amazon	4,000	Andes Mts. Peru	Atlantic Ocean

			Kunlun Mts.,	
3.	Changjiang		China	China Sea
	(Yangtze)	3,964		
4.	Huang (Yellow)	3,395	Kunlun Mts., China	Yellow Sea
5.	Ob-Irtysh	3,362	Altai Mts., China	Gulf of Ob
6.	Amur	2,744	Khingan Mts., China	Sea of Japan
7.	Lena	2,734	Baikal Mts., Russia	Laptev Sea
8.	Congo	2,718	Zaire	Atlantic Ocean
9.	Mekong	2,600	Tibet	S. China Sea
10.	Niger	2,590	Guinea	Atlantic Ocean
11.	Yenisey	2,543	Lake Baikal, Russia	Kara Sea
12.	Paraná	2,485	Brazil	Rio de la Plata
13.	Mississippi	2,340	Minnesota	Gulf of Mexico
14.	Missouri	2,315	Montana	Mississippi River
15.	Murray-Darling	2,310	Australia	Indian Ocean
16.	Volga	2,290	Valdai Hill, Russia	Caspian Sea
17.	Purus	2,100	S. America	Amazon River
18.	Madeira	2,013	Bolivia/Brazil	Amazon River
19.	São Francisco	1,988	Brazil	Atlantic Ocean
20.	Yukon	1,979	Yukon Territory	Bering Sea

If the Mississippi and the Missouri Rivers were combined, as many river systems in the world are, the total length would be 3,740 miles, the third **most** in the world. The Rio Grande, running across 1,900 miles of the American West, would rank number 21 above.

SOURCE: Geological Survey, U.S. Department of the Interior; U.S. Department of Commerce, National Oceanic and Atmospheric Administration, *Principal Rivers and Lakes of the World* (1982).

Old Man River and the Rest of 'Em

THE Mighty Mississippi is the biggest and the **most** known of the great American rivers. But did you know that the Missouri is only a few miles shorter? What and where are the rest of the **most** lengthy of North American rivers?

	River	Length (mi)	Upper Limit	Outflow
1.	Mississippi	2,340	Minnesota	Gulf of Mexico
2.	Missouri	2,315	Montana	Mississippi R.
3.	Yukon	1,979	Yukon Territory	Bering Sea
4.	Rio Grande	1,900	Colorado	Gulf of Mexico
5.	Arkansas	1,459	Colorado	Mississippi R.
6.	Colorado (AZ)	1,450	Colorado	Gulf of California
7.	Red	1,290	New Mexico	Mississippi R.
8.	Columbia	1,243	British Columbia	Pacific Ocean
9.	Peace	1,210	British Columbia	Slave River
10.	Snake	1,038	Wyoming	Columbia R., WA
11.	Mackenzie	1,025	Northwest Terr.	Arctic Ocean
12.	Churchill	1,000	Saskatchewan	Hudson Bay
13.	Ohio	981	Pittsburgh, PA	Mississippi R.
14.	Pecos	926	New Mexico	Rio Grande
15.	Brazos	923	Texas	Gulf of Mexico
16.	Canadian	906	Colorado	Arkansas River
17.	Upper Columbia	890	British Columbia	Snake River
18.	Tennessee–			
	French Broad	886	North Carolina	Ohio River
19.	S. Saskatchewan	865	Rocky Mts.	Saskatchewan R.
20.	Fraer	850	Continental Divide	Strait/Georgia

SOURCE: Geological Survey, U.S. Department of the Interior

Falling Waters

WATER that falls the **most** falls from waterfalls. Following is a list of the world's greatest waterfalls measured by the **most** vertical distance that water plunges.

	Waterfall	Location	Height (ft)
1.	Angel	Venezuela	3,281
2.	Tugela	Natal, So. Africa	3,000
3.	Cuquenan	Venezuela	2,000
4.	Sutherland	New Zealand	1,904
5.	Takkakaw	British Columbia	1,650
6.	Ribbon (Yosemite)	California	1,612
7.	Upper Yosemite	California	1,430

8.	Gavarnie	France	1,384
9.	Vettisfoss	Norway	1,200
10.	Widows' Tears (Yosemite)	California	1,170

Though Niagara Falls drops only 167 and 158 feet, it does rank first in terms of the **most** water that flows over it, twice as large, in terms of volume, as the next largest falls, Paulo Afonso in Brazil.

SOURCE: *The 1996 Information Please Almanac*

Mosts
from the World of
People

THIS CHAPTER CONTAINS **mosts** from the world of people, population, and demographics. So please read on and check out all the **mosts.** After all, **most** of the **mosts** in this chapter are attributable to all of us.

Most Populous Countries

MOST of the world's people live in the twenty most populous countries. Which ones are they?

	Country	1995 Population	Projected 2020 Population
1.	China	1,203,097,000	1,424,725,000
2.	India	936,546,000	1,320,746,000
3.	U.S.	263,814,000	326,322,000
4.	Indonesia	203,584,000	276,474,000
5.	Brazil	160,737,000	197,466,000
6.	Russia	149,909,000	159,263,000
7.	Pakistan	131,542,000	251,330,000
8.	Bangladesh	128,095,000	210,248,000
9.	Japan	125,506,000	126,062,000
10.	Nigeria	101,232,000	215,893,000
11.	Mexico	93,986,000	136,096,000
12.	Germany	81,338,000	82,385,000
13.	Philippines	73,266,000	115,988,000
14.	Iran	64,625,000	104,282,000
15.	Turkey	63,405,000	93,362,000
16.	Egypt	62,360,000	92,350,000
17.	Thailand	60,271,000	62,941,000
18.	United Kingdom	58,295,000	60,042,000

19.	Italy	58,262,000	57,844,000
20.	France	58,109,000	61,793,000

Canada's 1995 population was 28,435,000. Projected 2020 population is 34,347,000.

SOURCE: Bureau of the Census, U.S. Department of Commerce

Regional Populations

BASED on regions, similar in some respects to continents, **most** of the world's population lives in Asia. Check out what region follows on our list of **mosts.**

	Region	1995 Population	Projected 2020 Population
1.	Asia	3,246,600,000	4,360,221,000
2.	Africa	878,323,000	1,638,261,000
3.	Europe	509,254,000	528,823,000
4.	Latin America and Caribbean	481,365,000	651,163,000
5.	Former Soviet Union	297,508,000	335,119,000
6.	U.S. and Canada	292,375,000	360,820,000
7.	Oceania, incl. Australia	28,680,000	37,369,000
	World	5,734,106,000	7,911,776,000

SOURCE: Bureau of the Census, U.S. Department of Commerce

Your Tongue or Mine?

WHAT language is spoken the **most** in the world? If you guessed Chinese, you're partly right. The truth is that it is Mandarin, just one of several regional languages spoken within China. Can you guess what some of the other **most** commonly spoken languages in the world are?

	Language	Speakers
1.	Mandarin	975,000,000
2.	English	478,000,000
3.	Hindi	437,000,000
4.	Spanish	392,000,000

	Language	Speakers
5.	Russian	284,000,000
6.	Arabic	225,000,000
7.	Bengali	200,000,000
8.	Portuguese	184,000,000
9.	Malay-Indonesian	159,000,000
10.	Japanese	126,000,000
11.	French	125,000,000
12.	German	123,000,000

SOURCE: S. Culbert, University of Washington, Seattle, WA

Most Populous Cities

THIS section, the **most** populated cities in the world, is based on metropolitan areas rather than city limits. The United Nations calls these "urban agglomerations." See which cities are among our **most** populated agglomerations.

	City, Country	1994 Population	Projected 2015 Population
1.	Tokyo, Japan	26,518,000	28,700,000
2.	New York City, U.S.	16,271,000	17,600,000
3.	São Paulo, Brazil	16,110,000	20,800,000
4.	Mexico City, Mexico	15,525,000	18,800,000
5.	Shanghai, China	14,709,000	23,400,000
6.	Bombay, India	14,496,000	27,400,000
7.	Los Angeles, U.S.	12,232,000	14,300,000
8.	Beijing, China	12,030,000	19,400,000
9.	Calcutta, India	11,485,000	17,600,000
10.	Seoul, So. Korea	11,451,000	13,100,000
11.	Jakarta, Indonesia	11,017,000	21,200,000
12.	Buenos Aires, Argentina	10,914,000	12,400,000
13.	Osaka, Japan	10,585,000	10,600,000
14.	Tianjin, China	10,376,000	17,000,000
15.	Rio de Janeiro, Brazil	9,817,000	11,600,000

SOURCE: United Nations Department for Economic and Social Information and Policy Analysis

Most Densely Populated Cities

WHAT cities are not only big, but also have the **most** people living within them per square mile? The following do.

	City	People per Square Mile
1.	Manila, Philippines	108,699
2.	Shanghai, China	70,449
3.	Cairo, Egypt	63,373
4.	Paris, France	53,389
5.	Bombay, India	48,396
6.	Buenos Aires, Argentina	37,959
7.	Tokyo, Japan	36,874
8.	Seoul, So. Korea	35,755
9.	Osaka, Japan	32,137
10.	Naples, Italy	26,942
11.	Jakarta, Indonesia	25,811
12.	Lisbon, Portugal	25,384
13.	Moscow, Russia	23,891
14.	New York, U.S.	23,310
15.	Milan, Italy	22,925
16.	Taipei, China	22,171
17.	Lyons, France	21,519
18.	Busan, Philippines	19,459
19.	Athens, Greece	18,315
20.	Leningrad/St. Petersburg, Russia	18,188

Feeling like you need to come up for air? Not much living space, is there? Consider this: Have you ever been in New York City? If you have, or even if you've just seen it on TV or the news or even just in pictures, you know how crowded it can get. Imagine being in a city like Manila, which is more than four times as crowded.

SOURCE: George Thomas Kurian, *The New Book of World Rankings,* third edition

Most Expensive Cities

ON a budget but thinking of a taking a vacation? Then memorize the following and avoid them at all costs. They are the **most** expensive cities on our planet.

The index is based on retail prices for 1994.

	Country	Index
1.	Tokyo	183
2.	Lagos	134
3.	Geneva	133
4.	Tripoli	131
5.	Buenos Aires	119
6.	Vienna	116
7.	Bonn	113
8.	Brussels	112
9.	Montevideo	110
10.	Paris	108
11.	Beirut	107
	Copenhagen	107
	Seoul	107
14.	Brazzaville	105
15.	Nairobi	103
16.	The Hague	102
17.	Manila	100
	New York City	100
	Roseau	100
20.	Helsinki	99
	London	99

SOURCE: United Nations, *Monthly Bulletin of Statistics,* March 1995

Most-Seasoned Cities

EVER wonder what ten cities have been in existence for the **most** number of years? Certainly this list would not show any city on the North American continent, or even in the New World. Think instead of the continents where the ancestors of **most** of us have come from and you'll be on the right track.

	City	Age (years)
1.	Gaziantep, Turkey	Over 5,000
	Jerusalem, Israel	Over 5,000
	Kirkuk, Iraq	Over 5,000
	Zurich, Switzerland	Over 5,000

5.	Konya, Turkey	Over 4,600
6.	Giza, Egypt	Over 4,568
7.	Sian, Shensi, China	4,200
8.	Asyut, Egypt	Over 4,160
	Luxor, Egypt	Over 4,160
10.	Lisbon, Portugal	Over 4,000

SOURCE: *World Book Encyclopedia*

Where Most Immigrants Are Coming From

DURING the years 1981 to 1989, the years covered by the last census (1990), **most** immigrants to the U.S. came from the following countries and regions.

	Country	Immigrants	Percent of Total
1.	Mexico	974,000	16.79
2.	Caribbean (excluding the Dominican Republic and Jamaica)	777,000	13.40
3.	Philippines	432,000	7.44
4.	Vietnam	353,000	6.08
5.	Central America	313,000	5.39
6.	Korea	307,000	5.28
7.	China	296,000	5.09
8.	India	231,000	3.98
9.	Dominican Republic	210,000	3.61
10.	Jamaica	189,000	3.25

SOURCE: U.S. Immigration and Naturalization Service, *Statistical Yearbook*

Most Populous States

BEFORE reading on, try to guess what the five **most** populated states in the U.S. are. . . .

Were you correct, or even close to correct? If you weren't, read on to bone up on where **most** Americans live.

1990 Rank	State	1990 Population	1980 Population	1980 Rank
1.	California	29,760,021	23,667,902	1
2.	New York	17,990,455	17,558,072	2
3.	Texas	16,986,510	14,229,191	3
4.	Florida	12,937,926	9,746,324	7
5.	Pennsylvania	11,881,643	11,893,895	4
6.	Illinois	11,430,602	11,427,518	5
7.	Ohio	10,847,115	10,797,630	6
8.	Michigan	9,295,297	9,262,078	8
9.	New Jersey	7,730,188	7,364,823	9
10.	North Carolina	6,628,637	5,881,766	10
11.	Georgia	6,478,216	5,463,105	13
12.	Virginia	6,187,358	5,346,818	14
13.	Massachusetts	6,016,425	5,737,037	11
14.	Indiana	5,544,159	5,490,224	12
15.	Missouri	5,117,073	4,916,686	15
16.	Wisconsin	4,891,769	4,705,767	16
17.	Tennessee	4,877,185	4,591,120	17
18.	Washington	4,866,692	4,132,156	20
19.	Maryland	4,781,468	4,216,975	18
20.	Minnesota	4,375,099	4,075,970	21

The 1980 U.S. Census for all states was 226,576,825. The 1990 census was 248,691,873. That shows a population increase of 9.76 percent. The United Nations estimate of the 1995 U.S. population is 263,814,000.

SOURCE: Mark T. Mattson, *Atlas of the 1990 Census*

Most Space in the States

So you've had your eye on that two-acre lot in the suburbs. Probably seems like an entire world at this point. But to put it in perspective, consider the following states with the **most** square miles.

	State	Area (sq mi)
1.	Alaska	656,424
2.	Texas	268,601
3.	California	163,707
4.	Montana	147,046
5.	New Mexico	121,598

6.	Arizona	114,006
7.	Nevada	110,567
8.	Colorado	104,100
9.	Oregon	98,386
10.	Wyoming	97,818
11.	Michigan	96,705
12.	Minnesota	86,943
13.	Utah	84,904
14.	Idaho	83,574
15.	Kansas	82,282
16.	Nebraska	77,358
17.	South Dakota	77,121
18.	Washington	71,302
19.	North Dakota	70,704
20.	Oklahoma	69,903

SOURCE: U.S. Geological Survey, Dept. of the Interior

Most Crowded

CAN'T stop bumping into people? Always waiting in lines? Takes forever to get somewhere? The problem might be that you are residing in one of the **most** crowded states in the Union. To determine a state's population density, you measure the population per square mile—a much more telling indication of where the **most** crowds will be than the number of people alone, as the latter measurement doesn't account for land area. The **most** crowded major political subdivisions of the U.S., based on the 1990 census, have been ranked for you.

	State	Population per Square Mile
1.	District of Columbia	9,884.4
2.	New Jersey	1,042.0
3.	Rhode Island	960.3
4.	Massachusetts	767.6
5.	Connecticut	678.4
6.	Maryland	489.2
7.	New York	381.0
8.	Delaware	340.8
9.	Ohio	264.9
10.	Pennsylvania	265.1

	State	Population per Square Mile
11.	Florida	239.6
12.	Illinois	205.6
13.	California	190.8
14.	Hawaii	172.5
15.	Michigan	163.6
16.	Virginia	156.3
17.	North Carolina	136.1
18.	New Hampshire	123.7
19.	Tennessee	118.3
20.	South Carolina	115.8

Note that California, the **most** populated state in the U.S., ranks only thirteenth in terms of population density.

SOURCE: Mark T. Mattson, *Atlas of the 1990 Census*

Most Space

So, our description and list of the **most** crowded states got you thinking . . . thinking about life in the least-crowded states where you can enjoy the **most** space. And you know how that goes: everyone is interested in personal space these days. So, if you too are in need of it, look into the following. Remember, though, these figures are not based on total state populations, but on the population per square mile.

	State	Population per Square Mile
1.	Alaska	1.0
2.	Wyoming	4.7
3.	Montana	5.5
4.	South Dakota	9.2
5.	North Dakota	9.3
6.	Nevada	10.9
7.	Idaho	12.2
8.	New Mexico	12.5
9.	Nebraska	20.5
10.	Utah	21.0
11.	Oregon	29.6
12.	Kansas	30.3

13.	Colorado	31.8
14.	Arizona	32.2
15.	Maine	39.8
16.	Arkansas	45.1
17.	Oklahoma	45.8
18.	Iowa	49.7
19.	Mississippi	54.0
20.	Minnesota	55.0

SOURCE: Mark T. Mattson, *Atlas of the 1994 Census*

Big Time

LOOKING for the big time? Here's an idea, how about going to where **most** of the people live? If you're thinking somewhere in the United States, then following is a list of the biggest cities.

Note that in other places in this book, population numbers may differ from those below for the same metropolitan area. That has to do with two circumstances. The first is that the date of the census or projection may differ, and the second is that other accounts may be looking at an entire urban area without regard to state, county, or city lines. In the following, though, we are going straight by the book. The figures are facts, right from the 1990 Census and are for the areas within city boundaries only.

	City	Population
1.	New York, NY	7,322,564
2.	Los Angeles, CA	3,485,398
3.	Chicago, IL	2,783,726
4.	Houston, TX	1,630,553
5.	Philadelphia, PA	1,585,577
6.	San Diego, CA	1,110,549
7.	Detroit, MI	1,027,974
8.	Dallas, TX	1,006,877
9.	Phoenix, AZ	983,403
10.	San Antonio, TX	935,933
11.	San Jose, CA	782,248
12.	Baltimore, MD	736,014
13.	Indianapolis, IN	731,237
14.	San Francisco, CA	723,959
15.	Jacksonville, FL	635,230
16.	Columbus, OH	632,910

	City	Population
17.	Milwaukee, WI	628,088
18.	Memphis, TN	610,337
19.	Washington, DC	606,900
20.	Boston, MA	574,283

Surprised? You may have reason to be. Remember that the above population figures are for city residents only. **Most** people living in an urban area don't live in the city, but rather live in outlying suburbs. Take New York, for example: 7,322,564 people live within the city limits, but social scientists would argue that it has 16,271,000 residents in the total urban area inside and outside of those boundaries.

SOURCE: Bureau of the Census, U.S. Dept. of Commerce

Religious Groups with the Most Members

CHURCHES with the **most** membership in the U.S. are listed below.

	Religious Group	Membership
1.	Roman Catholic Church	52,893,217
2.	Southern Baptist Convention	14,477,364
3.	United Methodist Church	9,192,172
4.	Moslems	6,000,000+
5.	National Baptist Convention of the U.S.A.	5,500,000
6.	Evangelical Lutheran Church in America	5,341,452
7.	Church of Jesus Christ of Latter-Day Saints (Mormons)	3,860,000
8.	Church of God in Christ	3,709,661
9.	Church of Scientology	3,500,000
10.	Presbyterian Church (U.S.A.)	3,007,322
11.	National Baptist Church Convention in America	2,688,799
12.	Lutheran Church—Missouri Synod	2,630,588
13.	Episcopal Church in the U.S.A.	2,504,507
14.	African Methodist Episcopal Church	2,210,000
15.	Assemblies of God (General Council)	2,135,104
16.	Greek Orthodox, Archdiocese of North and South America	1,950,000
17.	United Church of Christ	1,676,105
18.	Church of Christ	1,623,754
19.	American Baptist Churches in the U.S.A.	1,576,483
20.	Baptist Bible Fellowship	1,500,000

21. Union of American Hebrew Congregations
        (Reform Judaism)   1,300,000
22. United Synagogue of America (Conservative Judaism)   1,250,000
23. African Methodist Episcopal Zion Church   1,195,173
24. Christian Church (Disciples of Christ)   1,106,692
25. Christian Churches and Church of Christ   1,063,469

The above memberships were based on 1989 data.

SOURCE: William B. Williamson, *An Encyclopedia of Religions in the U.S.: 100 Religions Speak for Themselves*

Where the Boys (and Girls) Are!

LOOKING for that special someone? Looking to replace that once-special someone? Then start looking in the states where **most** of the people are of the gender you're seeking. Here's a hint: if you're a guy looking for a gal, don't move to Alaska. And if you're a gal looking for a guy, stay clear of the District of Columbia (Washington, DC). The odds won't be in your favor.

So where do you find the **most** of what you're looking for? Read on.

Men to Women—Advantage Women

	State	Males/100 Females
1.	Alaska	111.41
2.	California	100.19 to 111.41
	Hawaii	
	Wyoming	
	Nevada	

Women to Men—Advantage Men

	State	Females/100 Males
1.	District of Columbia	114.47
2.	Mississippi	109.10

State	Females/100 Males
3. Alabama	108.70 to 106.43
Arkansas	
Florida	
Iowa	
Kentucky	
Louisiana	
Massachusetts	
Missouri	
New Jersey	
New York	
Ohio	
Pennsylvania	
Rhode Island	
South Carolina	
Tennessee	
West Virginia	
19. Connecticut	106.36 to 104.28
Georgia	
Illinois	
Indiana	
Maine	
Michigan	
Nebraska	
North Carolina	
Oklahoma	
Vermont	
Wisconsin	
30. Arizona	104.08 to 100.76
Colorado	
Delaware	
Idaho	
Kansas	
Maryland	
Minnesota	
Montana	
New Hampshire	
New Mexico	
North Carolina	
North Dakota	
Oregon	

Texas
Utah
Virginia
Washington

SOURCE: Mark T. Mattson, *Atlas of the 1990 Census*

All right, so it looks like guys actually might have an easier time of it when looking for a gal. So tell me, why are all my guy friends always complaining?

The Most Marriages

So you've met that special person and it's time to tie the knot. Well, where do **most** of us get married? Following is a list of countries where love is **most** likely to lead a couple down the aisle.

	Country	Marriage Rate per 1,000
1.	Anguilla	22.2
2.	Virgin Islands	12.9
3.	Benin	12.8
4.	British Virgin Islands	12.7
5.	Bermuda	12.2
6.	Guam	11.3
7.	Mauritius	11.0
8.	Liechtenstein	10.8
9.	American Samoa	10.7
	Pakistan	10.7
11.	Fiji	10.1
12.	Cayman Islands	10.0
13.	Soviet Union	9.8
	Tanzania	9.8
15.	United States	9.7
16.	Bangladesh	9.4
	Burkina Faso	9.4
	Egypt	9.4
19.	Albania	9.1
	Puerto Rico	9.1

Canada ranks fifty-fourth, with a marriage rate of 7.1. Ranking near the bottom is Afghanistan, at 0.4. The period covered was 1988.

SOURCE: *U.N. Demographic Yearbook*

Reverend Sun Myung Moon's Mosts

ON August 25, 1992, the Reverend Sun Myung Moon and his wife officiated at the wedding of over 30,625 couples, the **most** ever to be joined in a single ceremony. While the main ceremony uniting 20,825 couples took place at the Olympic Stadium in Seoul, South Korea, other participants around the world were linked via satellite.

SOURCE: *The Guinness Book of Records 1996,* Bantam, 1996

The Most Divorces

OK, so you've tried it, you got the seven-year itch, you made a silly mistake, you were only kids, you can't stand your in-laws. The reasons go on and on. So do the alimony payments.

What countries have the **most** divorces? The following do.

	Country	Divorces per 1,000
1.	Maldives	25.5
2.	Liechtenstein	7.3
3.	Peru	6.0
4.	U.S.	4.8
5.	Puerto Rico	4.0
6.	Bermuda	3.8
7.	Cuba	3.1
8.	East Germany (1988)	2.9
9.	Canada	2.8
	Denmark	2.8
	United Kingdom	2.8
12.	Greenland	2.7
	Hungary	2.7
14.	Austria	2.5
	Czechoslovakia (1988)	2.5
16.	Netherlands	2.3
	Sweden	2.3
18.	Iceland	2.2
19.	West Germany (1988)	2.1
20.	Austria	2.0

SOURCE: *U.N. Demographic Yearbook*

The Kids Are Taking Over

Do you have kids? Ever hear, "I'm bored." Well, maybe you might consider shipping your youngster off to one of the following countries, where kids are the **most** abundant and where there would be no lack of playmates.

For the purposes herein, "kids" are people under the age of fifteen. The period covered is for the year 1988.

	Country	Percent of Population
1.	Kenya	51
2.	Benin	49
	Syria	49
	Botswana	48
	Iraq	48
	Rwanda	48
	Solomon Islands	48
	Angola	48
	Uganda	48
	South Yemen	48
	Zimbabwe	48
12.	Belize	47
	Comoros	47
	Honduras	47
	Liberia	47
	Malawi	47
	Nicaragua	47
	Niger	47
	Trust Territory of the Pacific Islands	47
	North Yemen	47

The U.S. ranks 154 out of all nations, with kids constituting 22 percent of the total population. Canada and a good deal of Western Europe rank right after it, with youth populations of approximately 21 percent.

SOURCE: *World Population Prospects*

The Most Adoptions

IN 1994, approximately 50,000 children were adopted in the U.S., down considerably from the 1970 peak of 89,200. With birth control, abortion, and later marriages, fewer American children are available for adoption each year. As for children from outside the States, several countries have placed restrictions on the number of children available, making it more difficult for those seeking to adopt. For example, in 1991, adoptions from Romania totaled 2,552; in 1994, there were just 199. Adoptions from Korea were at their highest in 1986, with 6,188 children finding homes with U.S. families; in 1994, that total was just 1,795. In 1990, a record total of 10,097 children from outside the U.S. were adopted into American families. In 1994, there were just 8,195 such adoptions.

According to the National Council for Adoptions, these are the countries with the **most** children being adopted by families in the U.S.

	Country	No. of Children
1.	Korea	1,795
2.	Russian Federation	1,530
3.	People's Republic of China	787
4.	Paraguay	483
5.	Guatemala	436
6.	Other European countries (except the former U.S.S.R. and Romania)	409
7.	India	406
8.	Colombia	351
9.	Philippines	314
10.	Other former U.S.S.R.	268

SOURCE: National Council for Adoptions

The Most Common Organizations

THINK about the organizations to which you belong. How many monthly association or organization meetings do you attend, and how many newsletters or notices do you receive each week in the mail?

Following are the **most** common types of membership organizations in the U.S.

	Type of Organization	Number
1.	Commercial	3,768
2.	Health/medical	2,331

3.	Public affairs	2,169
4.	Cultural	1,904
5.	Social welfare	1,852
6.	Hobby/avocational	1,555
7.	Scientific/technological	1,347
8.	Educational	1,289
9.	Religious	1,227
10.	Agricultural	1,119

SOURCE: Gale Research, Inc., Detroit, Michigan

The Most Members

So you've been sending in that monthly or yearly dues payment. Ever wonder which organization has the most members in the U.S.? With 32,000,000 members in 1996, the American Association of Retired Persons (AARP) leads the list. Consider too that seniors are also well represented by the National Council of Senior Citizens with 5,000,000 members.

SOURCE: *Encyclopedia of Associations*, Gale Research, 1997

Mosts Among the Labor Unions

In 1955, 33.2 percent of all American workers belonged to labor unions. In 1995, this figure had fallen to 14.9 percent. This doesn't mean Americans have stopped working. We're working as hard as ever, if not harder. It's just another indication that times have changed.

Read on to see which labor unions have the **most** members (in the U.S.).

	Union	1995 Members
1.	National Education Association	2,000,000
2.	International Brotherhood of Teamsters, Chauffeurs, Warehousemen, and Helpers of America	1,400,000
	United Food and Commercial Workers' International Union	1,400,000
4.	American Federation of State, County, and Municipal Employees	1,300,000
	International Union of Automobile, Aerospace, and Agricultural Implement Workers of America	1,300,000

	Union	1995 Members
6.	International Union of Service Employees	1,084,720
7.	American Federation of Teachers	900,000
8.	International Brotherhood of Electrical Workers	800,000
9.	Laborers' International Union of North America	750,000
10.	Communications Workers of America	600,000

SOURCE: Bureau of Labor Statistics, U.S. Dept of Labor (taken from *The World Almanac at Book of Facts 1997*, World Almanac Books, New Jersey, 1996)

Where to Find the Most Environmentalists

PRIDE in our environment is nothing new. Consider the Audubon Society. It's been in existence for ninety years. The Sierra Club, founded by Scottish-born naturalist John Muir, celebrated its hundredth year in 1992. Both these organizations couldn't have gotten along without the help of people like you, naturalists in your own right every time you send in a donation or pay your membership dues.

Following are environmental organizations in the U.S. with the **most** members.

	Organization	Year Founded	Annual Budget	Membership
1.	National Wildlife Federation	1936	$100,000,000	4,400,000
2.	Greenpeace	1971	$50,000,000	1,700,000
3.	World Wildlife Fund	1961	$60,000,000	1,200,000
4.	The Nature Conservancy	1951	$131,000,000	800,000
5.	National Audubon Society	1905	$44,000,000	600,000
6.	Sierra Club	1892	$43,000,000	550,000
7.	National Parks and Conservation Association	1919	$14,000,000	350,000
8.	Environmental Defense Fund	1967	$24,000,000	300,000
9.	The Wilderness Society	1935	$14,700,000	270,000
10.	Natural Resources Defense Council	1970	$20,000,000	170,000

SOURCE: *Encyclopedia of Associations*, Gale Research, 1997

Where the Most Boy Scouts Are

SIR Robert Baden-Powell (1857–1941), a former British Army general, held a camp for boys on Brownsea Island, Dorset, England, from July 29 to August 9, 1907. This gathering was the beginning of the Scouting movement, and the following year, Baden-Powell founded the Boy Scouts organization. Today more than 23 million boys between the ages of 11 and 15 in 211 nations are members of the Scouts. In fact, there are just 13 countries worldwide in which Scouting does not exist or is banned for political reasons. One such country is China.

So where are **most** of the Boy Scouts? Read on.

	Country	Boy Scouts
1.	United States	4,882,700
2.	Philippines	2,350,710
3.	India	2,272,700
4.	Indonesia	2,134,368
5.	United Kingdom	657,466
6.	Bangladesh	368,063
7.	Pakistan	326,753
8.	South Korea	309,460
9.	Thailand	274,123
10.	Canada	269,425

SOURCE: Boy Scouts of America

Where the Most Girl Scouts Are

TOGETHER, Baden-Powell and his sister, Agnes (1858–1945), began the Girl Guides in 1910. Today, the World Association of Girl Guides and Girl Scouts has a membership of 8.5 million Scouts and Guides across the world in over 128 member organizations. The U.S. has the **most** Girl Scouts of any country, but it's interesting to see just how diverse and truly international the organization has become.

	Country	Girl Scouts
1.	United States	3,510,313
2.	Philippines	1,250,928
3.	India	758,575
4.	United Kingdom	707,651
5.	South Korea	184,993

	Country	Girl Scouts
6.	Pakistan	101,634
7.	Indonesia	98,656
8.	Malaysia	92,539
9.	Japan	88,331
10.	Australia	87,331

SOURCE: The World Association of Girl Guides and Girl Scouts

Cookies, Girl Scouts, and Where You'll Find the Most

WITH 3.5 million Girl Scouts in the U.S., we're looking at a lot of good deeds and about as many cookies.

Once each year, the Girl Scouts go knocking on their neighbors' doors, selling cookies to raise funds for their activities. But in 1996, for the first time ever, Girl Scout cookies are being sold via the Internet through the organization's web site. So log on and start thinking over whether it's going to be chocolate-covered mint, chocolate chip, or buttery sugar cookies. In the meantime, though, have a glance below to see where you'll find the **most** Girl Scouts in the U.S.

	State	Girl Scouts
1.	California	217,411
2.	New York	176,092
3.	Illinois	150,737
4.	Texas	150,561
5.	Pennsylvania	149,987
6.	Ohio	143,597
7.	Michigan	116,872
8.	New Jersey	94,901
9.	Florida	93,200
10.	Missouri	87,642

SOURCE: The World Association of Girl Guides and Girl Scouts

The Most Commonly Shared Surnames

THE **most** common surname in the English-speaking world is Smith. A survey conducted by the Social Security Administration some twenty years ago showed that in the U.S. alone, over 2,382,509 individuals share that particular last name. Although the SSA hasn't repeated its study, the ranking of the top ten surnames hasn't changed too much.

Following are the ten **most** common surnames in the U.S. today.

	Surname	Number of Persons
1.	Smith	2,238,400
2.	Johnson	1,634,300
3.	Williams/Williamson	1,348,000
4.	Brown	1,268,400
5.	Jones	1,230,500
6.	Miller	1,076,100
7.	Davis	972,500
8.	Wilson	737,300
9.	Anderson/Andersen	712,500
10.	Taylor	648,400

SOURCES: Social Security Administration; Elsdon C. Smith, *American Surnames*, Genealogical Publishing Co., Inc. 1995

What Most Are Naming Them

DECIDING what to name a baby can be an agonizing process for new parents. Which family member or friend should they honor? Will anyone be offended? Should the name reflect the child's ethnic or cultural background? Will the child be teased in school for the name bestowed upon it? Suggestions come from family and friends. Other ideas come from movies, television, and popular fiction. Names of favorite celebrities are always popular, as are biblical names. A case in point is Michael (an archangel and protector of Israel in the Bible), which has been the most popular boys' name in the U.S. for the last thirty years. The names James, John, and David ranked among the top ten in the 1950s, the 1970s, and now the 1990s, and all three ranked among the top fourteen in the 1920s and 1980s. On the other hand, not one name appearing among the top ten girls' names in the 1920s, 1950s, and 1970s (including the top names Mary, Linda, and Michelle) remains among the top ten today. Here are the current **most** popular girls' and boys' names in the U.S.

Girls' Names	Boys' Names
1. Ashley	**1.** Michael
2. Jessica	**2.** Christopher
3. Amanda	**3.** Joshua
4. Brittany	**4.** Matthew
5. Sarah	**5.** Andrew
6. Samantha	**6.** Ryan
7. Megan	**7.** Jacob
8. Emily	**8.** Nicholas
9. Kayla	**9.** Tyler
10. Elizabeth	**10.** James

SOURCE: Linda Rosenkrantz and Pamela Redmond Satran,
Beyond Jennifer and Jason, St. Martin's Press, 1988/1990/1994

The Most Notorious Deadbeat Dad

IN the U.S., deadbeat parents—usually Dad—owe an estimated $34 billion to over 23 million children in unpaid support. For six years, Jeffrey Nichols skipped town, ignored court orders, and schemed to hide his financial assets to avoid paying child support. At one point, he even lied about being the father of his own three children. Then, on August 18, 1995, New York State Supreme Court Justice Phyllis Gangel-Jacob ordered Nichols to pay his ex-wife, Marilyn Kane, $580,000, the **most** ever awarded under the 1992 Federal Child Support Recovery Act. Nichols was jailed until he came up with the money, making him the **most** notorious of "deadbeat dads."

Money Buying the Most Happiness or the Most Affairs

IF a wife wants to know whether her husband is having an affair, the first place to look just might be his paycheck. According to a study conducted by *American Couples,* husbands with the highest incomes are the **most** likely to have extramarital affairs.

Here's a list by income of the percentage of men who have affairs the **most.**

	Income	Percent Having Affairs
1.	$60,000 or more	70%
2.	$40,000–$50,000	67

3.	$30,000–$40,000	55
4.	$20,000–$30,000	45
5.	$10,000–$20,000	33
6.	$5,000–$10,000	25
7.	under $5,000	16

SOURCE: *American Couples*

Where Most Succumb

WHAT are the **most** common circumstances under which affairs occur? In a 1991 survey of over 2,000 Americans published in a book called *The Day America Told the Truth,* 31 percent admitted having had affairs and described how they took place.

So if you suspect anything, maybe you don't want to read on, or maybe you do?

	Circumstance	Percent of Total
1.	Casual meetings/a bar	28%
2.	Just happened/accident	12
3.	Growing friendship	10
4.	Introduced by a friend	7
	Sexual attraction	7
	Pursued by eventual lover	7
7.	Midlife crisis	2

SOURCE: James Patterson, *The Day America Told the Truth,* Dutton, 1992

The Most Likely Cohorts

THE same 2,000 Americans in *The Day America Told the Truth* also described with whom **most** of the affairs occurred.

	Partner in Affair	Percent of Total
1.	Friend	24%
2.	Co-worker	23
3.	Old flame	21
4.	Stranger	20

	Partner in Affair	Percent of Total
5.	Friend of spouse	15
6.	Prostitute	9
7.	Boss	7

SOURCE: James Patterson, *The Day America Told the Truth,* Dutton, 1992

Fears and Phobias: What Most of Us Dread the Most

FOR some of us, just thinking about our phobias can make our heart pound, bring out beads of sweat on our foreheads, and make our hands clammy. They are our greatest fears. Whether it's acrophobia (fear of heights), agoraphobia (fear of open spaces), or xenophobia (fear of strangers), fears can control our lives. Some people, for example, refuse to travel by airplane. Others become fearful at the thought of crossing a bridge. And many people have trouble just leaving their homes. As an extreme example, Howard Hughes was so fearful of germs that he became a complete recluse, refusing to cut his hair or fingernails and for years not leaving the confines of his rooms. He wouldn't even allow people to speak to him.

But what is it that most Americans fear the **most?** A poll of 3,000 people revealed the following top five fears:

	Fear	
1.	Speaking before a group	41%
2.	Heights	32%
3.	Insects and bugs	22%
	Financial problems	22%
	Deep water	22%

SOURCE: National Institute for Mental Health

The Most Get-Well Cards Work

WHEN nine-year-old Craig Shergold of Carlshalton, Great Britain, was diagnosed with a brain tumor in 1989, he had one wish to fulfill before he died. He wanted to be listed in the *Guinness Book of Records* for having received the **most** get-well cards ever. Volunteers in England contacted the Children's Wish Foundation in Atlanta, Georgia, which offered to solicit and count the cards, and soon Craig's story was widely publicized all over the world. So much mail arrived each day that it soon began filling whole rooms of the foundation's warehouse, and by 1991 Craig had received over 33 million cards.

Craig's wish was fulfilled when the *Guinness* editors included this new world's record in their 1992 edition. Craig and his family then asked that people please stop sending cards. But Craig's original story seems to have taken on a life of its own. The cards and gifts included everything from religious symbols and teddy bears to a smoked ham and continued to arrive each day.

The foundation estimates that Craig has now received over 70 million cards. Craig's story continues to be published all over the world and was even recently posted on the Internet. Having survived his battle with cancer, Craig is now sixteen years old and says simply, "I'm fine. Please help some other kid."

SOURCE: *The Guinness Book of Records 1992*, Facts on File, Inc. 1991

The Most Amazing Maize Maze

"IF you build it, they will come," said Don Frantz as he began dreaming of creating the world's **most** enormous cornfield maze. Covering three acres in the middle of a cornfield in Shippensburg, Pennsylvania, the Amazing Maize Maze is so large that the pattern can only be seen clearly from a plane. Fifteen volunteers carefully cut the two miles of paths through the corn over three months, and the maze was open to the public on weekends from August 19, 1995 through September 4 (Labor Day).

Frantz, teamed up with world-renowned maze designer Adrian Fisher of Great Britain to create the maze, coming complete with mailboxes containing hints, music playing in the background, and a Maze Master standing high above to help those who lose themselves inside. Fisher and Frantz also worked together on the previous record holder, a cornfield maze called the Stegosaurus, constructed as a charity fund-raiser at Lebanon Valley College in Annville, Pennsylvania, in 1993.

SOURCE: Shippenburg, Pennsylvania Chamber of Commerce

The Most Brains

WHO's the **most** intelligent person in the world? With a recorded IQ of 228, Marilyn vos Savant can claim that title. Vos Savant is a member of several international high IQ societies, including Mensa and the International Legion of Intelligence. Vos Savant has published several books, including *Brain Building* and *I've Forgotten Everything I Learned in School*. The **most** intelligent three-year-old, and the youngest member of Mensa, is Rhiannon Linington-Payne of Shropshire, England, who has an IQ of 155 and the reading level of children twice her age.

SOURCE: Mensa

The Most Miss America Titles

"THERE she is, Miss America. There she is, your ideal." Those words are sung each September in Atlantic City as an excited, sometimes tearful, newly crowned Miss America walks before an audience of cheering admirers. Since 1921 the Miss America Pageant has been the country's premier beauty and talent contest. Women between the ages of seventeen and twenty-six are judged on a variety of factors, including talent, intelligence, grace and poise, and, of course, looks. Although the pageant has changed in recent years, becoming Miss America is still a dream for many young women. Some view winning the pageant as a first step toward a career in show business, while others are more concerned with winning the scholarships and lucrative personal-appearance contracts, which together total over $180,000.

Only one woman, Mary Campbell of Columbus, Ohio, has been crowned Miss America twice, the **most** times in the history of the pageant. Mary served for both 1922 and 1923, the second and third years of the pageant.

Mosts
from the World of
Business

As NEARLY EVERYONE in the world has had some sort of job or another over the course of their lifetime, we can assume business is a large enough category to yield quite a few interesting **mosts**. Think about it. We admire those with the **most** money. We choose to live in areas with the **most** growth. We attempt to work for companies offering the **most** security. And all of us are constantly at work trying to make the **most** we can. All of these and many more fall within the scope of business. So please browse on and see just how much those with the **most** have.

Who Employs the Most on the Globe?

WHERE do you work? Chances are that you might work for one of the following companies. Why not?—these places are huge. Not only do they have more employees than **most**, but **most** employ more people than there are residents in some of North America's larger cities. Several employees are probably needed just to count the employees. How'd you like to have to take attendance every morning?

Following is a ranking of companies around the globe employing the **most** people as of the 1994 business year.

	Company	1994 Employees
1.	U.S. Postal Service	728,944
2.	General Motors	692,800
3.	Wal-Mart Stores	600,000
4.	PepsiCo	471,000
5.	Siemens (German)	382,000
6.	Sears, Roebuck	360,000
7.	Deutsche Bank (German)	357,324
8.	Deutsche Post (German)	340,000

	Company	1994 Employees
9.	Ford Motor Company	337,778
10.	K Mart	335,000
11.	Hitachi (Japan)	331,673
12.	Daimler-Benz (German)	330,551
13.	United Parcel Service	320,000
14.	AT&T	304,500
15.	Unilever	304,000
16.	IRI (Italy)	292,695
17.	Matsushita Electric Industries (Japan)	265,397
18.	Fiat (Italy)	248,810
19.	IBM	243,039
20.	Philips Electronics (Netherlands)	243,032

Keep in mind that if we considered the number of people working in government in any of the countries listed above, some of the above **mosts** wouldn't even have made the list.

SOURCE: "The Global 500," *Fortune* magazine, Aug. 7, 1995

Who Employs the Most in the U.S.?

WE'VE seen where people work around the world, so let's turn back toward home. The numbers remain staggering.

	Company	Employees
1.	General Motors Corporation	710,800
2.	U.S. Postal Service	691,723
3.	Wal-Mart Stores, Inc.	528,000
4.	PepsiCo, Inc.	423,000
5.	Sears, Roebuck and Company	359,000
6.	K Mart Corporation	344,000
7.	Ford Motor Company	322,213
8.	AT&T Corporation	308,700
9.	United Parcel Service of America, Inc.	286,000
10.	IBM	256,207
11.	General Electric	222,000
12.	J. C. Penny Company, Inc.	193,000
13.	The Kroger Company	190,000

14.	Dayton Hudson Corporation	174,000
15.	Philip Morris Companies, Inc.	173,000
16.	McDonald's Corporation	169,000
17.	United Technologies Corporation	168,600
18.	Lockheed Martin Corporation	163,700
19.	Marriott International, Inc.	163,440
20.	Sara Lee Corporation	146,000

SOURCE: *Hoover's Masterlist of America's Top 2,500 Employers* (1995)

1994 Most Billions

TALK about an aggressive sales force! Just have a look at the following, a list of the largest companies in the world ranked by the **most** sales in 1994.

	Company	Country	Employees	1994 Sales (billions)
1.	Mitsubishi	Japan	36,000	$175.8
2.	Mitsui	Japan	80,000	171.5
3.	Itochu	Japan	7,345	167.8
4.	Sumitomo	Japan	22,000	162.5
5.	General Motors	U.S.	692,800	155.0
6.	Marubeni	Japan	9,911	150.2
7.	Ford Motor Company	U.S.	337,778	128.4
8.	Exxon	U.S.	86,000	101.5
9.	Nissho Iwai	Japan	17,008	100.9
10.	Royal Dutch/Shell Group	U.K./Netherlands	106,000	94.9
11.	Toyota Motor	Japan	110,534	88.2
12.	Wal-Mart Stores	U.S.	600,000	83.4
13.	Hitachi	Japan	331,673	76.4
14.	Nippon Life Insurance	Japan	90,132	75.3
15.	AT&T	U.S.	304,500	75.1
16.	Nippon Telegraph & Telephone	Japan	194,700	70.8
17.	Matsushita Electric Industries	Japan	265,397	69.9
	Tomen	Japan	3,192	69.9
19.	General Electric	U.S.	221,000	64.7
20.	Daimler-Benz	Germany	330,551	64.2

Consider that the world's biggest company, ranked in revenues, is Mitsubishi. Now consider that it has achieved this with only 36,000 employees, giving it a "Global 500" ranking of only 294. Thus it doesn't always take the **most** to make the **most**.

SOURCE: "The Global 500," *Fortune* magazine, Aug. 7, 1995

1993 Most Billions

FORTUNES rise and fall, as you'll see by comparing the rankings of the world's largest companies in 1994 to the same rankings in 1993. As before, rankings are based on the **most** revenues.

	Company	Country	Employees	1993 Sales (billions)
1.	General Motors	U.S.	710,800	$133.6
2.	Ford Motor Company	U.S.	322,213	108.5
3.	Exxon	U.S.	91,000	97.8
4.	Royal Dutch/Shell Group	U.K./Netherlands	117,000	94.1
5.	Toyota	Japan	109,279	85.3
6.	Hitachi	Japan	330,637	68.6
7.	IBM	U.S.	267,196	67.7
8.	Matsushita	Japan	254,059	61.4
9.	General Electric	U.S.	222,000	60.8
10.	Daimler-Benz	Germany	366,736	59.1
11.	Mobil	U.S.	61,900	56.6
12.	Nissan	Japan	143,310	53.8
13.	British Petroleum	U.K.	72,600	52.5
14.	Samsung	So. Korea	191,303	51.3
15.	Philip Morris	U.S.	173,000	50.6
16.	IRI	Italy	366,471	50.5
17.	Siemens	Germany	391,000	50.4
18.	Volkswagen	Germany	251,643	46.3
19.	Chrysler	U.S.	128,000	43.6
20.	Toshiba	Japan	175,000	42.9

If you're thinking it would take more than a rock in a slingshot to bring any of the these companies down, you're right. Especially Exxon, which was the big winner with the **most** profits of $5,280,000,000. IBM had the **most** losses of any of the above, amounting to −$8,101,000,000 on the year.

SOURCE: "The Global 500," *Fortune* magazine, July 25, 1994

Where to Find a Behemoth

YOU'VE compared 1993's rankings of the largest companies in the world to 1994's and you've noticed the shift in fortunes. Now consider where **most** of the world's top companies are located and see which country hosts the **most**.

	Country	Number of Companies	Company with the Most Sales (rank)
1.	U.S.	151	General Motors (5)
2.	Japan	149	Mitsubishi (1)
3.	Germany	44	Daimler-Benz (20)
4.	France	40	Elf Aquitaine (46)
5.	Britain	33	British Petroleum (31)
6.	Switzerland	14	Nestlé (39)
7.	Italy	11	IRI (38)
8.	South Korea	8	Daewoo (52)
9.	Netherlands	8	Philips Electronics (58)
10.	Spain	6	INI (132)

SOURCE: "The Global 500," *Fortune* magazine, Aug. 7, 1995

The Most Profitable

REVENUE is nice and income ain't bad either, but when it comes to profit, there's nothing else like it. Who profited the **most** over the 1994 business year? Below is a top 10.

	Company	Country	Profit (billions)
1.	Royal Dutch/Shell Group	U.K./Netherlands	$6.2
2.	Ford Motor	U.S.	5.3
3.	Exxon	U.S.	5.1
4.	General Motors	U.S.	4.9
5.	General Electric	U.S.	4.7
	Philip Morris	U.S.	4.7
	AT&T	U.S.	4.7
8.	Standard Life Assurance	U.K.	4.3
9.	Chrysler	U.S.	3.7
10.	Citicorp	U.S.	3.4

SOURCE: "The Global 500," *Fortune* magazine, Aug. 7, 1995

Most Unhappy

WHO lost the **most** money? Take a cue from the executives who run the following companies and sit down. It won't be easy.

	Company	Company	1994 Losses (billions)
1.	Sony	Japan	3.0
2.	Sumitomo Bank	Japan	2.9
3.	Credit Lyonnais	France	2.2
4.	Digital	U.S.	2.2
5.	Nissan Motor	Japan	1.7
6.	Metallgesellschaft	Germany	1.6
7.	CNCF	France	1.5
	Air France Group	France	1.5
9.	Prudential Insurance	U.S.	1.2
10.	IRI	Italy	1.1

SOURCE: "The Global 500," *Fortune* magazine, Aug. 7, 1995

The Most Owners and Then Some

LOOKING to make a little investment, but you don't want to go into it alone? Well how about going along with the crowd and putting your money into the **most** widely held publicly traded companies in the U.S.? You won't be alone.

	Company	Number of Stockholders
1.	AT&T	2,344,160
2.	BellSouth	1,387,800
3.	NYNEX	1,093,200
4.	Bell Atlantic	1,064,792
5.	Ameritech	1,042,400
6.	Southwestern Bell	973,600
7.	Pacific Telesis	933,400
8.	General Motors	891,600
9.	US West	867,800
10.	IBM	764,600
11.	Exxon	620,500
12.	GTE	504,000

13.	Royal Dutch Petroleum	500,000
14.	General Electric	475,000
15.	Occidental Petroleum	463,000
16.	McDonald's	378,000
17.	Sears, Roebuck	331,800
18.	Mobil	286,600
19.	Ford Motor	282,600
20.	Pacific Gas & Electric	261,000

SOURCE: *S&P 500 Directory,* 1994

The Biggest of the Big

WHO makes, builds, refines, produces, and manufactures the **most**? The following do, by industry.

Industry	Company	Country	1994 Sales (billions)
Aerospace	Boeing	U.S.	$21.9
Airlines	American	U.S.	16.1
Banks	Deutsche Bank	Germany	33.1
Beverages	Coca-Cola	U.S.	16.2
Brokerages	Merrill Lynch	U.S.	18.2
Building Materials	Saint Gobain	France	13.4
Chemicals	DuPont	U.S.	35.0
Computers/Office Equip.	IBM	U.S.	65.1
Electronics/Equipment	Hitachi	Japan	76.4
Food	Philip Morris	U.S.	53.8
Food Services	PepsiCo	U.S.	28.5
Forest/Paper Products	Intern'l Paper	U.S.	15.0
General Merchandiser	Wal-Mart	U.S.	83.4
Industrial/Farm Equip.	Mitsubishi	Japan	28.7
Metal Products	Pechiney	France	12.9
Metals	IRI	Italy	45.4
Mining/Crude Oil Prod'n	Ruhrkohle	Germany	15.7
Motor Vehicle/Parts	General Motors	U.S.	155.0
Petroleum Refining	Exxon	U.S.	101.5
Pharmaceuticals	Johnson & Johnson	U.S.	15.7
Publishing/Printing	Dai Nippon Printing	Japan	12.0
Rubber/Plastic Products	Bridgestone	Japan	15.6

Industry	Company	Country	1994 Sales (billions)
Soaps/Cosmetics	Procter & Gamble	U.S.	30.3
Telecommunications	AT&T	U.S.	75.1
Tobacco	BAT Industries	U.K.	22.1

SOURCE: "The Global 500," *Fortune* magazine, Aug. 7, 1995

Who's Climbing the Most and the Highest

WE'RE talking change in profits here, and in this section you'll see which industries are climbing to the top the quickest. Not a bad thing to know if you're in the job market. To arrive at per-industry breakdowns, we've simply compared 1994 industry profits to those in 1993. The result yields a percentage increase in profits, and below we supply you with the **mosts**.

	Industry	Percent Change
1.	Computers/Office Equipment	87.7
2.	Wholesalers	75.6
3.	Motor Vehicles and Parts	59.5
4.	Electronics/Electrical Equipment	46.4
5.	Mail/Package/Freight Delivery	41.5
6.	Chemicals	37.2
7.	Petroleum Refining	36.1
8.	Industrial and Farm Equipment	33.8
9.	Publishing/Printing	31.0
10.	Metals	29.9
11.	Beverages	27.5
12.	Electric and Gas Utilities	26.6
13.	Telecommunications	26.4
14.	Forest and Paper Products	25.1
15.	Food	22.2
16.	Soaps/Cosmetics	21.2
17.	Aerospace	20.1
18.	Food and Drug Stores	19.9
19.	Tobacco	17.4
20.	Insurance	14.1
21.	Trading	10.5
22.	Scientific/Photo/Control Equipment	9.7
23.	Pharmaceuticals	9.2
24.	Metals Products	8.7

25.	Engineering/Construction	5.2
26.	General Merchandising	2.9
27.	Commercial Banks	−2.4
28.	Diversified Financials	−4.4
29.	Specialist Retailers	−7.3
30.	Airlines	−9.6

As a note, *Fortune* magazine's Global 500 median for all industries is 14.4 percent. All you students and job seekers out there compare that to the above industries first before making that big leap into any of the above.

SOURCE: "The Global 500," *Fortune* magazine, Aug. 7, 1995

The Most Likely to Be Seen

WHY is it that you're always noticing a McDonald's restaurant or a Subway or a KFC? Probably because of all the respective franchises. Following is a list of companies with the **most** franchises. Hard to miss them, isn't it? And that's the point.

	Franchise Chains	Number of Outlets
1.	McDonald's	14,298
2.	Subway	10,041
3.	KFC	8,187
4.	Burger King	6,826
5.	Tandy	6,600
6.	Century 21 Real Estate	6,000
7.	International Dairy Queen	5,348
8.	Domino's Pizza	5,300
9.	Jani-King	4,214
10.	ServiceMaster	4,181
11.	Hardee's	3,997
12.	Wendy's	3,928
13.	Snap-On Tools	3,657
14.	Baskin-Robbins	3,511
15.	Blockbuster Entertainment	3,473

Unlisted are the 7-Eleven Convenience Stores due to franchising policies. In 1993, 7-Eleven had 10,604 franchises in the U.S.

SOURCE: International Franchise Association, 1995

R-E-S-P-E-C-T

WHAT do Rodney Dangerfield and Aretha Franklin have in common? You're probably thinking not much, but the truth is that both are experts on the subject of respect, or lack thereof. Though they didn't compile the following, the good people working for *Hoover's Masterlist of America's Top 2,500 Employers* (1995) did, but whether you're a comedian, a performer or a consumer, it's best to know what companies are the **most** respected in America today.

Company
1. Rubbermaid
2. Microsoft
3. Coca-Cola
4. Motorola
5. Home Depot
6. Intel
7. Procter & Gamble
8. 3M
9. UPS
10. Hewlett-Packard

Making the Most from the Best

LOOKING to make the **most** from your money? Then consider going to the best analysts. Not the lie-on-the-couch type, but the ones who pick the best stocks **most** of the time. Following are the **most** respected stock research departments among some of Wall Street's **most** respected firms.

Firm
1. Goldman, Sachs
2. Merrill Lynch
3. Donaldson, Lufkin, Jenrette
4. Salomon Brothers
5. Smith Barney
6. Morgan Stanley
7. CS First Boston
8. Paine Webber
9. Lehman Brothers
10. Prudential Securities

SOURCE: *The 1996 Information Please Business Almanac and Sourcebook*

Big Winners Making You the Most!

LOOKING to make a big score? Well, not to sound too smug, but here's where you might have looked last year (we wish *we* did!). Below are the companies whose stocks made the **most** money for investors in 1995.

	Company/Stock	1995 High	1995 Low	Percent Change from '94
1.	Diana	26.88	3.81	386.4
2.	Continental Airlines "B"	47.50	6.50	370.3
3.	Corrections Corporation of America	38.88	8.00	360.4
4.	PHP Healthcare	28.88	4.81	334.8
5.	Safeguard Scientific	51.50	11.34	330.2
6.	National Media	21.13	4.50	309.8
7.	Culbro	51.88	11.75	267.3
8.	Aames Financial	36.88	7.75	237.9
9.	GRC International	39.63	11.38	237.4
10.	Keithley Instruments	18.00	4.81	235.0

SOURCE: *The New York Times,* January 2, 1996

The Most Money

WE'VE all heard of Rockefeller, Carnegie, Hearst, Getty, Ford, Vanderbilt, and a number of other legendary American millionaires and billionaires. And just as their fortunes were built on hard work and genius, other contemporary Americans are also hard at work building their own fortunes. Consider the richest man in America, and among the richest in the world, William "Bill" Gates. At only thirty-nine, he is already worth $15 billion, all of it built on hard work and foresight. See how others are out making their fortunes, perhaps placing their names among those of legend.

	Person (age)	Fortune In	Hometown	Net Worth (billions)
1.	William Gates III (39)	Microsoft	Bellevue, WA	$15.0
2.	Warren Buffet (65)	Stock market	Omaha, NE	12.0
3.	John Werner Kluge (81)	Metromedia	Charlottesville, VA	6.7

Person (age)	Fortune In	Hometown	Net Worth (billions)
4. Paul G. Allen (42)	Microsoft	Mercer Is., WA	6.1
5. Sumner Redstone (72)	Movie Theaters/ Viacom	Newton Centre, MA	4.8
6. Richard M. DeVos (69)	Amway	Ada, MI	4.3
Jay Van Andel (71)	Amway	Ada, MI	4.3
Samuel Newhouse, Jr. (67)	Publishing/ Cable TV	NYC	4.3
Donald Newhouse (65)	Publishing Cable TV	NYC	4.3
10. Helen Walton (76)	Wal-Mart	Bentonville, AR	
(shares with the following)			21.0
S. Robson Walton (51)	Wal-Mart	Bentonville, AR	
John T. Walton (49)	Wal-Mart	San Diego, CA	
Jim C. Walton (47)	Wal-Mart	Bentonville, AR	
Alice L. Walton (46)	Wal-Mart	Rogers, AR	
15. Ronald O. Perelman (52)	Revlon/ New World Communications	NYC	4.2
Lawrence J. Ellison (51)	Oracle Corp.	Atherton	4.2
17. David Packard (83)	Hewlett-Packard	Los Altos Hills, CA	3.7
18. Walter H. Annenberg (87)	Publishing	Wynnewood, PA	3.4
19. Keith Rupert Murdoch (64)	News Corp./Fox	Australia/London/ NYC/LA	3.3
20. Forrest Edward Mars, Sr. (80s)	Candy/Pet Food	Las Vegas, NV	
(shares with the following)			12.0
Forrest Edward Mars, Jr. (64)		McLean, VA	
John Franklyn Mars (59)		Arlington, VA	
Jacqueline Mars Vogel (age and residence unknown)			
24. Barbara Cox Anthony (72)	Newspapers/ Cable TV	Honolulu, HI	
(shares with the following and her family)			6.0
Anne Cox Chambers (75)	Newspapers/ Cable TV	Atlanta, GA	

SOURCE: "The Forbes 400," *Forbes Magazine,* Oct. 16, 1995

States with the Most Forbes 400 Members

So you've finally made the Forbes 400. Congratulations! You're worth somewhere between Bill Gates's $15 billion and a few dollars less than Oprah Winfrey's $340 million. But where do you live? Maybe with some of the other members of such an exclusive roster. Where do **most** of them live?

	State	Number of Forbes 400 Members
1.	California	99
2.	New York	70
3.	Texas	42
4.	Florida	27
5.	Illinois	22
	Ohio	22
7.	Massachusetts	20
8.	Pennsylvania	19
9.	Michigan	16
10.	Washington	14

SOURCE: "The Forbes 400," *Forbes Magazine,* Oct. 16, 1995

Cities with the Most Forbes 400 Members

HAVE a look at what cities **most** of the Forbes 400 members live in.

	City	Number of Forbes 400 Members
1.	New York City	55
2.	Los Angeles area	30
3.	San Francisco	26
4.	Dallas–Fort Worth	18
5.	Seattle	10

SOURCE: "The Forbes 400," *Forbes Magazine,* Oct. 16, 1995

More Money Please

IF you're visiting any of the below cities on your next business trip, make sure to put in for more per diem money, as they require the **most** internationally. For the business traveler, these are the **most** expensive cities in the world.

	City	Total Cost per Diem ($)
1.	Tokyo, Japan	464
2.	Hong Kong	433
3.	Paris, France	342
4.	London, England	337
5.	Brussels, Belgium	322

Per diems represent average costs for all meals and single-rate lodging in business-class hotels.

SOURCE: *Runzheimer Meal-Lodging Cost Index,* Runzheimer International, based on rates gathered between the second half of 1994 and the first quarter of 1995

Make That in Dollars

So you're planning on domestic travel for that business trip, then plan on getting as many dollars as you can. You might try guessing first, before you read on and learn what U.S. cities require the **most** in per diem money.

Per diems represent average costs for all meals and single-rate lodging in business-class hotels.

	City	Total Cost per Diem ($)
1.	New York, NY	289
2.	Washington, DC	260
3.	Honolulu, HI	246
4.	Chicago, IL	229
5.	Boston, MA	218

SOURCE: *Runzheimer Meal-Lodging Cost Index,* Runzheimer International, based on rates gathered between the second half of 1994 and the first quarter of 1995

Where to Go When They Cut Your Per Diem

YOUR company is cutting back, slashing budgets, really tightening its belt. The number crunchers are looking for opportunities in less expensive areas of the world. Where are they going to send you? Maybe to one of the following cities, where they plan to save the **most** money on your per diem.

	City	per Diem ($)
1.	Abidjan, Ivory Coast	85
2.	London, Ontario	99
3.	Panama City, Panama	109
4.	Bordeaux, France	118
5.	Guangzhou, China	121

SOURCE: *Runzheimer Meal-Lodging Cost Index,* Runzheimer International, based on rates gathered between the second half of 1994 and the first quarter of 1995

What a Savings!

WHERE do you get the **most** value for your money when on business travel domestically? You might consider the following.

	City	Total Cost per Diem ($)
1.	Wheeling, WV	79
2.	Johnson, TN	80
3.	Macon, GA	82
4.	Fort Smith, AR	84
5.	Lincoln, NE	86

SOURCE: *Runzheimer Meal-Lodging Cost-Index,* Runzheimer International, based on rates gathered between the second half of 1994 and the first quarter of 1995

What a Place!

WHERE do most people want to live? Well, in the towns and cities that offer the **most**. According to the July 1996 issue of *Money* Magazine, the following ten cities do just that. *Money* Magazine's criteria: the economy, health, crime, housing, education, weather, transit, and leisure arts.

Rank	City
1.	Madison, WI
2.	Punta Gorda, FL
3.	Rochester, MN
4.	Fort Lauderdale, FL
5.	Ann Arbor, MI
6.	Fort Myers-Cape Coral, FL
7.	Gainsville, FL
8.	Austin, TX
9.	Seattle, WA
10.	Lakeland, FL

Did you notice that Florida had five spots in the top ten? If the list continued, you'd see that Florida also contained ten cities in the top twenty. And just for your information, ranking in at 100 is Altoona, PA. At 200 is Columbus, OH. And at 300, Rockford, IL.

Where the Most Money Is Made

WHICH localities' residents are making the **most** money? The following places are on the basis of per capita income. Bear in mind that high per capita income doesn't necessarily mean the people are rolling in dough, because in some of these areas the living expenses are also more than **most,** but let's not concern ourselves with that for now.

	City	Nearest Commercial Center	1993 Income (dollars)
1.	San Francisco, CA	San Francisco	$32,927
2.	West Palm Beach–Boca Raton, FL	South Florida	32,230
3.	New Haven–Bridgeport–Stamford–Danbury–Waterbury, CT	New York City	31,151
4.	Bergen-Passaic Counties, NJ	New York City	30,298
5.	Trenton, NJ	Philadelphia	29,385
6.	Naples, FL	Naples	29,237
7.	Middlesex-Somerset-Hunterdon Counties, NJ	New York City	28,999
8.	Newark, NJ	Newark	28,687
9.	Nassau-Suffolk Counties, NY	New York City	28,630
10.	New York, NY	New York City	27,975

11.	Washington, DC, and neighboring parts of MD, VA, WV	Washington	27,761
12.	San Jose, CA	San Jose	27,360
13.	Reno, NV	Reno	26,671
14.	Anchorage, AK	Anchorage	26,619
15.	Hartford, CT	Hartford	26,147
16.	Seattle-Bellevue-Everett, WA	Seattle	26,121
17.	Monmouth-Ocean Counties, NJ	New York City	25,805
18.	Sarasota-Bradenton, FL	Sarasota	25,634
19.	Oakland, CA	Oakland	25,621
20.	Orange County, CA	L.A./San Diego	25,022
21.	Honolulu, HI	Honolulu	24,929
22.	Boston-Worcester-Lawrence-Lowell, MA	Boston	24,861
23.	Chicago, IL	Chicago	24,857
24.	Boulder-Longmont, CO	Denver	24,612
25.	Atlantic–Cape May Counties, NJ	Atlantic City	24,397

Figures are based on 1993 income, the latest date available.

SOURCE: U.S. Bureau of Economic Analysis, *Survey of Current Business,* May 1995

Where the Most Money Is, by County

To just consider where the **most** money is being made within American cities is not to consider the whole picture. **Most** people eventually choose to live in the suburbs, thus skewing the picture somewhat. These same people may work and make **most** of their money in the nearby city (or perhaps not), but their residence is listed in the suburbs. So let's take a look at which residents of what counties made the **most** per capita income in 1993 (the latest year with figures available).

1993 Rank	County	Per Capita Income	Percent of Nat'l Average
1.	New York, New York	$52,277	251.3%
2.	Sherman, Texas	42,373	203.7
3.	Sully, South Dakota	39,707	190.9
4.	Pitkin, Colorado	39,481	189.8
5.	Marin, California	38,310	184.2
6.	Fairfield, Connecticut	37,642	181.0
7.	Somerset, New Jersey	36,542	175.7
8.	Teton, Wyoming	35,983	173.0

1993 Rank	County	Per Capita Income	Percent of Nat'l Average
9.	Westchester, New York	35,945	172.8
10.	Greeley, Kansas	35,594	171.1
11.	Esmerelda, Nevada	35,465	170.5
12.	Bergen, New Jersey	34,658	166.6
13.	Morris, New Jersey	34,412	154.4
14.	Montgomery, Maryland	34,299	164.9
15.	Arlington, Virginia	34,216	164.5
16.	Alexandria City, Virginia	34,023	163.6
17.	Nantucket, Massachusetts	33,991	163.4
18.	Hartley, Texas	33,863	162.8
19.	Hamilton, Kansas	33,459	160.9
20.	Nassau, New York	32,966	158.5

SOURCE: U.S. Bureau of Economic Analysis, *Survey of Current Business,* May 1995

The Most Income by State

MAYBE you live in one of the following states, and hopefully you're making the average per capita income listed, or maybe even more! In any event, have you ever wondered what state's residents made the **most** money in 1995? You need not wonder any longer.

1995 Rank	State	Per Capita Income (dollars)	1990 Rank
1.	Connecticut	30,303	1
2.	New Jersey	28,858	2
3.	Massachusetts	26,994	4
4.	New York	26,782	3
5.	Maryland	25,927	5
6.	New Hampshire	25,151	10
7.	Nevada	25,013	9
8.	Illinois	24,763	11
9.	Hawaii	24,738	6
10.	Alaska	24,182	7
11.	Delaware	24,124	12
12.	California	23,699	8
13.	Washington	23,639	14
14.	Virginia	23,597	13

15.	Michigan	23,551	20
16.	Colorado	23,449	17
17.	Rhode Island	23,310	15
18.	Pennsylvania	23,279	16
19.	Minnesota	23,118	19
20.	Florida	22,916	18

Incidentally, the average U.S. per capita income is $22,788.

SOURCE: U.S. Bureau of Economic Analysis, *Survey of Current Business,* May 1996

Growing Income

ARE you finding that your income is growing? Maybe you're doing a great job at work or maybe you're living in a state that is growing, or maybe both. Read on to find out what states showed the **most** growth in per capita income between 1994 and 1995.

1995 Rank	State	Percent Growth
1.	Louisiana	6.9%
2.	Arizona	6.6
3.	Michigan	6.2
	New Hampshire	6.2
	Rhode Island	6.2
	Oregon	6.2
7.	Utah	6.1
	South Carolina	6.1
9.	New Mexico	6.0
	California	6.0

At the other end of the scale, South Dakota was the slowest growing state in 1995, with a percentage decrease of −0.3.

SOURCE: U.S. Bureau of Economic Analysis, *Survey of Current Business,* May 1996

States with the Most Bankruptcies

THINKING of going bankrupt? Well, if you live in one of the following states, you won't be alone. Below is a list of the states with the **most** bankruptcy filings in the 1994 legal-business year.

	State	Bankruptcies
1.	California	150,900
2.	New York	47,800
3.	Florida	41,900
4.	Texas	41,800
5.	Georgia	40,500
6.	Illinois	38,400
7.	Tennessee	35,600
8.	Ohio	32,500
9.	Virginia	24,400
10.	New Jersey	23,800

SOURCE: Administrative Office of the U.S. Courts, unpublished data

What Did You Call Me?

As the world gets more complicated, so do our titles. Have you ever wondered what an executive assistant or coordinator or office manager is? Well, they're a secretary.

The 1996 Professional Secretary's Handbook of Tips and Lists shows the following as the ten **most** common secretarial titles.

1. Secretary (general)
2. Secretary (specialized)
3. Executive Secretary
4. Executive Assistant
5. Administrative Assistant
6. Administrative Secretary
7. Office Manager
8. Senior Secretary
9. Educator/Instructor
10. Coordinator

Mosts
from the World of
Money

WE'VE TAKEN A good look at who's making money and how they're doing it, but now let's take a look at money itself—after all, it's what **most** of us spend **most** of our day pursuing.

The History of Notes and the Most Valuable Note

EVER wonder why portraits of statesmen are used on currency? In 1928, when the present design of American currency was adopted, a large percentage of the population was either illiterate or, in the case of new immigrants, did not speak English. Portraits were used to make it easier for those who could not read the numbers or words to determine the denomination of a note. The portraits chosen, particularly those of U.S. presidents, were thought to have a more permanent familiarity in the minds of the public.

What was the **most** valuable note ever printed by the Bureau of Engraving and Printing? Although it was never circulated among the general public, the $100,000 gold certificate, on which the portrait of President Woodrow Wilson appeared, was printed for just twenty-three days, from December 18, 1934, to January 9, 1935, and was issued only to Federal Reserve banks against an equal amount of gold bullion held by the Treasury. The **most** valuable denomination ever in general circulation was the $10,000 note bearing the portrait of Salmon P. Chase, who was secretary of the treasury during the Civil War and helped promote the National Banking System. Although denominations larger than $100 were no longer issued after 1969, approximately 345 of those $10,000 bills are still in circulation.

SOURCE: U.S. Treasury

The Most Wear and Tear

EVERY wonder which Federal Reserve note spends the **most** time in circulation? That all depends on the denomination. And what bills get passed around more than a single? None. So guess which wear out the quickest? Following is the average life of U.S. currency:

	Note	Average Life
1.	$100	9 years
2.	$50	9 years
3.	$20	4 years
4.	$10	3 years
5.	$5	2 years
6.	$1	18 months

SOURCE: U.S. Federal Reserve, Bureau of Engraving and Printing

Bills Printed the Most

OVER $380 billion in U.S. currency is in circulation today, two-thirds of it outside the country. The Bureau of Engraving and Printing produces approximately 9 billion notes each year, or about 35 million daily, which makes for the creation of a handy $465 million per day. What a money-maker!

A U.S. Federal Reserve Note is 0.0043 inch thick. Four hundred ninety bills make a pound. Now can you guess how high a stack of all the bills produced in a year would rise? And while you're at it, take a guess at how much this stack would weigh. But if you don't want to guess, we'll tell you. The stack of bills produced in one year would stand 610.8 miles tall, the distance between Salt Lake City, Utah, and Santa Fe, New Mexico, and would weigh 18,367,347 pounds.

Prior to 1993, about 95 percent of the new bills were printed to replace those removed from circulation. In the last few years, however, that figure has been reduced to about 90 percent because investors from other countries, particularly Russia, have been purchasing more U.S. currency than ever before.

Which denomination does the bureau print the **most** of each year? Based on the number of notes printed and the approximate percentages of each denomination, here's a chart of estimated annual U.S. currency production and costs.

Note	Percent of Production	Amount Produced	Dollar Value Produced	Total Cost
1. one	44	3,960,000,000	$3,960,000,000	$14,652,000
2. twenty	24	2,160,000,000	$43,200,000,000	$7,992,000
3. ten	12	1,080,000,000	$10,800,000,000	$3,996,000
4. five	12	1,080,000,000	$5,400,000,000	$3,996,000
5. fifty	4	360,000,000	$18,000,000,000	$1,332,000
6. hundred	4	360,000,000	$36,000,000,000	$1,332,000
TOTAL	100	9,000,000,000	$117,360,000,000	$33,300,000

To produce a note, the average cost is 3.7 cents.

SOURCE: U.S. Federal Reserve, Bureau of Engraving and Printing

The Most Counterfeiters Ever

BY the end of the Civil War, a full third of all U.S. paper currency in circulation was counterfeit, a devastating situation for a nation struggling to recover economically from such a divisive and destructive war. On July 5, 1865, the Secret Service was created as a part of the Department of the Treasury to help suppress counterfeit currency. Today, the Service estimates that just 0.001 percent of the currency in circulation is counterfeit and that approximately 90 percent of all known counterfeit currency is seized before it ever reaches the public. That means you can rest easy. **Most** of the money in your wallet should be the real thing.

SOURCE: Department of the Treasury, United States Secret Service

Making the Most Changes to Stop Counterfeiters

ACCORDING to the Secret Service, the **most**-passed counterfeit denomination of U.S. currency is the $20 bill, followed by the $100 bill, the $10 bill, the $50 bill, and the $1 bill. The $100 note is the **most** widely circulated bill in the world. It is also the **most** common foreign-produced counterfeit note, but this may not be the case for long. In 1996, after a five-year study of more than 120 different security features, the Treasury introduced a new $100 note designed to keep ahead of advances in reprographic technology which could be used in counterfeiting. The redesigned note incorporates security features such as a watermark depicting the same historical figure as the portrait, a security thread that glows red in ultraviolet light, color-shifting ink that changes from green to black when viewed from different angles, microprinting of words and figures that appear to the naked eye as a solid line, and concentric fine-line printing, all of which make the new bills extremely difficult to counterfeit. Other denominations will be introduced individually at intervals of 6 to 12 months over the next several years to provide the manufacturers of ATM, vending, and other money-handling machines time to modify their equipment.

SOURCES: Department of the Treasury, United States Secret Service;
Bureau of Engraving and Printing

The Most Change

THE U.S. Mint produced the **most** coins ever in fiscal year 1995 (October 1, 1994, through September 30, 1995). A total of 19,519,253,440 coins were minted, shattering a 1982 record of 19,467,902,440. Other records set in 1995 included the minting of the **most** of each individual coin except the penny, of which the **most** ever produced was in 1994, when a total of 13,459,075,000 pennies were made.

The Denver Mint produced the **most** coins of any individual facility in fiscal 1995, with a total of 10,307,156,440. This toppled the 1989 record of 10,108,272,000 coins set by the Philadelphia Mint, the largest mint in the world, which covers 11½ acres and has an annual production capacity of 12 billion coins.

Here's a list of 1995 coins minted. The list is arranged by percentage of total production:

	Coin	Percent of Production	Amount Produced	Dollar Value Produced
1.	Cents	68.8	13,418,625,000	$134,186,250.00
2.	Dimes	12.1	2,364,988,110	$236,498,811.00
3.	Quarters	10.6	2,070,174,110	$517,543,527.50
4.	Nickels	8.3	1,623,366,110	$81,168,305.50
5.	Half-Dollars	0.2	42,100,110	$21,050,055.00
	TOTALS	100	19,519,253,440	$990,446,949.00

SOURCE: Department of the Treasury, United States Mint

The Most Valuable Stack of Coins
for a Most Valuable Project

IT was a once-in-a-lifetime dream project. The YWCA of Se ittle, King County, Washington, wanted to raise $3.2 million to build the YWCA Family Village, a comprehensive program that combines transitional housing with on-site support services to help homeless families become self-sufficient. But it took the cooperation of the entire community to make that dream a reality. Businesses ranging from small neighborhood stores to software giant Microsoft donated to the project. Federal, state, and local municipal governments provided some of the funding. People even held parties and asked for donations to Family Village instead of presents. On May 28, 1992, the YWCA held a special celebration and ground-breaking ceremony during which all the coins that had been collected were delivered to the Redmond, Washington, site. At the end of the day, they counted an astounding 1,000,298 coins worth $126,463.61, the **most** valuable pile of coins ever.

The YWCA Family Village opened its doors in March 1993 and now provides critically needed services to over 300 people each year.

SOURCE: YWCA, Seattle, Washington

One Man with the Most Pennies

"RELIABLE banking since 1901" goes the slogan for Steel Valley Bank of Dillonvale, Ohio. And Steel Valley certainly proved it when one prospective customer asked for assistance in making a deposit. But this was no ordinary deposit. The unnamed man from Steubenville had been collecting pennies since he was five years old, and now, at age seventy, he had decided that he wanted to deposit his collection in a bank. No problem, until you consider that his collection amounted to an estimated 8 million pennies filling forty large trash cans. And what does that amount to? Well, $80,000 and the **most** pennies ever turned in by an individual at one time.

Reportedly, two other banks had refused when the elderly gentleman asked for assistance, but bank president George Hazlen visited the man and told him that the bank could indeed handle his deposit. Over a period of four days, a pickup truck retrieved the pennies from the man's home and carried them to the bank—no easy task considering that 8 million pennies weighs 48,000 pounds!

How does someone collect so many pennies? On average, each year for nearly sixty-five years, the man would have had to collect $1,230.77 in pennies, or about $3.37 in pennies each day (that is, of course, 337 pennies). A U.S. penny measures three-quarters of an inch in diameter, so that if all 8 million coins were laid side by side, the line would go on for about 96.7 miles. A penny is also one-sixteenth of an inch thick, so stacked one on top of the other, they would reach nearly eight miles high.

If collecting 8 million pennies was an amazing feat, so was counting them. It took a bank employee to monitor and feed the machine, which counts and bags 5,000 pennies in 5 to 10 minutes, three and one-half months to count all the coins. As the pennies were bagged, they were transported to the nearest Federal Reserve, and the amount was credited to the man's account. What's particularly remarkable about this deposit is that it occurred just five months after the Federal Reserve in Cleveland began rationing pennies because its inventory had fallen short.

Mosts
from the World of
Politics and
Government

ONE OF THE greatest privileges of living in the U.S. is that everyone has a say, provided you're a citizen and over the age of eighteen. Having a say is also called a vote, and in the following we're going to look at the people whom we've voted for **most** often. We'll also check out politics and government around the world.

The Most Electoral Votes Received

GEORGE Washington won the very first U.S. presidential election unanimously, receiving all 69 electoral votes. His 100 percent of the electoral votes was the **most** ever earned by any U.S. president.

SOURCE: Joseph Nathan Kane, *Facts About the Presidents,* Sixth Edition, H.W. Wilson Company, New York, 1993

By the election of 1936, the U.S. had 48 states and Franklin Roosevelt defeated Republican candidate Alfred M. Landon by 515 electoral votes (523 to 8), receiving 98.5 percent of the electoral votes, the second-highest percentage ever. In 1984, Ronald Reagan won the **most** electoral votes ever, 525 out of a possible 538, but this 97.6 percent of the total still ranks him third, behind Washington and Roosevelt.

SOURCE: Joseph Nathan Kane, *Facts About the Presidents,* Sixth Edition, H.W. Wilson Company, New York, 1993

Following are the presidents who won elections with the **most** electoral votes. Keep in mind, though, that the figures below do not represent the margin of victory over an opponent, just the number of electoral votes won (though there is a connection between the two).

	President	Party	Year	Electoral Votes
1.	Ronald Reagan	Republican	1984	525
2.	Franklin Roosevelt	Democrat	1936	523
3.	Richard Nixon	Republican	1972	520
4.	Ronald Reagan	Republican	1980	489
5.	Lyndon Johnson	Democrat	1964	486
6.	Franklin Roosevelt	Democrat	1932	472
7.	Dwight Eisenhower	Republican	1956	457
8.	Franklin Roosevelt	Democrat	1940	449
9.	Herbert Hoover	Republican	1928	444
10.	Dwight Eisenhower	Republican	1952	442

SOURCE: *The World Almanac and Book of Facts 1997*, Robert Famighetti, editor, World Almanac Books, New Jersey, 1996

One More Most for the Gipper!

SINCE the popular vote was introduced in 1872, the presidential candidate to win the **most** popular votes is Republican Ronald Reagan, who was re-elected in 1984 with 54,281,858 votes to Walter Mondale's 37,457,215. Reagan also won the **most** electoral votes that year, as you can see above.

SOURCE: *The World Almanac and Book of Facts*, Robert Famighetti, editor, World Almanac Books, New Jersey, 1996

Following is a list of the U.S. presidents who have received the **most** popular votes in any one election year.

	President	Party	Year	Votes
1.	Ronald Reagan	Republican	1984	54,455,075
2.	George Bush	Republican	1988	48,886,097
3.	Richard Nixon	Republican	1972	47,169,911
4.	Bill Clinton	Democrat	1992	44,909,889
5.	Ronald Reagan	Republican	1980	43,899,248
6.	Lyndon Johnson	Democrat	1964	43,129,484
7.	Jimmy Carter	Democrat	1976	40,830,763
8.	Dwight Eisenhower	Republican	1956	35,590,472
9.	John F. Kennedy	Democrat	1960	34,226,731
10.	Dwight Eisenhower	Republican	1952	33,936,234

Please keep in mind that our population is growing, and that is why modern-era presidents often receive more votes.

SOURCE: *The World Almanac and Book of Facts 1997,* Robert Famighetti, editor, World Almanac Books, New Jersey, 1996

Nixon's Most Substantial Win

"NIXON's the One!" The presidential candidate to win by the **most** popular votes over his opponent was Republican Richard M. Nixon. With a little help from his staff at CREEP (the Committee to Re-elect the President), Nixon was already plotting the cover-up of the Watergate break-in as he celebrated his 1972 re-election over George McGovern. Nixon's 17,994,460 lead (47,165,234 to 29,170,774), is the **most** ever, and his 47 million popular votes amount to the third highest of all-time and resulted in him carrying 49 states, the **most** ever until Ronald Reagan matched that total in 1984. Ironically, the question "What did the president know and when did he know it?" became better known than many of Nixon's campaign slogans.

Within two years Nixon resigned, explaining that he felt he could no longer lead the country with so much of his time and effort being spent responding to the Watergate investigation.

SOURCE: *The World Almanac and Book of Facts 1997.* Robert Famighetti, editor, World Almanac Books, New Jersey, 1996

With Whom the Land Slides the Most

"ALL the Way with LBJ." Richard Nixon may have won in 1972 by the largest number of votes, but he did not win by the highest percentage of the vote. In 1964 Democrat Lyndon Johnson took 61.05 percent of the popular vote to Barry Goldwater's 38.47 percent (43,126,506 to 27,176,799) in the greatest landslide ever. Johnson's 22.58 percent margin of victory over Goldwater was the **most** in presidential election history between the winner and his next-closest opponent.

SOURCE: *The World Almanac and Book of Facts 1997,* Robert Famighetti, editor, World Almanac Books, New Jersey, 1996

The Most Third-Party Votes

"ROSS for Boss!" Although no third-party candidate has ever been elected president, third-party presidential campaigns often serve as rallying points for those who support the candidates' views on particular issues. Certainly the campaigns of Alabama governor George Wallace (American Independent, 1968), Minnesota senator Eugene McCarthy (Democrat, 1968, 1988, and 1992; independent, 1972 and 1976), and **most** recently Texas billionaire H. Ross Perot (independent, 1992; Reform Party, 1996) prompted national debates on racism, the Vietnam War, and the economy.

The third-party candidate to win the **most** popular votes in any election is H. Ross Perot. His extraordinary total of 19,721,433 votes in 1992 was nearly twice that of any other third-party candidate in history and amounted to 18.9 percent of the popular vote. Although that total represented only the third-highest percentage for an independent candidate, it was the highest for any candidate who had not already served as president.

SOURCE: Joseph Nathan Kane, *Facts About the Presidents*, H.W. Wilson Company, New York, 1993

Incredibly, Perot and his supporters accomplished this without accepting any federal campaign funds. Perot himself kicked in $60 million for the campaign. Such an impressive finish hardly seemed possible on election eve, as Perot himself acknowledged when he and his wife danced to what had become his campaign's theme song, Patsy Cline's "Crazy."

Teddy Remains the Most Successful by Percentage

THE **most** successful third-party candidate in history is Theodore Roosevelt. In 1912, Roosevelt ran as a Progressive against Democratic candidate Woodrow Wilson and the Republican incumbent, President William Taft. Wilson won the election with 435 electoral votes and Taft received just 8. But as a former president, Roosevelt earned 27.4 percent of the popular vote, the highest percentage of any third-party candidate, and 88 of the 531 electoral votes.

SOURCE: *The World Almanac and Book of Facts 1997*, Robert Famighetti, editor, World Almanac Books, New Jersey, 1996

Making the Most Tries for a Third Party

AMONG third-party candidates, Norman Mattoon Thomas, who represented the Socialist Party six times between 1928 and 1944, has appeared the **most** often on the national ballot. In 1928, he received 267,420 votes as a candidate against Herbert Hoover. Running against Franklin Roosevelt, he received 881,951 votes in 1932; 187,720 votes in 1936; 99,557 votes in 1940; and 80,518 votes in 1944. He received 139,009 votes when he ran against Harry S. Truman in 1948.

SOURCE: Joseph Nathan Kane, *Facts About the Presidents,* Sixth Edition, H.W. Wilson Company, New York, 1993

States Where the Most Presidents Were Born

THE state of Virginia can claim the title of birthplace of the **most** presidents with eight: George Washington, Thomas Jefferson, James Madison, James Monroe, William Henry Harrison, John Tyler, Zachary Taylor, and Woodrow Wilson. Ohio is second, with seven presidents: Ulysses S. Grant, Rutherford B. Hayes, James A. Garfield, Benjamin Harrison, William McKinley, William Howard Taft, and Warren G. Harding. Third place is held by Massachusetts and New York, with four presidents each. Massachusetts is the birthplace of John and John Quincy Adams, John F. Kennedy, and George Bush. New York is where Martin Van Buren, Millard Fillmore, and both Theodore and Franklin Roosevelt were born.

SOURCE: Joseph Nathan Kane, *Facts About the Presidents,* Sixth Edition, H.W. Wilson Company, New York, 1993

Presidents Sharing the Most Blood Ties

THE **most** closely related presidents were John Adams and John Quincy Adams, who were father and son. William Henry Harrison was Benjamin Harrison's grandfather. James Madison and Zachary Taylor were second cousins. Franklin Delano Roosevelt was a fifth cousin of Theodore Roosevelt, but genealogists have shown that Franklin Roosevelt is remotely related to the **most** other presidents—a total of eleven, five by blood and six by marriage.

SOURCE: Joseph Nathan Kane, *Facts About the Presidents*, Sixth Edition, H.W. Wilson Company, New York, 1993

Presidents Sharing the Most First Names

BIBLICAL names predominate the list of presidential first names, with twenty-two presidents having names which appear in either the Old or New Testaments. The **most** common first name of the presidents is James. The six presidents named James were Madison, Monroe, Polk, Buchanan, Garfield, and Carter. Five were named John: John Adams, John Quincy Adams, Tyler, Coolidge (born John Calvin), and Kennedy. Four were named William: William Henry Harrison, McKinley, Taft, and Clinton. Next, there were two presidents named Thomas: Jefferson and Wilson (born Thomas Woodrow); two named Andrew: Jackson and Johnson; two named Franklin: Pierce and Franklin Delano Roosevelt; and two named George: Washington and Bush.

SOURCE: Joseph Nathan Kane, *Facts About the Presidents*, Sixth Edition, H.W. Wilson Company, New York, 1993

The Most Popular Presidential Alma Maters

IF you have any ambitions of being president one day, you should seriously consider enrolling at Harvard/Radcliffe University. (Of course, you have to be accepted, so your first ambition might be to study a little harder.) Among the 32 presidents who attended college, 12 of them went to Ivy League colleges (11 are on this list, and Theodore Roosevelt attended Columbia Law School) and 5 went to Harvard, the alma mater of the **most** future presidents.

Here are the colleges attended by two or more future presidents.

University	President (Graduation)
Harvard	John Adams (July 16, 1755)
	John Quincy Adams (July 18, 1787)
	Theodore Roosevelt (June 20, 1880)
	Franklin D. Roosevelt (June 24, 1903)
	John F. Kennedy (June 21, 1940)
Yale	William Taft (June 27, 1878)
	Gerald Ford (law school, 1941)
	George Bush (June 22, 1948)
	Bill Clinton (law school, 1973)
William and Mary	Thomas Jefferson (April 25, 1762)
	James Monroe (1776)
	John Tyler (July 4, 1807)

U.S. Military Academy	Ulysses S. Grant (July 1, 1843)
	Dwight D. Eisenhower (June 12, 1915)
Princeton	James Madison (September 25, 1771)
	Woodrow Wilson (June 18, 1879)

SOURCE: Joseph Nathan Kane, *Facts About the Presidents*, Sixth Edition, H.W. Wilson Company, New York 1993

Presidents Hitting the Books the Most

THE **most** educated U.S. president was Woodrow Wilson, who not only overcame dyslexia to graduate from Princeton and the University of Virginia Law School, but went on to earn a Ph.D. from Johns Hopkins in 1886. His first book, *Congressional Government,* served as his doctoral dissertation.

SOURCE: Joseph Nathan Kane, *Facts About the Presidents,* Sixth Edition, H.W. Wilson Company, New York 1993

The Jobs Most Presidents Have

THE **most** common occupation among future presidents is that of lawyer. Although they did not all attend law school, many served apprenticeships in law offices. Twenty-six of America's forty-two presidents have been members of the bar. Several presidents did graduate from law school, however, including Bill Clinton, the only future president to be selected as a Rhodes Scholar, allowing him to study at England's Oxford University, which he did from 1967 to 1968.

SOURCE: Joseph Nathan Kane, *Facts About the Presidents,* Sixth Edition, H.W. Wilson Company, New York, 1993

The Most Verbose President Suffers an Irony or Two

THE inaugural speech with the **most** words in history just might just have been responsible for the shortest presidency. William Henry Harrison stood in a driving rain for nearly two hours delivering his 8,445-word address. He soon developed pneumonia and died just 32 days later. A further irony is that Harrison had pledged in his speech that he would serve just one term.

SOURCE: Joseph Nathan Kane, *Facts About the Presidents,* Sixth Edition, H.W. Wilson Company, New York, 1993

The Most Presidents Alive at One Time

WHEN Bill Clinton was inaugurated on January 20, 1993, the U.S. had the **most** living former presidents ever for the longest time in history. The five men were George Bush, Jimmy Carter, Gerald Ford, Ronald Reagan, and Richard Nixon—until the latter's death some fifteen months later on April 22, 1994. The first time the U.S. could boast five living former presidents was at the inauguration of Abraham Lincoln on March 4, 1861. Presidents Martin Van Buren, John Tyler, Millard Fillmore, Franklin Pierce, and James Buchanan were all still living then. Tyler died ten months later, on January 18, 1862.

SOURCE: Joseph Nathan Kane, *Facts About the Presidents*, Sixth Edition, H.W. Wilson Company, New York, 1993

The Presence of the Most Presidents

THE **most** former or future presidents ever to appear together at a single gathering were among those assembled at the old House Chamber of the Capitol on December 30, 1834. The eight men were former presidents John Quincy Adams and Andrew Jackson; Vice President Martin Van Buren; Senators John Tyler and James Buchanan; and Representatives James K. Polk, Millard Fillmore, and Franklin Pierce.

On November 4, 1991, Ronald and Nancy Reagan welcomed those attending the dedication of the Ronald Reagan Presidential Library in Simi Valley, California. Their guests that day included President George Bush, First Lady Barbara Bush, Jimmy and Roslynn Carter, Gerald and Betty Ford, Richard and Pat Nixon, and Lady Bird Johnson. These eleven current and former presidents and first ladies were the **most** ever to attend the same gathering.

SOURCE: Joseph Nathan Kane, *Facts About the Presidents*, Sixth Edition, H.W. Wilson Company, New York, 1993

The Most U.S. Presidents in One Year

THREE men held the office of U.S. president in 1841, the **most** ever to serve in a single year. Defeated in the 1840 election, Martin Van Buren left office in March and was succeeded by William Henry Harrison, who caught pneumonia during his inauguration and died on April 4. Harrison's vice president, John Tyler, then became president.

SOURCE: Joseph Nathan Kane, *Facts About the Presidents*, Sixth Edition, H.W. Wilson Company, New York, 1993

Re-elected the Most, Serving the Longest

FRANKLIN D. Roosevelt was first elected president in 1933, and then went on to be re-elected three more times, the **most** of any president. Through his inspirational oratory, Roosevelt communicated to the American public a strength of conviction, a clarity of purpose, and an unfailing optimism which drew them out of the Great Depression. Roosevelt's sense of social justice and his firmly held conviction that government had the responsibility to redress social and economic inequities led him to promote programs like the New Deal, of which Social Security was a major piece of legislation. "The test of our progress is not whether we add more to the abundance of those who have much, it is whether we provide enough for those who have too little," he said in his second inaugural address.

Roosevelt collapsed and died of a stroke on April 12, 1945, having served as president for twelve years and thirty-nine days, the most years of any American president. A constitutional amendment was later ratified limiting future presidents to two terms, so for now it looks like this record will stand.

SOURCE: Joseph Nathan Kane, *Facts About the Presidents,* Sixth Edition, H.W. Wilson Company, New York, 1993

Presidents Hitting the Most High and the Most Low

THE Gallup Presidential Approval Poll has been checking on the political health of U.S. presidents since 1947. All presidents get high approval ratings during the "honeymoon" immediately after their inauguration, but typically the ratings fall as disenchantment begins to set in.

The **most** consistently popular presidents have been John Kennedy (70 percent average), Franklin Roosevelt (68 percent average), and Dwight Eisenhower (65 percent average).

George Bush has the distinction of winning the **most** approval points of any president, and nearly the fewest. In March 1991, after the Persian Gulf War victory, Bush's soaring 89 percent approval rating far surpassed the prior record of 82 percent, held by John F. Kennedy. However, a sluggish economy in the summer of 1992 plunged Bush's approval to 30 percent, not far from the record low of 23 percent, shared by Presidents' Nixon and Truman.

SOURCE: Gallup Organization

Presidents and Their Most Unusual Pets

U.S. presidents and their families have certainly had their share of unusual pets. Thomas Jefferson had a trained mockingbird; John Quincy Adams, an alligator; William McKinley, a Mexican parrot; and Calvin Coolidge, a raccoon. During John F. Kennedy's presidency, Caroline Kennedy had a pony, which she named Macaroni. Theodore Roosevelt turned the White House into a veritable zoo. During his presidency, the home of the nation's first family was also home to bear cubs, a young lion, a macaw, a donkey, raccoons, snakes, cats, dogs, rats, and guinea pigs! Many presidents, however, have had more conventional pets. Lyndon and Lady Bird Johnson had two beagles, named Him and Her. Bill and Hillary Clinton brought their daughter Chelsea's cat, Socks, with them to the White House, despite the president's allergy. However, it is Millie, the beautiful dog owned by George and Barbara Bush, who earns the title of **most** popular presidential pet. The royalties for Millie's "as told to" book by Barbara Bush, were reportedly greater than her president-owner's $200,000 annual salary. Of course, Millie's earnings were donated to charity.

SOURCES: Margaret Truman, *White House Pets*, D. McKay Company, New York, 1969; Joseph Nathan Kane, *Facts About the Presidents*, Sixth Edition, H.W. Wilson Company, New York 1993

Republicans Have the Most Victories and the Most Consecutive Years

SINCE 1856, when the Republican Party nominated John C. Frémont as their first presidential candidate, Republicans have won the **most** presidential elections and have served as president for the **most** overall terms of office. A total of 15 Republicans have served 21 terms as president over 84 years. Just 9 Democratic presidents have been elected to 14 terms for a total of 56 years.

During that same period, Republicans have also held the office of president for the **most** consecutive years. Beginning with the inauguration of Abraham Lincoln on March 4, 1861, and ending on March 4, 1885, with the inauguration of Democrat Grover Cleveland, the U.S. had a Republican in the White House for 24 straight years. More recently, the longest consecutive occupancy of the White House was by the Democrats, beginning with the inauguration of Franklin D. Roosevelt on March 4, 1933, and lasting through Harry Truman's presidency, just under 20 years total, until Republican Dwight Eisenhower took office on January 20, 1953.

SOURCE: Joseph Nathan Kane, *Facts About the Presidents,* Sixth Edition, H.W. Wilson Company, New York, 1993

The Most Ballots Cast for the Nominee

EARLY presidential candidates were selected by political caucuses that met in secret. But the mystery and political intrigue behind who received each party's nomination for president and vice president didn't go away with the advent of national political conventions in 1830. Differences among the party members often boil to the surface during the conventions, giving rise to everything from shouting matches to fistfights on the convention floor. Delegates sometimes withhold their votes during early ballots, cast their votes for someone they know cannot win in order to block the leading candidate, or nominate someone for the sole purpose of enabling that person to give a speech.

The Democratic convention of 1924, which lasted an exhausting fourteen days, took the **most** ballots ever to nominate a presidential candidate. When the first ballot was taken, William Gibbs McAdoo of California received 431 votes, nearly twice that of the next-closest candidate, but far less than the 731 votes required. Voting continued until finally, on the 103rd ballot, John William Davis of West Virginia, who had only received 31 votes on the first ballot, was nominated with 844 votes. Davis ran unsuccessfully against Calvin Coolidge.

The president requiring the **most** ballots to secure his nomination was Democrat Franklin Pierce, who was finally nominated on the 49th ballot in 1852. Woodrow Wilson, another Democrat, is next, receiving his nomination on the 46th ballot at the 1912 convention. The Republican president who required the most ballots to win the nomination was James A. Garfield, who received his party's nomination on the 36th ballot in 1880.

SOURCE: Joseph Nathan Kane, *Facts About the Presidents,* Sixth Edition, H.W. Wilson Company, New York, 1993

Chicago Hosts the Most

CHICAGO, Illinois, has hosted the **most** Republican and Democratic national conventions of any city, with a grand total of 24 of the 82 conventions held since 1832. Of the 14 candidates nominated at the Republican conventions held there, 8 were elected president: Lincoln (1860), Grant (1868), Garfield (1880), Benjamin Harrison (1888), Theodore Roosevelt (1904), Taft (1908), Harding (1920), and Eisenhower (1952). Of the 6 candidates nominated at the 10 Democratic conventions held in Chicago, just 2 of them became president: Cleveland (1884 and 1892) and Franklin D. Roosevelt (1932, 1940, and 1944).

SOURCE: Joseph Nathan Kane, *Facts About the Presidents.* Sixth Edition, H.W. Wilson Company, New York, 1993

The Presidents Vetoing and Overridden the Most

ALTHOUGH the Constitution doesn't specifically use the word "veto," the president can refuse to sign into law any bills sent to him by Congress that don't advance his policies (or political life). No president in history has exercised this veto power more than Franklin D. Roosevelt. During his twelve years in office (1933 to 1945), Roosevelt vetoed 635 of the bills Congress sent to him, the **most** of any president, for an average of 53 vetoes each year, with Congress overriding just 9 of them. Roosevelt sent 372 bills back to Congress, but the Constitution also provides for a "pocket veto," meaning a president can simply ignore any bill sent to him ten days before Congress adjourns. Roosevelt also holds the record for the **most** "pocket vetoes," with a grand total of 263.

On an annual basis, though, it is Grover Cleveland who vetoed the **most** legislation. During his eight years in office (1885–1889 and 1893–1897), Cleveland vetoed 584 bills, or an average of 73 each year he was in office.

Congress, of course, can override a presidential veto by a two-thirds vote of each house. The president to have the **most** vetoes overridden by Congress was Andrew Johnson. During his presidency (1865–1869), Johnson vetoed just 28 bills, but 15 of them were overridden by Congress.

SOURCE: Joseph Nathan Kane, *Facts About the Presidents,* Sixth Edition, H.W. Wilson Company, New York, 1993

Birthplace of the Most Vice Presidents

WHILE more presidents were born in Virginia than any other state, New York can claim the title of birthplace of the **most** vice presidents. In fact, the number of vice presidents born in New York is more than any two other states combined. The eight vice presidents born there were George Clinton (who served under both Jefferson and Madison), Daniel D. Tompkins (under Monroe), Martin Van Buren (under Jackson), Millard Fillmore (under Taylor), Schuyler Colfax (under Grant), William Wheeler (under Hayes), Theodore Roosevelt (under McKinley), and James Sherman (under Taft). Of the fourteen vice presidents who went on to become president, three of them were from New York: Van Buren, Fillmore, and Theodore Roosevelt.

SOURCE: Joseph Nathan Kane, *Facts About the Presidents,* Sixth Edition, H.W. Wilson Company, New York, 1993

The Most Musically Gifted Vice President

VICE President Charles Gates Dawes, who served during Calvin Coolidge's second term, wrote the **most** hit songs of any U.S. vice president. A classical composer, Dawes wrote Melody in A Major in 1912. In 1951 Carl Sigman added lyrics to the tune, and in 1958 Tommy Edwards recorded "It's All in the Game." The song soon reached number one on the pop charts and has been recorded by a number of artists over the years.

The Most Cabinet Jobs

SERVING in four different cabinet posts under two presidents, Elliot L. Richardson has held the **most** different posts of any cabinet officer. During Richard Nixon's presidency, he served as secretary of health, education and welfare, secretary of defense and as attorney general. He was also secretary of commerce under Gerald Ford from 1976 to 1977.

SOURCE: Joseph Nathan Kane, *Facts About the Presidents,* Sixth Edition, H.W. Wilson Company, New York, 1993

Cabinet Member Employed by the Most Presidents

THOUGH he held only two separate cabinet positions, Henry L. Stimson was a member of the cabinet during five different administrations, the **most** of any cabinet officer. He was secretary of war from 1911 to 1913 under Presidents William Taft and Woodrow Wilson, and held the same position from 1940 to 1945 under Franklin D. Roosevelt and Harry Truman. He also served as secretary of state under Herbert Hoover from 1929 to 1933.

SOURCE: *The World Almanac and Book of Facts 1997.* Robert Famighetti, editor, World Almanac Books, New Jersey, 1996

The Most-Experienced Cabinet Member

THE cabinet member to spend the **most** years in office was James Wilson of Iowa. Wilson took office as secretary of agriculture under William McKinley from March 5, 1897, and remained in that post through McKinley's first and second administrations, Theodore Roosevelt's two administrations, and William Taft's administration. He was finally replaced with a new Woodrow Wilson appointee on March 6, 1913. Overall, he held his cabinet post for sixteen consecutive years and one day.

SOURCE: Joseph Nathan Kane, *Facts About the Presidents,* Sixth Edition, H.W. Wilson Company, New York, 1993

Party Holding the Most Congressional Seats

THE Republican Party was formed in 1854 in opposition to the expansion of slavery, mainly by Northerners from the two major political parties of the time, the Democrats and the Whigs. But which party has controlled the House of Representatives and Senate the **most** since then? Of the 71 elections between 1854 and 1994, the Democrats retained a majority of seats in the House of Representatives 42 times, and the Republicans, 29. The situation is reversed in the Senate, however, with Republicans holding the majority 38 times, and the Democrats, 33.

SOURCE: Joseph Nathan Kane, *Facts About the Presidents,* Sixth Edition, H.W. Wilson Company, New York, 1993

Most Aged Senator

U.S. Senator Strom Thurmond was reelected to the U.S. Senate in November 1996 at the age of 93 years, 11 months.

SOURCE: Senate of the United States

Records Set for the Most Years in Congress

SINCE the First Congress in 1879, over 11,000 men and women have served as senators or representatives. However, no one has served longer in Congress than Arizona Democrat Carl Hayden (1877–1972). Hayden's record 42 years in the Senate from 1927 to 1969 is the **most** years of service by any senator. Combined with his 15 years in the House of Representatives from 1912 through 1926, Hayden represented Arizona for almost 57 years, the **most** total years of service in Congress.

SOURCE: Congress of the United States

Mississippi Democrat Jamie Whitten was first elected to the House of Representatives in November 1941. When he finished his last term of office at the end of 1993, he had served for the **most** years of any representative, a total of 53 years.

SOURCE: *Congressional Quarterly Weekly Report,* Sept. 16, 1995

Among women who have served in Congress, Maine Republican Margaret Chase Smith served for the **most** years in the Senate. During her 24 years as a senator, from 1949 to 1973, Smith also set a record for the **most** consecutive roll-call votes. Smith cast 2,941 votes between 1955 and September 7, 1968, when she was hospitalized and missed one vote. Her dedication is even more remarkable considering that it wasn't until 1993 that a new Senate women's room was opened to accommodate a growing number of women senators—eight as of the 1994 election.

SOURCE: *People,* June 12, 1995 and *Congressional Quarterly Weekly Report,* June 3, 1995

Voting the Most

ON average, members of the Senate and the House have good to excellent voting records. In 1992, the average senator voted 97 percent of the time; the average House member, 95 percent. The record for the most consecutive votes in the House is held by Kentucky Democrat William H. Natcher (1909–94), who cast 18,401 straight votes over forty years without missing a single recorded vote, often at considerable personal sacrifice.

SOURCE: *Congressional Quarterly Weekly Report,* December 31, 1994

The **most** consecutive votes in the Senate were cast by Wisconsin Democrat William Proxmire, who didn't miss a single roll-call vote during the final 21 years of his 30-year career.

SOURCE: *The New York Times*, Aug. 28, 1987

The Most Years as Speaker of the House

LEGENDARY Texas Democrat Sam Rayburn served the **most** years as Speaker of the House, a total of over 17 years between 1940 and 1961. Another Democrat, Thomas P. "Tip" O'Neill Jr. of Massachusetts, served the **most** continuous years as Speaker, 10 years from 1977 to 1987.

SOURCE: Congress of the United States

Mosts in the World of the Filibuster

MEMBERS of the Senate are allowed nearly unlimited debate on bills. When they use this benefit to delay or block action on a bill, it becomes a filibuster. In August 1957, legendary South Carolina Democrat (and now Republican) Strom Thurmond spoke for a record 24 hours and 19 minutes against proposed civil rights legislation, interrupted only by the swearing in of a new senator. This was the **most** lengthy filibuster in Senate history, but not the most lengthy continuous filibuster. Oregon Democrat Wayne Morris (1900–74) spoke for a straight 22 hours and 26 minutes on the Tidelands Oil Bill on April 24–25, 1953, without resuming his seat.

SOURCE: Senate of the United States

The Most Bills, the Most Laws

MEMBERS of the 90th Congress (1967–1969) introduced the **most** bills ever, a total of 26,460. Of all these bills, just 1,002 were passed into law. The 84th Congress (1955–1957) enacted the **most** public laws, a record 1,028.

SOURCE: U.S. House of Representatives

Spending the Most to Win and Lose

IF you'd like to run for the U.S. Senate, be prepared to spend somewhere between $800,000 and $14 million in order to win, and twice that to lose! If the 1994 Senate race between California Democrat Dianne Feinstein and Republican congressman Michael Huffington is any example, spending more money doesn't always guarantee a win.

Two years earlier, in 1992, Feinstein was elected to fill the two remaining years of the Senate seat vacated by Republican Pete Wilson when he resigned to become governor of California after beating her in the 1990 gubernatorial race. That same year, Huffington won his House seat after having spent $5.4 million in the **most** expensive congressional campaign ever.

By 1994, during the senatorial campaign, Huffington began attacking Feinstein's support of President Clinton's health plan and later her opposition of California's Proposition 187, which would deny public services to illegal immigrants. Feinstein countered by revealing that Huffington had once employed an undocumented alien, but the Huffington campaign soon disclosed that Feinstein had an illegal immigrant working for her in 1980. When the ballots were counted in November, Feinstein had been reelected by a margin of just 165,562 votes. She had spent over $14 million to win 3,977,063 votes, at a cost of $3.62 per vote, making hers the **most** expensive winning Senate campaign of all time (but not the **most** expensive per vote total, a record that belongs to Jay Rockefeller). But Huffington had spent just under $30 million, more than twice what Feinstein had spent, to win 3,811,501 votes, at a cost of $7.86 per vote, and $28.4 million of that was his own money, the **most** ever contributed by a candidate to his own Senate campaign. Even after the votes were tallied, Huffington still refused to concede the election. But following allegations of election fraud, he finally gave up in February, after having waged the **most** expensive losing Senate campaign of all time.

SOURCES: *Esquire,* October 1994 and *Newsweek,* 11/7/94; *New York Times,* 11/8/94; *The World Almanac and Book of Facts* 1995, World Almanac Books, 1994

Spending the Most per Vote to Win That Senate Seat

JOHN D. "Jay" Rockefeller IV moved to West Virginia as a young VISTA volunteer in 1964. Two years later, he entered state politics as a Democrat and won election to the West Virginia House of Delegates. In 1968 he won the office of West Virginia's secretary of state, where he served through 1973.

Rockefeller lost his first bid for the governorship in 1972, then spent the next few years serving as president of West Virginia Wesleyan College. In 1976, he ran for governor again, and this time won by nearly two to one over his opponent. Rockefeller took no chances with his 1980 re-election campaign, spending almost $12 million on a media blitz that won him a second term.

In a state that restricts its governors to two consecutive terms, it seemed certain that Rockefeller would run for the Senate at the end of his term, and he did. But in 1984, West Virginia had the country's highest unemployment rate and was facing a slow-down in its largest industries— steel, glass, and coal. Under these circumstances, Rockefeller's election seemed far from assured when he entered the campaign. Bolstered by Ronald Reagan's popularity at the top of the Republican ticket, Rockefeller's opponent, John Raese, was running nearly even in the polls at election time. However, Rockefeller won the election, having launched another $12 million campaign, more than ten times Raese's $1.15 million. To win his 374,233 votes, Rockefeller had spent a record $32.21 per vote, the **most** ever for each vote in a winning Senate campaign.

Closer Races Than Most, If Not All

WHO says your vote doesn't count? It can't be called a victory, but the 1974 Senate race in New Hampshire between Republican Louis Wyman and Democrat John Durkin resulted in the **most** narrow margin ever in a Senate race. When the ballots were counted, Wyman led Durkin by just 2 votes, 110,926 to 110,924. Durkin challenged the results in the Senate, and after a long, heated dispute, the Senate finally declared itself unable to determine a winner. In a special election held the next year, Durkin won the Senate post with 53.6 percent of the vote.

The 1912 race between Democrat Key Pittman of Nevada and three challengers resulted in the **most** narrow winning margin of victory ever in a Senate election. Pittman won by just 89 votes and was elected to the Senate by the smallest number of votes ever, just 7,942.

The Senate Seats Costing the Most

How much does it cost to run the U.S. Senate? According to the *Report of the Secretary of the Senate* for the year from October 1994 through September 1995, salaries and expenses amounted to just over $433.4 million. This included $16.4 million in salaries for the vice president and the senators, $33.4 million in salaries for Senate officers and employees (including the Senate chaplain, the secretary of the senate, and the sergeant at arms), just under $63.2 million in salaries and expenses for Senate committees (like the Armed Services, Appropriations, and Judiciary Committees), and $33.1 million in salaries for the Capitol Police. But by far the biggest chunk of the money, $199 million, went to pay the staff salaries and operating expenses of the senators' Washington and field offices. Senators from more populous states are allocated larger budgets in order to maintain more field offices in the states they represent, so it's no surprise that the senators who spend the **most** to maintain their offices are from California, Texas, New York, and Florida.

Following are the **most** expensive Senate offices that taxpayers maintain. Figures are based on the six months from October 1, 1994, to September 1995.

	Senator	State	Salaries (dollars)	Expenses (dollars)	Total (dollars)
1.	Barbara Boxer	CA	2,388,494	140,638	2,529,132
2.	Dianne Feinstein	CA	2,327,506	123,841	2,451,347
3.	Phil Gramm	TX	2,064,943	150,352	2,215,295
4.	Alfonse D'Amato	NY	2,004,413	168,655	2,173,067
5.	Daniel Patrick Moynihan	NY	1,995,349	173,212	2,168,561
6.	Kay Baily Hutchison	TX	1,876,363	139,439	2,015,802
7.	Arlen Specter	PA	1,860,046	69,303	1,929,349
8.	Carol Moseley-Braun	IL	1,760,618	145,114	1,905,732
9.	Connie Mack	FL	1,821,181	83,660	1,904,840
10.	Paul Simon	IL	1,772,968	92,949	1,865,916

SOURCE: *Report of the Secretary of the Senate*

PAC Mosts

FEDERAL law prohibits corporations and labor unions from giving money directly to political campaigns, so they and other special-interest groups form political action committees (PACs) to provide funds for candidates whose ideas and policies they support. According to the Federal Election Commission, today over 4,600 PACs contribute to Democratic and Republican candidates, especially those who advocate particular stands on issues like abortion, gun control, or welfare.

Whatever your politics, you're likely to find a PAC supporting candidates who agree with you on important issues. During the two years 1993–94, more than 3,000 PACs contributed over $189 million to candidates. The largest portion, $136 million, went to House candidates, with the remaining $53 million going to Senate candidates. Incumbents continued to receive the bulk of PAC contributions, a full 73 percent, compared to 10 percent for challengers and 17 percent for those running for open seats. Contributions to Democratic candidates far outweighed those to Republicans 62.4 percent to 37.6 percent ($117.5 million to $71.5 million), with just $322,985 going to support third-party candidates.

Corporate-sponsored PACs contributed the **most** to candidates in 1993–1994, and the following list shows the largest contributor to federal candidates in each category from January 1993 to December 1994.

1. **Corporate:**   1,461 PACs contributed a total of $69,581,799. United Parcel Service (UPSPAC) was the largest contributor, giving $2,647,113.

2. **Trade/Member/Health:**   628 PACs contributed a total of $52,799,649. American Medical Association was the largest contributor, giving $2,386,947.

3. **Labor:**   255 PACs contributed a total of $41,825,927. American Federation of State, County, and Municipal Employees was the largest contributor, giving $2,529,682.

4. **Non-Connected Organization:**   500 PACs contributed a total of $18,049,730. The National Committee for an Effective Congress was the largest contributor, giving $775,126.

5. **Corporate, Without Stock:**   112 PACs contributed a total of $4,071,108. The Aircraft Owners and Pilots Association was the largest contributor, giving $481,100.

6. **Cooperative:**   50 PACs contributed a total of $3,042,328. The Committee for Thorough Agricultural Political Education of Associated Milk Producers, Inc., was the largest contributor, giving $788,231.

Totaling all of the above amounts to 3,006 PACs coming up with a combined sum of $189,370,541.

SOURCE: Federal Election Commission

Among the 3,006 PACs that contributed to candidates in 1993–94, only 30—just 1 percent of the total—contributed in excess of $1 million each. Of those 30 PACs, 16 are sponsored by labor organizations, 12 by trade/membership associations, and 2 by corporations. However, contributions from those 30 organizations equaled 25.5 percent of the total dollars, or $48.2 of the $189 million.

Here are the 10 PACs that contributed the **most** to federal candidates between January 1993 and December 1994.

	PAC Name	Category	Total Contribution
1.	United Parcel Service (UPSPAC)	Corporate	$2,647,113
2.	American Federation of State, County, and Municipal Employees	Labor	$2,529,682
3.	Democratic Republican Independent Voter Education Committee	Labor	$2,487,152
4.	American Medical Association Political Action Committee	Trade/Member	$2,386,947
5.	National Education Association Political Action Committee	Labor	$2,260,850
6.	Association of Trial Lawyers of America Political Action Committee	Trade/Member	$2,164,035
7.	UAW-V-CAP (United Auto Workers Voluntary Community Action Program)	Labor	$2,147,190
8.	National Rifle Association Political Victory Fund	Trade/Member	$1,853,038
9.	Realtors Political Action Committee	Trade/Member	$1,851,978
10.	Dealers Election Action Committee of the National Automobile Dealers Association	Trade/Member	$1,832,570

SOURCE: Federal Election Commission

Mosts Among Women in Government

THE world's parliament with the **most** women members is the German Parliament, with 177 out of its 672 MPs being women. However, the country with the **most** women as a percentage of its total MPs is Sweden. Of Sweden's 349 members of Parliament, 141 of them are women, representing 40.4 percent of the total. With 62 women out of 651 MPs, the British Parliament has just 9.5 percent.

Overall, only eighteen countries have more than 20 percent women MPs. The top ten, those with the **most** by percentage, are:

	Country	Women MPs	Total MPs	Percent Women
1.	Sweden	141	349	40.4
2.	Norway	65	165	39.4
3.	Denmark	60	179	33.5
4.	Finland	67	200	33.4
5.	Netherlands	47	150	31.3
6.	Seychelles	9	33	27.3
7.	Germany	177	672	26.3
8.	Mozambique	63	250	25.2
9.	South Africa	100	400	25.0
10.	Iceland	15	63	23.8

Eleven Women Ministers in Sweden Is a Most

THE country with the **most** women cabinet members is Sweden. Currently, there are eleven women ministers out of a total of twenty-two.

SOURCE: *The Guinness Book of Records 1996,* Bantam, 1996

The States with the Most Women Legislators

A 1994 study by the National Women's Political Caucus determined that a candidate's sex did not affect his or her chances of winning an election. The reason there aren't more women politicians, the study found, is that there are so few women candidates. Compounding this is the fact that the overwhelming bias in politics is in favor of incumbent candidates, the majority of whom are men, meaning that men will continue to enjoy that advantage for some time. However, the study showed that when women run, particularly for open seats, they win as often as men. In 1994, women represented 20.6 percent of state legislators, or 1,529 of the total 7,424. This is a vast improvement over the situation twenty-five years ago, when only 4.0 percent of all state representatives were women.

The states with the **most** women legislators are listed below by the percentage they represent in each state's legislature.

State	Percent Women Legislators
1. Washington	39.6
2. Colorado	35.0
3. Vermont	33.9
4. New Hampshire	33.5
5. Arizona	33.3
6. Maine	31.7
7. Idaho	30.5
8. Kansas	29.1
9. Wisconsin	27.3
10. Nevada	27.0

SOURCE: National Women's Political Caucus

The World Leaders Targeted the Most

BEING a head of state can be hazardous to your health! In the two hundred years between 1718 and 1918, the **most** frequently assassinated heads of state were the czars of Russia. Four czars and two heirs apparent were assassinated, and there were numerous failed attempts. Charles de Gaulle, president of France from 1958 to 1969, was said to have survived more than thirty-one plots against his life, the **most** known failed assassination attempts against any head of state. A fictionalized account of one such attempt against de Gaulle was presented in Frederick Forsyth's *The Day of the Jackal.*

SOURCE: *The Guinness Book of Records 1996,* Bantam Books, 1996

The Most Likely Successor to the British Throne

ELIZABETH II began her reign as queen of England upon the death of her father, King George VI, in 1952. Although the question of who will succeed her to become Britain's next monarch has been the subject of tabloid newspaper and television headlines for years, the rules governing succession to the crown have been in effect for centuries. Being born out of wedlock or becoming a Roman Catholic (for example, by marrying into that faith) are the only two real disqualifiers. But social and political pressures can also take their toll, as they did with King Edward VIII, who abdicated the throne in 1936 when it became clear that he could not marry the woman he loved, an American divorcée named Wallis Simpson, and remain king.

The British royal line of succession begins with the monarch's eldest son, then that son's sons in descending order by age, followed by that son's daughters. Next is the monarch's second-eldest son, followed by his sons and daughters, and so on, ending with the monarch's daughters and her children. Following all the children and their offspring are the monarch's brothers and their children, then finally the sisters and their children, and so on. The line then continues with uncles, aunts, and cousins.

The ten individuals listed below are the **most** likely to succeed Queen Elizabeth II to the British throne.

1. HRH The Prince of Wales (Prince Charles). First son of Queen Elizabeth II. Born Nov. 14, 1948.

2. HRH Prince William of Wales. First son of Prince Charles. Born June 21, 1982.

3. HRH Prince Henry of Wales. Second son of Prince Charles. Born Sept. 15, 1984.

4. HRH The Duke of York (Prince Andrew). Second son of Queen Elizabeth II. Born Feb. 19, 1960.

5. HRH Princess Beatrice of York. First daughter of Prince Andrew. Born Aug. 8, 1988.

6. HRH Princess Eugenie of York. Second daughter of Prince Andrew. Born Mar. 23, 1990.

7. HRH Prince Edward. Third son of Queen Elizabeth II. Born Mar. 10, 1964.

8. HRH The Princess Royal (Princess Anne). Daughter of Queen Elizabeth II, the highest-ranking officially divorced heir to the throne. Born Aug. 15, 1950.

9. Peter Phillips. The highest-ranking commoner. Son of Princess Anne. Born Nov. 15, 1977.

10. Zara Phillips. Daughter of Princess Anne. Born May 15, 1981.

SOURCES: John Cannon and Ralph Griffiths, *The Oxford Illustrated History of the British Monarchy,* Oxford University Press, N.Y., 1988; Peter Fearon, *Behind the Palace Walls,* Carol Publishing Group, Inc., 1993 by Boron Hall, Inc.

The Most Legislators for the Most People

NOT surprisingly, the world's **most** populous country also has the world's largest legislative body. The National People's Congress of the People's Republic of China has the **most** members of any legislative assembly in the world. A total of 2,978 members representing a single party are indirectly elected to serve for a five-year term of office.

SOURCE: Consulate of China

Fixing an Election the Most

HOW do you tell if an election's been "fixed"? One good clue is when the number of votes exceeds the total number of eligible voters. The 1927 election of Liberian president D. B. King (1875–1961) is certainly the **most** crooked election of all time. King was returned to office with an official margin of victory over his opponent, Thomas J. R. Faulkner, of 234,000 votes, 15.5 times greater than the entire electorate.

SOURCE: United Nations

The Legislators Making the Most

JAPANESE legislators are the **most** highly paid in the world. Including monthly allowances and bonuses, Prime Minister Tomichi Murayama receives an annual salary of 38,463,360 yen, the equivalent of $343,000. Japan's Diet (Parliament) consists of a House of Representatives, with 511 members elected for four years, and a House of Councillors, with 252 members, half of whom are elected every three years for six-year terms. Each member of the Diet receives an annual salary of 23,633,565 yen, or $211,000, including bonuses, which is more than the $200,000 salary of the U.S. president.

SOURCE: Consulate of Japan

The Sheriff Makes the Most

WITH an annual salary of $212,259 per year, Los Angeles County sheriff Sherman Block may just be the U.S.'s **most** highly paid public official. "I don't feel any need to apologize," he says. "I'm worth it. I've never accepted my paycheck with my head down." Block earns more than President Clinton, whose annual salary is $200,000, and more than California's Governor Wilson, who earns $120,000 a year. In fact, Block earns 43 percent more than the nation's loftiest law-enforcement officer, U.S. Attorney General Janet Reno, whose annual salary is $148,400.

A December 1995 *Los Angeles Times* analysis of the salaries paid by the nation's largest county government shows that the ten highest paid L.A. County officials earn between $150,000 and Block's $212,259 per year. An estimated 1,225 of the county's 85,000 employees earn over $100,000 in base salary alone. Three-quarters of those earning these six-figure salaries are either doctors who work in the county's health services department, or lawyers and judges who work in the county's justice system. How did this happen in a county facing a budget crisis so severe that its largest public hospital, County USC Medical Center, was on the verge of shutting down? Well, in 1987, the county moved from a civil-service-based compensation program to a performance-based system more commonly used in corporations. The theory was that the county could neither attract nor keep good department heads or managers if it couldn't pay them what they might earn in the private sector. Merit raises of from 20.4 to 34 percent between 1988 and 1995 gradually allowed the salaries of even second-tier administrators to increase to these levels. In November 1994, voters approved a charter amendment allowing county supervisors to lower the salaries of the sheriff, district attorney, and county assessor when those offices are vacated. Then in July 1995, county supervisors voted to replace the performance-based pay system with one in which employee evaluations aren't directly linked to raises. Still, the county anticipates years of holding the line on raises and other benefits like transportation allowances before the salary crisis is over.

SOURCE: *The Los Angeles Times*, 12/95

Mosts
from the World of
War

NATURAL DISASTERS OCCUR, and there is little we can do about them other than to pay attention to and respect our surroundings. Man-made disasters occur because of human error or equipment failures or some combination of the two. But since the dawn of man, there have been wars, and the resultant casualties are staggering. Consider some of the following **mosts** and remember that each number represents an aggregate of individuals—people like you and me.

Also in this section you'll see what armies around the world have the **most** recruits and what countries spend the **most** and even who makes the **most** in the U.S. armed services.

The World's War Dead

THE following wars have been the **most** devastating the human race has ever waged. The number of deaths are utterly monstrous. Let's hope that we are never faced with such catastrophe again.

	Date	War	Involvement	Deaths
1.	1939–1945	World War II	28 countries	15,843,000
2.	1914–1918	World War I	15 countries	8,545,800
3.	1950–1953	Korean War	16 countries	1,893,100
4.	A.D. 66–70	Jewish Wars of the Roman Empire		1,000,000
5.	1701–1714	War of the Spanish Succession	France–Holy Roman Empire states	1,000,000
6.	1937–1941	Sino-Japanese War	Japan-China	1,000,000
7.	1861–1865	Civil War	US	647,528
8.	1936–1939	Civil War	Spanish	611,000
9.	1961–1973	Vietnam War	US-Vietnam-China	546,000

	Date	War	Involvement	Deaths
10.	1813–1814	The Wars of Liberation	Russia, France and 13 other countries	545,000

Some estimates of overall deaths of combatants and non-combatants in World War II reach as high as 55,000,000.

Of interest is the fact that the United States has been involved in five of the bloodiest wars of all times.

SOURCE: Jay Robert Nash, *Darkest Hours* (1976)

World War I Casualties

EVERYONE suffered during World War I, but what country suffered the **most** in terms of casualties and deaths?

	Country	Mobilized Forces	Killed or Died	Wounded	POW/MIA	Total Casualties
1.	Russia	12,000,000	1,700,000	4,950,000	2,500,000	9,150,000
2.	Germany	11,000,000	1,773,700	4,216,058	1,152,800	7,142,558
3.	Austria-Hungary	7,800,000	1,200,000	3,620,000	2,200,000	7,020,000
4.	France	8,410,000	1,357,800	4,266,000	537,000	6,160,800
5.	Britain	8,904,467	908,371	2,090,212	191,652	3,190,235
6.	Italy	5,615,000	650,000	947,000	600,000	2,197,000
7.	Turkey	2,850,000	325,000	400,000	250,000	975,000
8.	Romania	750,000	335,706	120,000	80,000	535,706
9.	Serbia	707,343	45,000	133,148	152,958	331,106
10.	U.S.	4,734,991	116,516	204,002	—	320,518

The U.S. casualty figures would undoubtedly have been higher if it had joined the war from its inception, as several of the countries above had.

SOURCE: *The 1996 Information Please Almanac*

World War II Casualties

ONLY twenty years after the signing of the Armistice, a second, even greater conflict was beginning—World War II. Read on to see again what countries suffered the **most** in terms of casualties.

	Country	Troops	Killed	Wounded	Total Casualties
1.	U.S.S.R.	n/a	6,115,000	14,012,000	20,127,000
2.	Germany	20,000,000	3,250,000	7,250,000	10,500,000
3.	China	17,250,521	1,324,516	1,762,006	3,086,522
4.	Japan	9,700,000	1,270,000	140,000	1,410,000
5.	Poland	n/a	664,000	530,000	1,194,000
6.	U.S.	16,112,566	291,557	670,846	962,403
7.	Yugoslavia	3,741,000	305,000	425,000	730,000
8.	Britain	5,896,000	357,116	369,267	726,383
9.	Austria	800,000	280,000	350,117	630,117
10.	France	n/a	201,568	400,000	601,568

n/a = not available

Other countries participating in the war that also suffered casualties include Australia, Belgium, Brazil, Bulgaria, Canada, Czechoslovakia, Denmark, Finland, Greece, Hungary, India, Italy, the Netherlands, New Zealand, Norway, Romania, and South Africa. Thus World War II has the distinction of having had the **most** participants in any war ever. And so much of this brought about by one very ambitious man—Adolf Hitler.

SOURCE: *The 1996 Information Please Almanac*

Casualties in Major U.S. Wars

THE following is based on what wars, foreign and at home, caused the **most** American deaths. We could rank according to what war the **most** American troops participated in, but historically the **most** representative number of a war is the casualties caused by it. As you can see, however, American troop involvement was at its **most** in World War II, followed in order by Vietnam, Korea, World War I, and the Civil War.

	War	Troops	Killed	Wounded	Total Casualties
1.	World War II Dec. 7, 1941– Dec. 31, 1946	16,353,659	407,316	670,846	1,078,162
2.	Civil War (Union) 1861–65	2,213,363	364,511	281,881	646,392

War	Troops	Killed	Wounded	Total Casualties
(Confederate) 1861–66	600,000– 1,500,000	133,821	—	—
3. World War I Apr. 6, 1917– Nov. 11, 1918	4,743,826	116,708	204,002	320,710
4. Vietnam War Aug. 4, 1964– Jan. 27, 1973	8,744,000	58,168	153,303	211,471
5. Korean War June 25, 1950– July 27, 1953	5,764,143	33,651	103,284	136,935
6. Mexican War 1846–48	78,718	13,283	4,152	17,435
7. Revolutionary War 1775–83	184,000– 250,000	4,044	6,188	—
8. War of 1812 1812–15	286,730	2,260	4,505	—
9. Spanish- American War 1898	306,760	2,446	1,662	4,108
10. Persian Gulf War 1991	467,539	293	467	760

You'll note that some of the above numbers do not match corresponding numbers for the same information in other areas of this chapter. That is because the above account for all deaths, on the battlefield and otherwise, plus Coast Guard participation (active in World Wars I and II, Korea, and Vietnam, with deaths in all but the Korean War), whereas other numbers take into account only battlefield deaths and sometimes discount Coast Guard involvement.

Accurate statistics do not exist for Confederate forces, thus wounded and total casualties figures have been left blank.

The Korean War death and total casualties figures are higher, and the U.S. Department of Defense is reestimating U.S. deaths that occurred off the battlefield.

No figures exist for an exact or even an authoritative approximation of the number of Americans who died off the battlefield during and due to the Revolutionary War. For this reason, total casualties has been left blank. The same case exists with the War of 1812.

SOURCE: U.S. Department of Defense

The Most Troops

WHAT countries around the world have the **most** active-duty troops? You may not be surprised. Figures are based on the 1994 year.

	Country	Active Troops	Reserve Troops
1.	China	2,930,000	1,200,000
2.	Russia	1,714,000	20,000,000
3.	U.S.	1,650,500	2,048,000
4.	India	1,265,000	300,000
5.	No. Korea	1,128,000	540,000
6.	So. Korea	633,000	4,500,000
7.	Pakistan	587,000	313,000
8.	Vietnam	572,000	3,000,000– 4,000,000
9.	Ukraine	517,000	1,000,000
10.	Iran	513,000	350,000
11.	Turkey	503,800	952,300
12.	Egypt	440,000	254,000
13.	Taiwan	425,000	1,657,500
14.	France	409,600	339,800
15.	Syria	408,000	400,000
16.	Iraq	382,000	650,000
17.	Germany	367,300	442,700
18.	Brazil	336,800	1,115,000
19.	Italy	322,300	584,000
20.	Myanmar	286,000	n/a

n/a = not available

SOURCE: International Institute for Strategic Studies, *The Military Balance, 1994–95* (published by Brassey's U.K.)

Heavy Recruiting

WE'VE looked at which countries in the world have the **most** active-duty troops. But let's consider which armies have the **most** troops per capita, that is, which countries call up or employ the highest proportion of their population in the military.

	Country	Percent of Population in Military
1.	No. Korea	5.30
2.	Israel	3.68
3.	Syria	2.85
4.	Jordan	2.62
5.	Oman	2.13
6.	Iraq	2.12
7.	Taiwan	2.10
8.	Greece	2.03
9.	Singapore	1.98
10.	Libya	1.74
11.	So. Korea	1.68
12.	Cuba	1.60
13.	Russia	1.51
14.	Vietnam	1.19
15.	Turkey	1.13

SOURCE: U.S. Arms Control and Disarmament Agency

The Most Military Sales

THE U.S. is one of the **most** prolific, if not *the* **most** prolific, arms manufacturers in the world. The American companies that make armaments sell not only to the U.S. government but to many foreign governments as well. Under very tight restrictions and government monitoring, the U.S. defense industry made the **most** sales in 1993 to the following countries.

	Country	1993 Sales (in dollars)	Percent Distribution
1.	Saudi Arabia	3,701,000,000	32.0
2.	Egypt	1,340,000,000	11.6

3.	Kuwait	913,000,000	7.9
4.	Israel	780,000,000	6.7
5.	Turkey	751,000,000	6.5
6.	Taiwan	731,000,000	6.3
7.	Germany	347,000,000	3.0
8.	Japan	327,000,000	2.8
9.	So. Korea	315,000,000	2.7
10.	Australia	245,000,000	2.1

SOURCE: U.S. Defense Security Assistance Agency, *Foreign Military Sales, Foreign Military Construction Sales, and Military Assistance Facts*

What Joe Is Paid

WE'VE all heard of our troops being referred to as "Joe," but do you know much about Joe's average pay? If you're a good guesser or know anything about the military, then you know that a general or admiral makes the **most,** but pay is also rated on how long a Joe has been in the service. Let's take a look at what any of the following would be paid at twenty years of service.

Commissioned Officers

	Army/Marines/Air Force	Navy	Salary
1.	General	Admiral	$108,201.60
2.	Lieutenant General	Vice Admiral	95,000.40
3.	Major General	Rear Admiral	90,014.40
4.	Brigadier General	Commodore	81,396.00
5.	Colonel	Captain	62,326.80
6.	Lieutenant Colonel	Commander	56,382.00
7.	Major	Lieutenant Commander	48,787.20
8.	Captain	Lieutenant	42,195.60
9.	First Lieutenant	Lieutenant Junior Grade	31,305.60
10.	Second Lieutenant	Ensign	24,696.00

Among enlisted personnel, a private in the Army or Marines is equivalent to a seaman recruit in the Navy or an airman basic in the Air Force. If after twenty years of service they had not advanced beyond this initiation grade, their yearly salary would be $10,252.80. If, however, a recruit had advanced to the top grade of command sergeant major or sergeant major in the Army, a master chief petty officer in the Navy, a sergeant major or master gunnery sergeant in the Marines, or a chief master sergeant in the Air Force, the recruit would make $34,268.40.

Other benefits exist in the services, though the above accounts for cash payments only.

SOURCE: U.S. Department of Defense

The Congressional Medal of Honor

THE Congressional Medal of Honor is the United States' highest military award and is given to recipients for conduct "above and beyond the call of duty." Often, the medal is awarded posthumously, including the restoration of it to William F. "Buffalo Bill" Cody in 1989 for his newly recognized scouting activities during the Indian Wars. He is perhaps the **most** famous recipient.

The Medal of Honor was awarded the **most** times during the following U.S. wars.

	War/Conflict/Other Period	Number of Medals Awarded
1.	Civil War	1,520
2.	World War II	433
3.	Indian Wars (1861–1898)	428
4.	Vietnam War	239
5.	Korean War	131
6.	World War I	124
7.	Spanish-American War	109
8.	Peacetime (1871–1898)	103
9.	Philippines-Samoa	91
10.	Boxer Rebellion	59

SOURCE: The Congressional Medal of Honor Society, Mount Pleasant, South Carolina

The Most Deaths in a Family Leads to a Better Policy

ON November 13, 1942, during the Battle of Guadalcanal, Frank, Joseph, Albert, George, and Matthew Sullivan of Waterloo, Iowa, were killed when a Japanese submarine sank the ship on which they served, the USS *Juneau*. The five Sullivan brothers were the most blood relatives ever killed while serving in a combat zone on the same U.S. naval vessel. This incident caused the U.S. military to change its policy regarding family members being assigned to the same unit or the same ship during military combat operations. Today only one member of a family may serve in an individual combat unit at any given time. However, there are no restrictions on family members being assigned to the same non-combat unit. A film, *The Fighting Sullivans*, was made about the brothers, and the Navy recently christened the USS *The Sullivans* in New York.

Mosts
from the World of
Natural and Man-made Disasters

FROM THE BEGINNING of man's time on earth, we have had to brave the elements. Part of that has been surviving natural disasters. And that hasn't changed. We are still combating such forces as earthquakes, pestilence, floods, tornadoes, and volcanic eruptions. But with education, information, and early warning devices, we are learning to control our losses, though it remains that we are confronted daily with the earth's awesome power.

Compounding this is the fact that our world has grown more complicated, and we are finding ourselves confronting disasters brought on by ourselves and our evolving technologies. There are now shipwrecks and airplane crashes, chemical leaks and gas-pipeline explosions, fires and mining disasters. And likely there will always be human and mechanical error, so these too, like natural catastrophes, are here to stay.

Read on to see which specific events have been the **most** lethal to mankind and perhaps to learn what kinds of circumstances to avoid.

Notable Hurricanes, Typhoons, and Storms Since 1900

THE devastating effects hurricanes, typhoons, and tropical storms have on people are enormous. Death can occur by drowning, exposure, starvation, disease, or other causes. The **most** deaths attributable to hurricanes, typhoons, and storms are listed below.

	Date	Classification	Location	Deaths
1.	Nov. 13, 1970	Cyclone	Bangladesh	300,000
2.	April 30, 1991	Cyclone	Bangladesh	139,000
3.	Oct. 15–16, 1942	Hurricane	Bengal, India	40,000

4.	June 1–2, 1965	Windstorm	Bangladesh	30,000
5.	May 28–29, 1963	Windstorm	Bangladesh	22,000
6.	May 11–12,1965	Windstorm	Bangladesh	17,000
7.	Sept. 18, 1906	Typhoon	Hong Kong	10,000
	Dec. 15, 1965	Windstorm	Bangladesh	10,000
	May 25, 1985	Cyclone	Bangladesh	10,000
10.	Aug–Sept. 1900	Hurricane	Galveston, TX	6,000
	Oct. 4–8, 1963	Hurricane	Caribbean	6,000

SOURCE: *The 1996 World Almanac and Book of Facts*

Floods and Tidal Waves Over Time

THE American writer Stephen Crane once described water as being indifferent, meaning that it could supply life or take it without conscience. Consider the number of deaths attributable to floods and tidal waves and you might find yourself in agreement. Rankings are based on the **most** human casualties.

	Date	Location	Deaths
1.	Aug. 1931	Huang He River, China	3,700,000
2.	1887	Huang He River, China	900,000
3.	1642	China	300,000
4.	1939	North China	200,000
5.	1228	Holland	100,000
	1911	Chang Jiang River, China	100,000
7.	Aug. 27, 1883	Indonesia	36,000
8.	Aug. 11, 1979	Morvi, India	15,000
9.	Oct. 10, 1960	Bangladesh	6,000
10.	Sept. 8, 1900	Galveston, TX	5,000
11.	Oct. 31, 1960	Bangladesh	4,000

SOURCE: *The 1996 World Almanac and Book of Facts*

Earthquakes

Most of us have grown accustomed to hearing about earthquakes, but have you ever researched the **most** deaths brought about by one? Perhaps you'll be amazed at the enormous devastation that can occur during and after an earthquake.

	Date	Location	Deaths	Richter Scale Magnitude
1.	Jan. 24, 1556	Shaanxi, China	830,000	n/a
2.	Oct. 11, 1737	Calcutta, India	300,000	n/a
3.	May 20, 526	Syria	250,000	n/a
4.	July 28, 1976	Tangshan, China	242,000	8.2
5.	Sept. 1, 1923	Yokohama, Japan	200,000	8.3
	May 22, 1927	Nan-Shan, China	200,000	8.3
7.	Dec. 30, 1730	Hokkaido, Japan	137,000	n/a
8.	Sept. 27, 1290	Chihli, China	100,000	n/a
9.	Dec. 16, 1920	Gansu, China	100,000	8.6
10.	Dec. 28, 1908	Messina, Italy	83,000	7.5

n/a = not available

Some of the **most** recent earthquakes have also taken the **most** lives. Consider the 1988 quake in Armenia that killed 55,000 people and the 1990 Iranian quake that took more than 40,000 lives.

SOURCE: Global Volcanism Network, Smithsonian Institution; U.S. Geological Survey, Department of the Interior

Volcanic Eruptions

THE number of fatalities caused by a volcanic eruption is often difficult to determine, since accounts may vary. Sometimes the historical record is incomplete, and casualties do not in all cases occur immediately after an eruption. Often there are accompanying diseases, starvation, or a poisoning effect brought on by the venting of toxic gases. Thus, no ranking is provided here—just a list of some of the **most** notoriously lethal eruptions of history.

1628 or 1645 B.C.: Santorini (Thera) Island explodes in the Mediterranean Sea. The number of attributable deaths is unknown. The eruption causes the evacuation of the island of Crete, 75 miles away, in effect ending the Minoan civilization.

Aug. 24–26, A.D. 79: Mt. Vesuvius, near Naples, Italy, explodes. The ancient towns of Pompeii and Herculaneum are destroyed. Approximately 16,000 people are killed.

260: Mt. Ilopango in El Salvador erupts and terminates the early Maya civilization. The number of deaths is unknown.

1586: Mt. Kelut on Java Island, Indonesia, erupts. As many as 10,000 people killed.

Sept. 4, 1618: Volcanic landslides kill 2,420 in Chiavenna Valley, Italy.

Dec. 15, 1631: Mt. Vesuvius, Italy, erupts. Casualties listed at over 4,000.

March 25, 1669: Mt. Etna in Catania, Sicily, erupts. About 20,000 die.

June 8, 1783: Mt. Skaptar in Iceland erupts. Casualties number 9,350.

May 21, 1792: Mt. Unzen in Japan erupts and causes a harbor wave. About 14,500 die.

April 10–12, 1815: Mt. Tambora in Sumbawa, Indonesia, erupts and kills 92,000.

May 8, 1902: Mt. Pelée in Martinique erupts and pours a cloud of flaming gas on the city of St. Pierre, where 28,000 die.

May 19, 1919: A boiling crater lake on Mt. Kelud on Java Island, Indonesia, breaks through and kills 5,000.

Jan. 17–21, 1951: Mt. Lamington on New Guinea produces a cloud of hot gas and dust (similar to that of Mt. St. Helens in 1980). About 3,000 die.

May 18, 1980: Mt. St. Helens in Washington State erupts and kills 57.

March 28, 1982: El Chichon in Mexico erupts and sends clouds of volcanic ash around the world. In the vicinity of the volcano, 1,880 die.

Nov. 13, 1985: Nevado del Ruiz erupts and causes a massive snow and mud slide that buries the town of Armero. Approximately 23,000 are killed.

Aug. 21, 1986: Carbon dioxide from an underwater volcano in Lake Nyos, Cameroon, vents and kills 1,700.

June 15, 1991: Mt. Pinatubo in the Philippines erupts and kills 800. Thousands of people are saved by evacuation.

Feb. 2, 1993: Mayon volcano in the Philippines produces a hot cloud of dust and gas that kills 70.

Thousands of volcanic eruptions have occurred throughout the history of the earth. And, as mentioned, records exist for only a relative handful of eruptions, with the vast majority of them occurring before man was even present on earth. Consider one of the prevailing theories in paleontology, that it was volcanic activity that killed off the dinosaurs a few hundred million years ago.

SOURCE: *Volcanoes of the World,* Geoscience Press; Global Volcanism Network, Smithsonian Institution, as of June 1995

Plagues, Epidemics, Famines, and Droughts

THE invisible killers. Unlike other natural disasters that can be seen, heard, touched, or smelled (but generally not tasted), plagues, epidemics, famines, and droughts come on invisibly and are spread silently. Consequently, the effects are far worse than other disasters.

Since no exact figures can be determined for such large-scale devastations, no numerical rankings exist here; rather, they are set down chronologically. Nevertheless, the events listed below remain the **most** lethal the world has ever seen.

Date	Location	Cause	Deaths
A.D. 558	Europe-Asia-Africa	bubonic plague	millions
987–1059	France	famine	millions
1333–1337	China	famine	6,000,000
1348–1666	Europe	bubonic plague	25,000,000
1520	Mexico	smallpox	3,000,000
1560	Brazil	smallpox	millions
1669–1670	India	famine	3,000,000
1745–1752	India	famine	millions
1769–1770	Hindustan, India	famine	3,000,000
1782–1784	India	famine	millions
1792	Egypt	plague	800,000
1810	China	famine	millions
1811	China	famine	millions
1812–1813	India	famine-locusts-rats	millions

1816–1817	Ireland	famine	737,000
1826–1837	Europe	cholera	millions
1840–1862	worldwide	cholera	millions
1846	China	famine	millions
1849	China	famine	millions
1863–1875	worldwide	cholera	millions
1866	India	famine	1,500,000
1876–1877	India	famine	6,000,000
1877–1878	China	famine	9,000,000
1889–1890	worldwide	influenza	millions
1892–1894	China	drought-famine	1,000,000
1896–1897	India	famine-drought	5,000,000
1898	India	great mortality	1,000,000
1899–1900	India	drought-disease	1,250,000
1899–1901	India	famine	1,000,000
1904	India	plague	1,000,000
1907	India	plague	1,316,000
1910–1913	China, India	bubonic plague	millions
1914–1924	Russia	famine-influenza	20,000,000
1917–1921	Russia	typhus	3,000,000
1917–1919	worldwide	influenza	25,000,000
1921–1922	Russia	drought	millions
1921–1923	India	bubonic plague	millions
1928–1929	China	famine	3,000,000
1932–1934	U.S.S.R.	famine	5,000,000
1936	West China	drought-famine	5,000,000
1943	India	wartime famine	millions
1943	Kwangtung, China	famine-disease	1,000,000
1968	Nigeria	famine	800,000

Deaths from recent famines in Africa could number in the hundreds of thousands or more.

SOURCE: Jay Robert Nash, *Darkest Hours* (1976)

Notable Fires Since 1845

FIRES are set by man or by naturally occurring phenomena such as lightning. We can't go back through all of time to see what areas have been plagued by the **most** fire disasters, but we can tell you where fires have occurred since 1845 and which have been the **most** destructive in terms of loss of life.

	Date	Location	Place	Deaths
1.	May 1845	Canton, China	theater	1,670
2.	Oct. 8, 1871	Wisconsin	forest fire	1,182
3.	Dec. 8, 1881	Vienna, Austria	Ring Theater	850
4.	Dec 30, 1903	Chicago	Iroquois Theater	602
5.	Nov. 2, 1994	Durunka, Egypt	burning fuel flood	500
6.	Nov. 28, 1942	Boston	Coconut Grove	491
7.	Oct. 14, 1913	Wales	colliery	439
8.	Sept. 1, 1894	Minnesota	forest fire	413
9.	Oct. 12, 1918	Minnesota	forest fire	400
10.	June 30, 1900	Hoboken, NJ	docks	326
11.	Dec. 17, 1961	Brazil	circus	323
12.	May 22, 1967	Brussels, Belgium	store	322
13.	April 21, 1930	Columbus, OH	penitentiary	320
14.	Dec. 10, 1994	Karamay, China	theater	300
15.	Dec. 5, 1876	Brooklyn, NY	theater	295

SOURCE: *The 1996 World Almanac and Book of Facts*

The Most in the Mines

No doubt about it, mining always has been and always will remain one of the **most** dangerous of all occupations. Following are the occurrences of the **most** deaths attributable to underground mining in the U.S. since 1900.

	Date	Place	Lives Lost
1.	Dec. 6, 1907	Monongah, WV	361
2.	Oct. 22, 1913	Dawson, NM	263
3.	Nov. 13, 1909	Cherry, IL	259
4.	Dec. 19, 1907	Jacobs Creek, PA	239
5.	May 1, 1900	Scofield, UT	200
6.	May 19, 1928	Mather, PA	195
7.	May 19, 1902	Coal Creek, TN	184
8.	April 28, 1914	Eccles, WV	181

| **9.** | Jan. 25, 1904 | Cheswick, PA | 179 |
| **10.** | March 8, 1924 | Castle Gate, UT | 171 |

The **most** workers ever killed in a mining disaster perished on April 25, 1942, in Manchuria, when 1,549 miners died. The **most** recent mining disaster took place on December 7, 1992, in Norton, Virginia. Eight miners lost their lives.

SOURCES: Bureau of Mines, U.S. Department of the Interior; Mine Safety and Health Administration, U.S. Department of Labor

Shipwrecks

SHIPS have gotten bigger over time, thus the casualties from shipwrecks have kept pace. What are the **most** disastrous shipwrecks over the past century and probably of all time?

1. **Nov. 1948.** A Chinese army evacuation ship, name unknown, explodes off of southern Manchuria. Loss of life is 6,000.

2. **Feb. 26, 1916.** The *Provence,* a French cruiser, sinks in the Mediterranean. Loss of life is 3,100.

3. **Dec. 6, 1917.** The *Mont Blanc,* a French ammunition ship, and the *Imo,* a Belgium steamer, collide. Loss of life is 1,600.

4. **April 14–15, 1912.** The *Titanic,* British passenger steamer, hits an iceberg in the North Atlantic. Loss of life is 1,503.

5. **May 7, 1915.** The *Lusitania,* a British steamer, is torpedoed by a German submarine off Ireland. Loss of life is 1,198.

6. **Dec. 26, 1954.** The *Toya Maru,* a Japanese ferry, sank in the Tsugaru Straits of Japan. Loss of life is 1,172.

7. **Dec. 3, 1948.** The *Kiangya,* a Chinese refugee ship, explodes south of Shanghai. Loss of life is more than 1,100.

8. **June 15, 1904.** The *General Slocum,* an American excursion steamer, burns in New York City's East River. Loss of life is 1,030.

9. **May 29, 1914.** The *Empress of Ireland,* a British steamer, sinks after a collision with a Norwegian collier in the St. Lawrence River. Loss of life is 1,014.

10. **March 18, 1921.** The *Hong Kong* is wrecked in the South China Sea. Loss of life is 1,000.

SOURCE: *The 1996 World Almanac and Book of Facts*

Aircraft Disasters

THIS section is dedicated to the **most** deaths attributable to aircraft disasters worldwide.

1. **March 27, 1977.** Two 747s collide on a runway in the Canary Islands. Loss of life is 582.

2. **Aug. 12, 1985.** A 747 crashes into Mt. Ogura in Japan. Loss of life is 520.

3. **March 3, 1974.** A DC-10 crashes near Paris. Loss of life is 346.

4. **June 23, 1985.** A 747 crashes into the Atlantic Ocean south of Ireland. Loss of life is 329.

5. **Aug. 19, 1980.** A Tristar burns after an emergency landing in Riyadh, Saudia Arabia. Loss of life is 301.

6. **July 3, 1988.** An Iranian A300 Airbus is shot down by the U.S. Navy warship *Vincennes* over the Persian Gulf. Loss of life is 290.

7. **May 25, 1979.** A DC-10 crashes after takeoff at O'Hare International Airport in Chicago. Loss of life is 275.

8. **Dec. 21, 1988.** A 747 explodes over and crashes in Lockerbie, Scotland. Loss of life is 270.

9. **Sept. 1, 1983.** A 747 is shot down after violating Soviet airspace. Loss of life is 269.

10. **April 26, 1994.** An Airbus A300-600R crashes at Japan's Nagoya Airport. Loss of life is 264.

SOURCE: *The 1995 Information Please Almanac*

Railroad Disasters

THE **most** destructive railroad disasters in the world are chronicled here. Like other disasters noted in this book of **mosts,** only those with the **most** fatalities are included.

	Date	Location	Deaths
1.	Dec. 12, 1917	Modane, France	543
2.	March 2, 1944	Salerno, Italy	521
3.	June 6, 1981	Bihar, India	500+
4.	Jan. 16, 1944	León Province, Spain	500
5.	April 3, 1955	Guadalajara, Mexico	300
6.	Sept. 22, 1994	Tolunda, Angola	300
7.	Sept. 29, 1957	Montgomery, W. Pakistan	250
8.	Feb. 1, 1970	Buenos Aires, Argentina	236
9.	May 22, 1915	near Gretna, Scotland	227
10.	Jan. 4, 1990	Sindh Province, Pakistan	210+

SOURCE: *The 1996 World Almanac and Book of Facts*

Explosions

FOLLOWING are the **most** notorious and **most** lethal of the world's explosions since around the turn of the century. As you'll see, explosions can occur in a number of ways.

	Date	Location	Accident Site	Deaths
1.	Dec. 3, 1984	Bhopal, India	chemical plant	3,849
2.	Nov. 2, 1982	Afghanistan	Salan Tunnel	1,000–3,000
3.	Dec. 6, 1917	Halifax, Can.	Halifax Harbor	1,654
4.	Aug. 7, 1956	Cali, Colombia	dynamite trucks	1,100
5.	April 14, 1944	Bombay, India	Bombay Harbor	700
6.	June 3, 1989	USSR	gas pipeline	650+
7.	April 16, 1947	Texas City, Texas	pier	576

SOURCE: *National Geographic Atlas of the World*

Airship Disasters

As the world's first transatlantic commercial airliner, the German zeppelin *Hindenburg* once carried a combined total of 117 passengers and crew members, the **most** ever to cross the Atlantic in an airship. On May 6, 1937, while attempting what should have been a routine landing at Lakehurst, New Jersey, the *Hindenburg* exploded into flames. Of the 97 passengers and crew aboard that trip, 35 were killed, along with one member of the ground crew. Contrary to popular opinion, however, this was not the world's worst airship disaster. In 1931 the U.S. Navy airship, the *Akron,* flew with 207 people aboard, the **most** ever carried on an airship. Two years later, on April 3, 1933, the *Akron* crashed into the sea during a storm off the Atlantic coast, leaving just 3 survivors and killing 73, the **most** ever to die in an airship tragedy.

Mosts
from the World of
Charity

WHO GIVES THE **most** and just how much is the **most?** Frankly, it's a lot. Read on and see what corporations, wealthy people, and people just like you and me are giving away. You might be pleasantly surprised.

Corporate Philanthropy

IF you love to give, give through your favorite companies by buying **mostly** from them. Following are the companies that love to give the **most.** Rankings were based on the percent of pre-tax income donated to charity (money and in-kind contributions).

	Company	Percent of Income Donated
1.	Ben & Jerry's Homemade	7.2%
2.	Hewlett-Packard	5.2
3.	Cummins Engine	5.0
	Dayton-Hudson	5.0
	H. B. Fuller	5.0
	Herman Miller	5.0
7.	Polaroid	4.0
	Stride Rite	4.0
9.	Quaker Oats	3.0
10.	Sara Lee	2.9
11.	General Mills	2.7
12.	J. P. Morgan	2.6
13.	Digital Equipment	2.5
	Merck	2.5
	Rouse	2.5
16.	Procter & Gamble	2.2
17.	ARCO	2.1
	Chambers Development	2.1

	Company	Percent of Income Donated
19.	Ashland Oil	2.0
	Chase Manhattan	2.0
	Colgate-Palmolive	2.0
	Curtice-Brown	2.0
	Huffy	2.0
	Norwest	2.0
	New York Times	2.0
	Tasty Baking	2.0
	Tektronix	2.0
	Tennant	2.0
	Texas Instruments	2.0
	Yellow Freight Systems	2.0

SOURCE: *The 1994 Business Almanac and Desk Reference*

Charities with the Most Income

YOU'VE decided to make a donation to charity and you're wondering which of the thousands of charitable organizations are the **most** funded. Following is a ranking of charities based on the **most** income derived from public support (contributions), government support, investments, and member dues.

	Charity	Location	Year Organized	Income (millions)
1.	Catholic Charities	Alexandria, VA	1910	$1,934
2.	American Red Cross	Washington, DC	1887	1,796
3.	YMCA of the U.S.A.	Chicago, IL	1851	1,763
4.	Salvation Army	Alexandria, VA	1865	1,297
5.	Goodwill Industries	Bethesda, MD	1902	849
6.	Shriners Hospitals	Tampa, FL	1922	601
7.	Boy Scouts of America	Irving, TX	1910	504
8.	Association for Retarded Citizens	Arlington, TX	1950	478
9.	United Cerebral Palsy	Washington, DC	1948	462
10.	Girl Scouts of the U.S.A.	New York, NY	1912	457
11.	CARE	Atlanta, GA	1945	451
12.	Planned Parenthood Federation	New York, NY	1916	446

13.	Second Harvest	Chicago, IL	1979	439
14.	United Jewish Appeal	New York, NY	1938	408
	YWCA of the U.S.A.	New York, NY	1906	408
16.	American Cancer Society	Atlanta, GA	1913	388
17.	National Easter Seal Society	Chicago, IL	1919	352
18.	Metropolitan Museum of Art	New York, NY	1870	339
19.	Boys/Girls Clubs of America	Atlanta, GA	1906	302
20.	Catholic Relief Services	Baltimore, MD	1943	296

SOURCE: *The Non Profit Times*, Nov. 1994

Better to Give Than to Receive

So we've seen which are the biggest charities based on all forms of support, but maybe you're wondering which charities take in the **most** in contributions alone?

	Charity	Contributions (millions)
1.	Salvation Army	$682.9
2.	American Red Cross	535.7
3.	Second Harvest	430.6
4.	United Jewish Appeal	408.2
5.	YMCA of the U.S.A.	361.2
6.	American Cancer Society	359.1
7.	Catholic Charities U.S.A.	344.1
8.	American Heart Association	239.9
9.	YWCA of the U.S.A.	239.6
10.	Public Broadcasting Service	229.9

SOURCE: *Chronicle of Philosophy*, Nov. 1, 1994

Givers with the Most

WE'VE seen what charities receive the **most** contributions and which have the **most** money, but have you ever wondered where all those contributions are coming from? Well, besides you and me, there are some pretty deep pockets out there that exist just for philanthropic purposes. These organizations are known as foundations, and most were funded by good-hearted folks and families with some even deeper pockets themselves. So read on to see what multimillionaires and billionaires have done with their money, and in the process see who has endowed the most money for charitable purposes.

	Foundation	Endowment
1.	Ford Foundation	$263,620,911
2.	W. K. Kellogg Foundation	173,158,573
3.	Pew Charitable Trusts	143,537,605
4.	J. D. and C. T. MacArthur Foundation	137,000,000
5.	Lilly Endowment	118,907,952
6.	Robert Wood Johnson Foundation	103,124,020
7.	Andrew W. Mellon Foundation	95,865,156
8.	Rockefeller Foundation	93,070,397
9.	DeWitt Wallace–Reader's Digest Foundation	72,324,761
10.	Kresge Foundation	67,678,493

SOURCE: The Foundation Center, *Foundation Giving,* 1994

Mosts
from the World of
Crime

THE "**MOST** WANTED." The **most** notorious. The **most** dangerous. The ones you should probably want to run from the **most** . . . We're referring to criminals, and if it's a subject that fascinates you, or even one that you abhor, you should read on and see who you should be afraid of the **most**.

The FBI's Ten Most Wanted

THEY are known as the FBI's "Ten **Most** Wanted Fugitives." Carefully chosen by special agents of the FBI's Criminal Investigation Division, the men and women appearing on the list must be career criminals or have committed crimes that make them particularly dangerous to society. Also the FBI must believe that national publicity will help in their apprehension of these men and women of the underworld.

In 1949 a newspaper reporter asked the FBI for the names and descriptions of the "toughest guys" it wanted to capture, and the story was so well received that Director J. Edgar Hoover implemented the "Ten **Most** Wanted" program on March 14, 1950. Since that time the names and faces of 445 fugitives, including those of 7 women, have appeared on the list. Thus far, 415 of them have been located, 129 as a direct result of citizen involvement; 15 were removed because legal proceedings were dismissed against them; and 4 were removed because they no longer met the criteria for the list; the remaining 398 fugitives have been captured. It's interesting to note how the list has changed over the years. In the 1950s, the top ten fugitives were mainly bank robbers, burglars, and car thieves. The 1960s saw political revolutionaries being added to the list for acts of sabotage, kidnapping, and destruction of government property. In the 1980s, members of organized crime and terrorist organizations began showing up, along with serial killers and those involved in drug-related crimes.

Over the years the state where the **most** top ten fugitives have been apprehended is California, with 58. Of the 19 fugitives located outside the U.S., **most,** a total of 10, were tracked down in Canada.

The FBI relies on the public to help locate these fugitives. In recent years, television programs such as Fox's *America's Most Wanted* and NBC's *Unsolved Mysteries* have helped by broadcasting information about the people on the list and their identities. For those who have access to the Internet, the list is now posted on the FBI's web site, including full descriptions and photographs. The current FBI's "Ten **Most** Wanted" list contains the names of just eight fugitives. Two others were taken into custody in January 1996. Undoubtedly, two more names will crop up to round the list out to ten names again.

SOURCE: Federal Bureau of Investigation, Criminal Investigation Division

The Most Time on the "Most Wanted List"

ON January 16, 1968, officers from Nashville, Tennessee, intercepted a car as it was leaving a house believed to be the gathering place for a ring suspected of cashing stolen money orders. As the two officers attempted to stop the vehicle, they were met with gunshots from a high-powered rifle. One of the officers died instantly, the other two months later. Police identified one of the four occupants of the car as Charles Lee Herron, who just three months earlier had been charged with arson in Cincinnati, Ohio. Herron was added to the FBI's "Ten **Most** Wanted Fugitives" list on February 9, 1968. Eighteen years later, on June 17, 1986, William Allen, a close associate of Herron's and a former "Top Ten" fugitive, tried to renew a false driver's license at a Department of Motor Vehicle office in Jacksonville, Florida. A quick-thinking examiner had him arrested, and Florida Highway Patrol officers soon identified the man they had in custody as Allen. A few hours later, Herron's whereabouts were established, and when FBI agents arrested him at 4:45 the next morning, Charles Lee Herron had spent eighteen years, four months, and nine days on the FBI's **most** wanted list, the **most** time of any fugitive.

SOURCE: Federal Bureau of Investigation, Criminal Investigation Division

The Most Time on "The List" by a Woman

BY 1970, protests against the Vietnam War had grown more violent than ever. On September 23, 1970, former Brandeis University student Katherine Ann Power and four other activists robbed the State Street Bank and Trust Company in Boston in order to finance their continued antiwar activities. As they fled the bank with over $26,000 in loot, they gunned down Boston police officer Walter Schroeder, who was responding to the robbery in progress. He died in a hail of submachine-gun fire. Power became one of only seven women ever to be placed on the FBI's "**Most** Wanted List" on October 17, 1970, where she remained until her name was removed on June 15, 1984. Power's tenure on the list was 13 years, 7 months, and 29 days, the **most** time of any woman. By 1993 Power was 44 years old and had spent 23 years as a fugitive. Under the name Alice Louise Metzinger, she had built a new life for herself. She was married, had a fourteen-year-old son, and was a restaurateur in the small town of Lebanon, Oregon. Stating that she wanted to deal with the events of her past life, Power surrendered to the FBI and Boston Police on September 15, 1993, and eventually pleaded guilty to manslaughter and bank robbery charges. In a statement, Power maintained that her crimes were not motivated by the desire for personal gain, but by a deep conviction that she had to take active steps to stop a war she believed was wrong. We're not sure what Officer Walter Schroeder's convictions were.

SOURCE: Federal Bureau of Investigation, Criminal Investigation Division

States with the Most Men on Death Row

As of October 31, 1995, there were 3,046 inmates under sentence of death in U.S. prisons in thirty-nine states. The NAACP Legal Defense and Educational Fund, which monitors death-row cases, reports that 48 percent of these death-row inmates are Caucasian, 41 percent are African American, 8 percent are Latino/Latina, 2 percent are Native American, and just under 1 percent are either Asian or of unreported racial heritage.

According to a list of death row inmates by state, California has the **most** prisoners awaiting execution. The states that follow are listed below (as of January 16, 1996).

	State	Inmates
1.	California	432
2.	Texas	417
3.	Florida	340
4.	Illinois	197
5.	Pennsylvania	161

SOURCE: The NAACP Legal Defense and Educational Fund

States with the Most Women on Death Row

To many, it came as no surprise when, in July 1995, Susan Smith received a life sentence after being convicted of the October 1994 drowning of her two young sons by leaving them strapped inside her car and allowing it to roll and sink into a lake. Though Smith will be eligible for parole in thirty years, her life's story mirrors those of several less fortunate women (in terms of harsher sentencing) now on death row. Like many of these forty-seven women in sixteen states (at the end of 1995), Smith's childhood was difficult at best. Her father had committed suicide, she was subsequently molested by her stepfather, and later, as a teenager, she failed a suicide attempt.

Of the 313 executions that have taken place in the United States since 1976, only one woman had been put to death by the end of 1995. According to Victor Streib, a Cleveland State University professor of law and an expert on death-penalty issues involving women, the state with the **most** women on death row is California.

	State	Inmates
1.	California	7
2.	Texas	6
3.	Florida	5
	Illinois	5
	Oklahoma	5
6.	Alabama	4
	Pennsylvania	4
8.	Missouri	2
	North Carolina	2
10.	Arizona	1
	Idaho	1
	Indiana	1
	Louisiana	1
	Mississippi	1
	Nevada	1
	Tennessee	1

SOURCE: Victor Streib, Cleveland State University

The Most Time Spent on Death Row

IN 1948 Sadamichi Hirasawa was convicted of poisoning twelve employees of a bank he was robbing for what turned out to be a grand total of $403. Hirasawa spent the next thirty-nine years awaiting execution in Sendai Jail, Japan, the **most** time anyone has ever been on death row. Hirasawa died in prison at the age of ninety-four.

SOURCE: *The Guinness Book of Records 1994,* Bantam, 1994

The Most Time on Death Row in the U.S.

IN the United States, Howard Virgil Lee Douglas served seventeen and a half years on death row, the **most** time by any prisoner in American penal history. On May 15, 1991, his death sentence was commuted to life in prison.

SOURCE: *The Guinness Book of Records 1994,* Bantam, 1994

States Executing the Most

SINCE the U.S. Supreme Court reinstated the death penalty in 1976, a total of 257 people had as of 1994 been executed in twenty-six of the forty jurisdictions with capital punishment statutes, including the U.S. military and the U.S. government. Thirteen states have no capital punishment statutes: Alaska, the District of Columbia, Hawaii, Iowa, Maine, Massachusetts, Michigan, Minnesota, North Dakota, Rhode Island, Vermont, West Virginia, and Wisconsin. Of those executed, **most,** approximately 55 percent, were Caucasian, 39 percent were black, and 5 percent were Latino. Just one individual was Native American. A list of executions by state shows that the large majority have occurred in southern states. With nearly one-third of all executions having taken place within its prisons, Texas is the state with the **most** executions.

Following is a list of states that have performed the **most** executions.

	State	Executions
1.	Texas	85
2.	Florida	33
3.	Virginia	24
4.	Louisiana	21
5.	Georgia	18
6.	Missouri	11
7.	Alabama	10
8.	Arkansas	9

	State	Executions
9.	North Carolina	6
10.	Nevada	5
11.	Delaware	4
	Mississippi	4
	South Carolina	4
	Utah	4
15.	Arizona	3
	Indiana	3
	Oklahoma	3
18.	California	2
	Illinois	2
	Washington	2
21.	Idaho	1
	Maryland	1
	Nebraska	1
	Wyoming	1

SOURCES: U.S. Law Enforcement Assistance Administration;
U.S. Bureau of Justice Statistics, *Correctional Populations in the United States Annual*;
U.S. Bureau of Justice Statistics, *Capital Punishment 1994*, Dec. 1994

The Most Common Method of Execution

AMONG the forty jurisdictions with capital punishment statutes, the **most** common legally prescribed method of execution is by lethal injection. Six states—Maryland, Montana, North Carolina, Utah, Virginia, and Washington—have two different methods of execution. In some states, a condemned prisoner may choose the method of execution; in others, the prisoner is executed by whatever method was legally sanctioned either when the crime was committed or when the death sentence was imposed.

Following are the **most** common methods of execution by state.

	Method of Execution	Number of States
1.	Lethal injection	32
2.	Electrocution	11
3.	Lethal gas	7
4.	Hanging/firing squad	4
5.	Firing squad	2

SOURCE: Bureau of Justice Statistics

Those Murdered the Most

THE 302 people who were executed between 1976 and October 1995 were convicted of murdering 408 people. **Most** of those victims, 82.6 percent, were Caucasian, 12.7 percent were black, 3.4 percent were Latino, and 1.2 percent were Asian. **Most** of the victims, 55.6 percent, were male, while 44.4 percent were female.

SOURCE: Bureau of Justice Statistics

The Handgun Takes the Most

IN the United States alone 22,540 people were murdered in 1992, amounting to one person in every 11,034. Only 2 percent of those who were convicted of murder in 1992 were sentenced to death. Not surprisingly, the **most** common murder weapon in the U.S. is the handgun. A total of 12,489, or 55.4, of all murders were committed with handguns. Altogether, firearms (including handguns, rifles, and shotguns) were used in 69.2 percent of the nation's murders.

SOURCE: Bureau of Justice Statistics, Department of Justice

Where the Bank Robbers Hit the Most

ALTHOUGH recent years have shown a dramatic decline in bank robberies, Los Angeles County, California, remains the "Bank Robbery Capital" of the United States. Nationwide, 7,029 bank robberies occurred in 1994, along with 355 other bank crimes (burglaries, larcenies, etc.). Loot, including cash, securities, and other property, was taken in 6,804 of these crimes totaling $58,428,792, of which investigators recovered almost 25 percent ($14,261,800). In L.A. County alone, 784 banks were robbed, representing over 11 percent of the national total. California, the state with the **most** bank robberies, had a total of 2,125, more than three times that of Florida, whose 662 robberies place it second among individual states. Amazingly, Los Angeles had more bank robberies than the entire state of Florida!

SOURCE: FBI Bank Crime Statistics Report for Federally Insured Financial Institutions

Bank Robbery Mosts

THE annual *FBI Bank Crime Statistics Report for Federally Insured Financial Institutions* contains some very revealing information about bank robberies. Men committed the **most** bank crimes in 1994, representing 97 percent of the 8,855 perpetrators. As one might expect, handguns were the **most** frequent weapon of choice, with knives, clubs, and explosive devices representing only a small portion of the weapons used. However, bank employees were the **most** frequent target of violence during bank robberies, accounting for 88 of the 167 people who were injured, which also included 25 perpetrators, 23 customers, 16 law officers, 12 guards, and 3 other individuals.

Interestingly, the people killed **most** often during bank robberies were the perpetrators themselves. Of the 23 deaths, 16 were those of perpetrators, followed by those of 3 guards, 2 employees, and 2 law enforcement officers.

SOURCE: Federal Bureau of Investigation

When Most Bank Robberies Occur

IT'S not surprising that **most** bank robberies occur at the branch offices of large commercial banks located in the business districts of metropolitan areas, since there are more branch banks in these locations than in rural or residential areas. But when do **most** bank robberies occur? Well, you just might want to avoid doing your banking on Fridays between nine and eleven A.M. Actually, the FBI's chart showing the occurrence of bank robberies by day of the week and time of day makes home banking and direct deposit seem very appealing.

Following are the days and time of day a bank robber is **most** likely to strike.

	Day	Occurrences
1.	Friday	1,677
2.	Monday	1,370
3.	Tuesday	1,329
4.	Thursday	1,246
5.	Wednesday	1,210
6.	Saturday	443
7.	Sunday	61
8.	undetermined	48
	TOTAL	7,384

Time of Day	Occurrences
1. 9–11 A.M.	1,854
2. 1–3 P.M.	1,824
3. 11 A.M.–1 P.M.	1,726
4. 3–6 P.M.	1,456
5. 6 P.M.–6 A.M.	273
6. 6–9 A.M.	159
7. undetermined	92
TOTAL	7,384

SOURCE: FBI Bank Crime Statistics Report for Federally Insured Financial Institutions

The Most Lucrative Bank Robbery Ever

THESE thefts seem small-time, though, compared to the single **most** lucrative bank robbery in history. The streets of Beirut, Lebanon, were filled with gunfire, explosions, and the worst civil unrest ever during the winter of 1975–76. On January 22, 1976, a guerrilla force blasted its way into the vaults of the British Bank of the Middle East in Bab Idriss, cleaning out the safe deposit boxes of cash and other valuables estimated by former finance minister Lucien Dahdah at $50 million.

SOURCE: Federal Bureau of Investigation

A $6 Billion Drug Seizure Makes It a Most

ON the night of September 28, 1989, Drug Enforcement Agency personnel and officers of the Tri-Cities Narcotics Task Force of the Los Angeles County cities of Bell, Huntington Park, and Maywood converged on a warehouse in the city of Sylmar, north of Los Angeles. After arresting three suspects, the officers executed a search warrant resulting in the seizure of over $10 million in cash and 20 tons of cocaine with an estimated street value of $6 billion to $7 billion, the **most** valuable drug seizure ever. The investigation was prompted by a tip-off from a local resident who had complained about heavy truck traffic and people leaving the warehouse "at odd hours and in a suspicious manner." The morning after the bust DEA special agent in charge, John M. Zienter, said, "This narcotics seizure of the largest amount of cocaine in the world should put to rest any further speculation about whether or not Los Angeles has in fact become the cocaine capital of the United States."

SOURCE: Drug Enforcement Agency

Requiring the Most Bail

ON October 16, 1989, four accused armed robbers and their attorneys appeared for a bail hearing before Judge David L. Tobin in the Dade Country Courthouse in Miami, Florida. The four defendants were arrested wearing jackets with the letters "FBI" emblazoned on the back and carrying phony FBI identification badges, while trying to stage a "bust" at the home of a known drug dealer. They were quickly apprehended by real FBI agents who already had the house under surveillance. During the hearing, the prosecutor maintained that the charges against the defendants were not "bailable" offenses, but after several minutes of heated argument with defense attorneys, he finally agreed to bail for each defendant in the amount of $100 billion! The defense attorneys stipulated to that amount, and with the single word "Done!" Judge Tobin set a world's record for the **most** bail ever demanded. Defense attorneys subsequently filed a motion for bail reduction, but Judge Tobin denied the request, reminding them that they had originally agreed to that amount.

Suffering the Most Crime by Income

CRIME doesn't always hit the innocent randomly. In 1994, violent crime hit the people with the lowest incomes hardest. Read on to see what people (aged 12 years or older) suffered the **most**, by income.

Annual Income	Victims per 1,000 people
Less than $7,500	88.3
$7,500–14,999	60.8
$15,000–24,999	51.7
$25,000–34,999	51.3
$35,000–49,999	49.3
$50,000–74,999	47.6
$75,000 or more	42.7

SOURCE: U.S. Bureau of Justice Statistics, *Criminal Victimization 1994,* April 1996

Suffering the Most Crime by Race

BESIDES the poor being subjected to a disproportionately high percentage of crime, African Americans suffer the **most** in terms of being victimized by criminals.

Race	1994 Victims per 1,000 people
Black	65.4
Hispanic	63.3
Non-Hispanic	51.9
White	51.5
Other	49.1

SOURCE: U.S. Bureau of Justice, *Criminal Victimization 1994*, April 1996

Citizens Victimized the Most in the Industrialized Countries

IN which country are you **most** likely to be a victim of crime? According to a study published in 1991, the United States leads the list of industrialized countries with 28.8 percent of the population claiming to have been victims of crime. Canada is second, with 28.1 percent, followed by Australia, with 27.8 percent.

With 11,085 crimes per 100,000 residents in 1994, Washington, DC, has the highest crime rate in the United States. But New Orleans, Louisiana has the highest murder rate, with 85.8 murders per 100,000, giving it the distinction of being one of the **most** dangerous cities in the United States.

SOURCE: *Crime in the United States*, annual, U.S. Federal Bureau of Investigation

The Most Inmates Worldwide

IN 1990–1991, the United States had the **most** people incarcerated per 100,000 citizens of any industrialized nation. The countries with the highest per capita incarceration rates are ranked below.

	Nation	Incarceration Rate per 100,000
1.	United States	455
2.	South Africa	311
3.	Venezuela	177
4.	Hungary	117
5.	Canada	111
	China	111
7.	Australia	79
8.	Portugal	77
9.	Czechoslovakia	72
10.	Denmark	71

SOURCE: Bureau of Justice Statistics, Department of Justice

Mosts
from the World of
Legal Matters

SOME OF US think of legal matters as a career opportunity, a golden egg, a respectable pursuit. Others of us cringe. "Am I going to get sued?" "Are they going to take my house or just everything in it?" It's a common enough worry, and whether you just accidentally ran a red light—right into the path of a Rolls Royce Silver Cloud—or mistakenly ran over your neighbor's freshly sodded lawn, you might find yourself wondering where you can find a good lawyer. And if you're interested in seeing who's found a really good lawyer, and settled for the **most**, then read on. You'll also discover where all the lawyers are and a few other **mosts** in the world of legal matters along the way.

The U.S. Has the Most Lawyers

ALTHOUGH the United States has just 5 percent of the world's population, it has **most** of the world's lawyers—70 percent, in fact. The American Bar Association estimates that by the year 2000, the U.S. will have one million lawyers. Compared to other countries, the United States also has the **most** per capita lawyers.

SOURCE: American Bar Association

The Most Attorneys and the Fewest Attorneys

ALL right, so we've seen that the United States is the **most** litigious of all societies, but where within the States might there be the **most** lawyers?

Washington, DC, has the **most** lawyers per capita in the United States. There is actually 1 lawyer for every 17 people. North Carolina has the fewest, with only 1 lawyer for every 704 residents.

SOURCE: American Bar Association

The Most Litigious States

IN 1994, *Forbes* magazine ranked the fifty states and the District of Columbia from the **most** to the least litigious. The ten states where plaintiffs were the **most** abundant in 1994 were:

1. District of Columbia
2. Rhode Island
3. Massachusetts
4. New Mexico
5. Nevada
6. Delaware
7. Florida
8. New York
9. New Hampshire
10. Washington

SOURCE: *Forbes* Magazine

Where to Find the Most Cases

IN 1991, a total of 18,971,437 civil cases were filed in state courts, including those of the District of Columbia and Puerto Rico. The states in which the **most** cases were filed were:

	State	1991 Civil Suits Filed
1.	California	1,906,188
2.	New York	1,569,457
3.	Virginia	1,427,105
4.	Florida	924,067
5.	Maryland	913,698
6.	New Jersey	911,714
7.	Texas	857,322
8.	Ohio	853,533
9.	Illinois	726,359
10.	Michigan	725,517

Keep in mind that the states above are also some of the more populous in the U.S.

SOURCE: American Bar Association

The States Handing Over the Most

IF you choose to file a civil suit, in which state would your award likely to be the **most**? *The Lawyer's Almanac* published a list of the ten states with the **most** awards over $1 million being granted between 1962 and 1989.

	State	Million-Dollar-Plus Awards
1.	New York	707
2.	California	540
3.	Florida	504
4.	Texas	320
5.	Illinois	216
6.	Michigan	202
7.	Pennsylvania	177
8.	Ohio	100
9.	Missouri	96
10.	New Jersey	86

SOURCE: *The Lawyers Almanac*

The States Granting the Most Divorces

THE "divorce capital" of the United States is still Nevada. Leading the country with the **most** per capita divorces annually, Nevada's divorce rate is 14.1 per 1,000. And in case you're wondering, the United States ranks fourth on the list of countries granting the **most** per capita divorces. Canada ranks ninth. And who beat Canada and the United States (where 1,187,000 divorces were granted in 1992, the **most** overall)? We suggest you turn to the chapter "MOSTS FROM THE WORLD OF PEOPLE," where we tell all. Following though are the states with the highest divorce rate annually.

	State	Divorces per 1,000
1.	Nevada	14.1
2.	Arizona	7.1
	Oklahoma	7.1
4.	Arkansas	7.0

State	Divorces per 1,000
5. Alaska	6.9
Wyoming	6.9
Tennessee	6.9
8. Florida	6.3
9. Kansas	6.2
10. Idaho	6.0

SOURCE: National Center for Health Statistics

Walking Away With the Most

THE **most** money ever awarded in a divorce settlement went to Soraya Khashoggi, the former wife of Adnan Khashoggi, the Saudi Arabian arms dealer. In 1982, Khashoggi's ex was awarded nearly a billion dollars—$950 million plus property, to be exact. With that amount of money, the former Mrs. Khashoggi would, in three months or so, at average interest rates, earn more than Princess Di received in her recent divorce settlement.

SOURCE: *The Guinness Book of Records 1996,* Bantam, 1996

The Most Money Rejected

THE **most** money ever rejected in a divorce settlement was an offer of $535 million by Texan Sid Bass to his wife Ann, who said that it would be inadequate for her to continue living in the style to which she had become accustomed.

SOURCE: Texas State Bar

The Most Pinstripes

THE law firm with the **most** employees in the world is Baker and McKenzie. Founded in Chicago in 1949, the firm had 1,651 lawyers in 28 countries as of 1993.

SOURCE: American Bar Association

Mammoth Companies Need the Most

WITH 342 attorneys working for it, Exxon has the **most** attorneys of any corporate legal department.

SOURCE: Exxon Corporation, Irving, TX

A Bankruptcy Most

WITH seven hundred attorneys, Finley, Kumble, Wagner, Heine, Underberg, Manley, Myerson and Casey was once the fourth-largest law firm in the United States. When it filed for bankruptcy in 1988, the New York firm claimed debts, exclusive of malpractice claims, totaling $108 million, the **most** ever claimed in a law firm bankruptcy case. Although the FDIC has a claim of $10.4 million against the firm's assets, it anticipates receiving only 20 cents on the dollar. However, the bankruptcy has proven quite lucrative for the accountants, lawyers, and trustees involved in representing the firm, who, by 1992, had received fees exceeding $37 million.

SOURCES: *New York Times,* Feb. 17, 1988; *New York Times,* October 28, 1988

All of OJ's Mosts

CALLED "the Trial of the Century," the murder trial of football legend and Hollywood celebrity O. J. Simpson held both the media and public transfixed for over a year. Simpson was arrested on June 17, 1994, for the brutal slashing murder of his ex-wife Nicole Brown Simpson and her friend, Ronald Goldman. Broadcast on local, network, and cable television, images of the arrest, the slow-speed chase down Los Angeles freeways, the bloody gloves that didn't fit Simpson's hands, and Nicole's chilling 911 calls have burned themselves into our public consciousness. Many of the trial's central figures have become household names: Judge Lance Ito, prosecutors Marcia Clark and Christopher Darden; defense attorneys Johnnie Cochran Jr., Robert Shapiro, Barry Scheck, and F. Lee Bailey; discredited LAPD detective Mark Fuhrman; Simpson houseguest Brian "Kato" Kaelin; and the outspoken victims' family members Fred Goldman and Denise Brown. Based on the number of satellite trucks and the hours of constant trial coverage, the Simpson trial was the **most** watched trial in history. Through CNN's daily gavel-to-gavel broadcasts, the world had an unblinking view into the criminal justice system. CNN, Court TV, and E! (Entertainment Television) saw their ratings triple during the trial, while U.S. businesses lost millions on employees taking time out to watch the trial on television during work hours. An astounding 150 million people were tuned in when, just after four hours of deliberation, the jury delivered its not-guilty verdict at 10:00 A.M. Pacific Time on October 3, 1995. Only two events in television history have earned that high a share of the viewing audience: the aftermath of the assassination of President John F. Kennedy and the Apollo 11 lunar landing. As the Simpson verdict was being read, there was a reported 58 percent drop in U.S. long distance telephone calls.

Jury selection in the Simpson case began on September 26, 1994. On January 11, 1995, a panel of twelve jurors and twelve alternates were sequestered in a downtown Los Angeles hotel. By the time the verdict was delivered on October 3, ten of the jurors had been replaced with alternates, thus leaving twelve jurors and two alternates who had spent 266 days—almost nine months—under the protection of L.A. County deputies, the **most** days sequestered of any jury in U.S. history. During that time, jurors were permitted occasional visits from spouses, were allowed to watch videos (but no broadcast television), and were taken as a group for brief outings occasionally. But no one can imagine what the lasting effects of this lengthy sequestration will have on the lives of the jurors, though if experience tells us anything, the jurors who were sequestered for the second **most** lengthy period of time ever are still feeling the aftereffects. We're referring to the members of the Los Angeles jury who found Charles Manson guilty of the 1969 Tate-Labianca murders and who were sequestered for a total of 227 days. Over the years many of them have said that their lives have not been the same since.

SOURCES: Nielsen Media Research and *U.S. News and World Report,* Oct. 16, 1995; *Newsweek,* October 16, 1995

The Most Costly Trial in U.S. History

IN terms of cost and length, however, the Simpson trial pales beside the Los Angeles McMartin Pre-School trial. Legal proceedings in the case began with the arraignment of Ray Buckey on September 7, 1983. Ultimately, Ray and Peggy Buckey were charged with fifty-two counts of child molestation and conspiracy at a Manhattan Beach, California, preschool. A lengthy preliminary hearing started on June 8, 1984, and jury selection for the trial began two years and ten months later on April 20, 1987. When both defendants were acquitted on January 18, 1990, the trial itself had taken over two years and eight months and had cost Los Angeles County over $15 million to prosecute, making this both the **most** protracted and the **most** expensive criminal trial in U.S. legal history. In contrast, the Simpson trial took just over a year and cost Los Angeles County $9 million.

SOURCE: *The Guinness Book of Records 1996,* Bantam, 1996

Guilty Gets the Most Leniency

ACCUSED criminals who plead guilty in U.S. courts receive the **most** lenient sentences. On average, for example, convicted murderers who plead guilty receive sentences half the length of those whose cases are tried before a jury.

SOURCE: American Bar Association

Mosts
from the World of
Education

Most, MOSTS, AND more **mosts** in the world of education. It's the first stage in a person's life when competition becomes a factor and someone actually keeps score. Read on and see how students are doing, who's having the **most** success, where you can go to make the **most** money after graduation, where you'll get the **most** respect. They're all factors in the world of education. So go ahead, read on and educate yourself.

If you are going onto college or continuing college or just plain pondering college, here are a few more **mosts** to tuck away in the **mosts** of the **mosts** lobe of your brain.

Have you ever wondered where you'll get the **most** education for your money? That is, the biggest bang for your buck! Or how about the **most** money for your degree? Don't kid yourself, students really are going on to good jobs after graduation these days.

SATs

I think we all know what this acronym stands for. We feared it as high school students and now either we hold our numbers close to our chests or we flaunt our scores, making sure to steer conversations toward them. Or some of us may even take the liberty of adding a hundred points—maybe even more—for conversational purposes only, of course.

The following ranking is of states with the **most** impressive average SAT scores during the 1995 school year.

	State	Average Score	Percent of High School Students Taking the Test
1.	North Dakota	1107	5
2.	Iowa	1099	5
3.	Minnesota	1085	9
4.	Utah	1076	4

5.	Wisconsin	1073	9
6.	South Dakota	1068	5
7.	Kansas	1060	9
8.	Nebraska	1050	9
9.	Illinois	1048	13
10.	Missouri	1045	9

The national average for 1995 was 910. The states above have among the lowest percentages of high school students taking the test in the nation.

SOURCE: College Entrance Examination Board

Taking the Most SATs

THE following states have, on a percentage basis, the **most** high school students taking the SATs. College Entrance Examination Board officials feel that the number of students taking the test is as important a number as test scores when looking at results on a state-by-state basis.

	State	Percent of High School Students Taking the Test	SAT Scores
1.	Connecticut	81	908
2.	Massachusetts	80	907
3.	New York	74	892
4.	New Hampshire	70	935
	New Jersey	70	898
	Pennsylvania	70	880
	Rhode Island	70	888
8.	Delaware	68	897
	Maine	68	896
	Vermont	68	901

SOURCE: College Entrance Examination Board

Most Agree, They're the Best

YOU just got your SAT scores back and they're outstanding! You've also just received your report card and you've done better than you, or anyone else for that matter, had suspected you would. What comes next? Well, you start looking at the **most** prestigious colleges and universities in the country (and you quickly apply before your parents have a chance to look over their tuition costs).

So, what are the **most** prestigious undergraduate schools in the nation? According to *The Gourman Report, a Rating of Undergraduate Programs in American and International Universities,* they are:

Institution
1. Princeton University
2. Harvard University
3. University of Michigan
4. Yale University
5. Stanford University
6. Cornell University
7. University of California at Berkeley
8. University of Chicago
9. University of Wisconsin—Madison
10. University of California at Los Angeles (UCLA)
11. Massachusetts Institute of Technology (MIT)
12. California Institute of Technology (Cal Tech)
13. Columbia University
14. Northwestern University
15. University of Pennsylvania
16. University of Notre Dame
17. Duke University
18. Brown University
19. Johns Hopkins University
20. Dartmouth College

SOURCE: Dr. Jack Gourman, *The Gourman Report, A Rating of Undergraduate Programs in American and International Universities*

Some Don't Agree

RESEARCHING top schools is like asking for an opinion. Everyone's got one. So as to widen our spectrum of the **most** prestigious universities in the U.S., we are including rankings from *U.S. News and World Report*'s "America's Best Colleges, 1996 Annual Guide," Sept. 18, 1995.

Institution
1. Harvard University
2. Princeton University
3. Yale University
4. Stanford University
5. Massachusetts Institute of Technology (MIT)
6. Duke University
7. California Institute of Technology (Cal Tech)
8. Dartmouth College
9. Brown University
10. Johns Hopkins University
11. University of Chicago
12. University of Pennsylvania
13. Cornell University
14. Northwestern University
15. Columbia University
16. Rice University
17. Emory University
18. University of Notre Dame
19. University of Virginia
20. Washington University (MO)

Liberal Arts Your Thing?

FOLLOWING are the **most** respected liberal arts colleges in the U.S.

College
1. Amherst College (Massachusetts)
2. Swarthmore College (Pennsylvania)
3. Williams College (Massachusetts)
4. Bowdoin College (Maine)
5. Haverford College (Pennsylvania)
6. Wellesley College (Massachusetts)
7. Middlebury College (Vermont)
8. Pomona College (California)
9. Bryn Mawr College (Pennsylvania)
10. Smith College (Massachusetts)
11. Carleton College (Minnesota)
12. Wesleyan College (Connecticut)
13. Vassar College (New York)
14. Grinnell College (Iowa)

College

15.	Washington and Lee University (Virginia)
16.	Claremont McKenna College (California)
17.	Colgate University (New York)
18.	Bates College (Maine)
19.	Colby College (Maine)
20.	Mount Holyoke (Massachusetts)

SOURCE: "America's Best Colleges, 1996 Annual Guide," *U.S. News and World Report,*
Sept. 18, 1995

The Most Difficult to Get Into

JUST so you don't get your hopes too high, even if you do have great SAT scores and you did study right through high school, be aware that the following schools are among the **most** difficult of all schools to get into. You may not see them on any of the other lists in here for one reason on another, but they continue to break hearts with their **most** difficult admissions standards.

Institution

1.	Harvard University
2.	Radcliffe College
3.	Princeton University
4.	Yale University
5.	The Cooper Union (strong in visual arts)
6.	Dartmouth College
7.	Brown University
8.	Deep Springs College
9.	The Juilliard School (strong in performing arts)
10.	Stanford University
11.	Massachusetts Institute of Technology (MIT)
12.	Williams College
13.	Rice University
14.	Duke University
15.	Amherst College
16.	Harvey Mudd College
17.	Swarthmore College
18.	Columbia University
19.	Wesleyan University
20.	University of Pennsylvania

If you plan to apply to any of the above, you should have SAT scores of at least 1300 and be in or very close to being in the top 10 percent of your high school class.

Please note that, on a percentage basis, fewer are admitted to the U.S. Naval Academy, the U.S. Military Academy, and the U.S. Air Force Academy than to any of the above.

SOURCE: The Princeton Review, Student Access Guide, *The Best 306 Colleges,* 1995 edition

The Most Students

WHERE can you find the **most** students? If you answered at school, you're right. But at which schools? And, particularly, at which colleges. Following are the universities in North America that had the **most** students enrolled during the 1995–96 academic year.

Enrollment figures pertain to main campuses.

	University	Students Enrolled
1.	Ohio State University—Columbus	36,166
2.	University of Indiana—Bloomington	35,551
3.	University of Texas—Austin	34,746
4.	Texas A&M University—College Station	34,278
5.	Pennsylvania State University—University Park	31,732
6.	Arizona State University	31,198
7.	Michigan State University	31,056
8.	University of Florida	28,479
9.	Brigham Young University	28,282
10.	Purdue University	27,750
11.	University of Arizona	26,468
12.	University of Madison—Madison	26,207
13.	University of Illinois—Urbana-Champaign	25,348
14.	University of Minnesota—Twin Cities	25,238
15.	University of Washington	24,592
16.	University of California at Los Angeles	23,649
17.	University of South Florida	23,622
18.	University of Michigan—Ann Arbor	23,088
19.	University of Georgia	22,832
20.	University of Akron	22,755

SOURCE: *The Guidance Information System,* Riverside Publishing Company (a Houghton Mifflin Company)

Paying the Most

WHAT colleges and universities are charging students the **most** these days? Below are the culprits, based on annual tuition, fees, and room and board.

We say "culprits" in jest, as the education provided is generally regarded as outstanding.

	College	Tuition per Year (dollars)
1.	Brandeis University	26,130
2.	Barnard College	25,492
3.	Massachusetts Institute of Technology (MIT)	25,400
4.	Hampshire College	25,210
5.	Yale University	25,110
6.	Bard College	25,044
7.	Tufts University	24,962
8.	Sarah Lawrence College	24,960
9.	Harvard University	24,880
10.	Bennington College	24,850

SOURCES: Gilbert and Jersey, *Money's Guide to 1,003 Colleges;*
also, *Money Guide: Best College Buys Now,* Time Inc.

So You Like School and You Like Money?

THINKING about adding a few more years to your education? Thinking about getting your MBA? Then think about these top business schools ranked according to whose graduates make the **most** money.

	Business School	Avg. Starting Income of Graduates (dollars)	Academic Rank
1.	Harvard University	102,630	5
2.	Stanford University	100,800	4
3.	Columbia University	100,480	8
4.	Dartmouth College (Amos Tuck)	95,410	13
5.	University of Pennsylvania (Wharton)	89,930	1
6.	Northwestern University (Kellogg)	84,640	2
7.	University of Chicago	83,210	3
8.	MIT (Sloan)	80,500	10

9.	University of Virginia (Darden)	74,280	12
10.	UCLA (Anderson)	74,010	9
11.	Cornell University (Johnson)	71,970	15
12.	U.C. at Berkeley (Haas)	71,970	19
13.	New York University (Stern)	70,660	16
14.	Duke University (Fuqua)	70,490	11
15.	Carnegie Mellon University	69,890	14
16.	University of North Carolina at Chapel Hill (Kenan-Flagler)	69,880	18
17.	University of Michigan	67,820	6
18.	University of Texas at Austin	61,890	17
19.	Indiana University	58,520	7
20.	Purdue University (Krannert)	54,720	20

SOURCE: Business Week, *Guide to the Best Business Schools* (1995), 4th edition

What's Your Sign?

MAYBE you didn't get into a business school whose graduates are making the **most** money. Life is not over. Why not apply to a business school where students do the **most** dating? Makes sense, right? According to *The Princeton Review,* you are likely to date the **most** at the following business schools (in no particular order):

> Brigham Young University
> Ohio State University
> Pennsylvania State University
> Southern Methodist University
> Tulane University
> University of California at Berkeley
> University of Denver
> University of Maryland
> University of North Carolina at Chapel Hill
> Wake Forest University

SOURCE: Gilbert Nedda, *The Princeton Review Student Access Guide to the Best Business Schools,* 1994 edition

Reading and Writing

So you'd rather read and write than make the **most** money? Then a graduate degree in English might be the answer. Of course, you might graduate and write a best-seller, then you too would be among those that are pulling in the **most** dollars. Where are the best graduate programs to learn the craft? Read on.

	Institution
1.	University of California at Berkeley
	Yale University
3.	Stanford University
	Harvard University
	Cornell University
	Johns Hopkins University
7.	University of Chicago
	Duke University
	Princeton University
10.	Columbia University
	University of Virginia
12.	University of California at Los Angeles
	University of Pennsylvania
14.	University of Michigan
15.	University of California at Irvine
	Brown University

SOURCE: "Best Graduate Schools: Liberal Arts," *U.S. News and World Report,* March 23, 1992

Law School and the Most $

THINKING about law school, but also thinking about the income you'll need to pay off the debts you accumulated to get your education? Then may we suggest you go to a law school where you'll get the **most** money after graduation and entry into the bar?

Following are top law schools whose students went on to make the **most** in salaries after graduation.

	Law School	1995 Median Starting Salaries	Academic Rank
1.	New York University	85,000	6
2.	Columbia University	83,000	5
3.	Yale University	82,000	1
4.	University of Virginia	75,000	9

5.	Georgetown University	73,000	12
6.	Harvard University	72,000	2
7.	Stanford University	71,000	3
8.	University of Chicago	70,000	4
	University of Michigan—Ann Arbor	70,000	7
	University of Pennsylvania	70,000	8
	Cornell University	70,000	11
	Northwestern University	70,000	14
	University of Southern California	70,000	15
	University of California at Los Angeles	70,000	17
15.	Boston University	68,000	29
16.	Fordham University	67,500	28
17.	University of California at Berkeley	67,000	12
18.	George Washington University	66,000	22
	University of California at Hastings	66,000	45
20.	Duke University	63,000	10

SOURCE: "America's Best Graduate Schools, 1996 Annual Guide,"
U.S. News and World Report, March 18, 1996

The Most Prestigious Medical Schools

WHETHER you're thinking of going to medical school or just plain thinking of going to a doctor (check his or her diploma on the wall to see if his or her school makes the list), consider the following. Barron's *Guide to Medical and Dental Schools,* 6th edition, ranks these schools as among the **most** prestigious of all medical schools (in alphabetical order).

Albert Einstein (New York)
Baylor College of Medicine (Texas)
Columbia University (New York)
Cornell University (New York)
Duke University (North Carolina)
Harvard University (Massachusetts)
Johns Hopkins University (Maryland)
New York University (New York)
Stanford University (California)
University of California at Los Angeles
University of California at San Diego
University of California at San Francisco
University of Chicago

University of Michigan
University of Minnesota—Minneapolis
University of Pennsylvania
University of Texas—Dallas
Vanderbilt University (Tennessee)
Washington University (Missouri)
Yale University (Connecticut)

Going to School to Stay in School

You like school. You really, really like school. So stay in school . . . forever. Following are the average salaries of college professors, according to field of study, for the 1993–94 academic year. See which ones are making the **most** money.

	Discipline	1993–94 Average Salary (dollars)
1.	Law	89,777
2.	Engineering	77,985
3.	Health Sciences	77,913
4.	Business and Management	77,535
5.	Computer and Information Science	75,964
6.	Physical Sciences	65,914
7.	Mathematics	63,776
8.	Psychology	62,567
9.	Public Affairs	62,435
10.	Social Sciences	62,351
11.	Library Science	61,827
12.	Interdisciplinary Studies	61,808
13.	Architecture	59,322
14.	Agribusiness	59,178
15.	Communications	58,933

SOURCE: "Plus Ça Change: The Annual Report on the Economic Status of the Profession, 1993–1994," *Academe*, March-April 1994

Mosts
from the World of
Sports

WELCOME TO THE wide, wide world of sports. Something for everyone here. That's why this chapter goes on and on. Also, because sports are competitive in nature, athletes are always striving for records, which, in our book, is a lot of **mosts.**

So go ahead and dive in. This one is for couch potatoes *and* players. It's the quickest way of locating what player or team has the **most** going for him, her, and/or them.

Summer Olympic Games

IN addition to the regular summer Olympic games, the International Olympic Committee organized the 1906 Intercalated Games in Athens to celebrate the tenth anniversary of the revival of the Olympics. Although the IOC doesn't officially recognize the results from those games, the medals won during that year are included in the totals below for the Summer Games (through 1996). Only the countries winning the **most** are included.

	Country	Gold	Silver	Bronze	Total
1.	United States	832	634	553	2,019
2.	USSR/UT/Russia[1]	466	381	343	1,190
3.	Germany[2]	360	375	390	1,125
4.	Great Britain	169	223	218	610
5.	France	175	179	206	560
6.	Sweden	132	151	174	457
7.	Italy	166	135	144	445
8.	Hungary	142	129	155	426

	Country	Gold	Silver	Bronze	Total
9.	Finland	99	80	113	292
	Australia	86	85	121	292

1. Includes Czarist Russia, the Unified Team of 1992, and the Russian team of 1996
2. Includes all of Germany, West Germany, and East Germany totals.

SOURCE: *The 1997 Information Please Sports Almanac,* Houghton Mifflin, 1996

Winter Olympic Games

IN 1924, the first Winter Olympics were held in Chamonix, France. Through the 1994 games, the countries with the **most** medals are:

	Country	Gold	Silver	Bronze	Total
1.	USSR/UT/Russia[1]	99	71	71	241
2.	Germany[2]	84	80	72	236
3.	Norway	73	77	64	214
4.	United States	53	56	37	146
5.	Austria	36	48	44	128
6.	Finland	36	45	42	123
7.	Sweden	39	26	34	99
8.	Switzerland	27	29	29	85
9.	Italy	25	21	21	67
10.	Canada	19	20	25	64

1. Includes Czarist Russia and the Unified Team of 1992.
2. Includes all of Germany, West Germany, and East Germany totals.

SOURCE: *The 1997 Information Please Sports Almanac.* Houghton Mifflin, 1996

The Olympic Athlete Winning the Most

THE 1956 Olympics in Melbourne, Australia, were the first games in which the Soviets outmedaled the U.S., winning their first track and field titles and dominating the gymnastics competition. That year, Soviet gymnast Larissa Latynina won the first 6 of her record 18 Olympic medals, the **most** won by an athlete in Olympic competition. In three Summer Games (1956, 1960, and 1964) Latynina won a total of 9 gold, 5 silver, and 4 bronze medals. With 14 of her medals won in individual competition, Latynina also holds the record for the **most** individual medals (6 gold, 5 silver, and 3 bronze). Her 9 gold medals are also the **most** earned by a female Olympic athlete.

SOURCE: *The 1997 Information Please Sports Almanac*, Houghton Mifflin, 1996

The Most 10s

No, we're not talking about a room full of Bo Derek clones. We're talking about perfect scores and a fourteen-year-old Romanian gymnast named Nadia Comaneci, who holds that Olympic record. In the 1976 Olympic Games in Montreal, Nadia scored seven perfect 10s in competition on her way to winning three gold medals. That's a **most** that captivated the games' worldwide audience and made little Nadia a celebrity.

SOURCE: International Olympic Committee

The Male Athlete with the Most Medals

Also in the 1976 Montreal Games, Soviet gymnast Aleksandr Dityatin became the first athlete ever to win 8 medals in a single Olympics. Through the 1980 Games in Moscow, Aleksandr Dityatin brought his overall total to 15 Olympic medals (7 gold, 5 silver, 3 bronze), the **most** ever won by a male athlete and the second-highest overall total. This outstanding feat also includes 3 medals won in Munich in 1972. Moreover, 12 of Dityatin's medals (6 gold, 3 silver, and 3 bronze) were won in individual competition, the **most** individual medals won by a male athlete.

SOURCE: International Olympic Committee

The Baseball Players Playing the Most

These guys like baseball. They really, really like baseball. They are those who have had the luck, the talent, and the stamina to have played the **most** career games, and they are:

	Player	Games
1.	Pete Rose	3,562
2.	Carl Yastrzemski	3,308
3.	Hank Aaron	3,298
4.	Ty Cobb	3,034
5.	Stan Musial	3,026

	Player	Games
6.	Willie Mays	2,992
7.	Dave Winfield	2,973
8.	Eddie Murray	2,971
9.	Rusty Staub	2,951
10.	Brooks Robinson	2,896

SOURCE: *The 1997 Information Please Sports Almanac,* Houghton Mifflin, 1996

Playing the Most Consecutive Games

YOU just can't keep some guys off the field. And following are the baseball players who have played the **most** consecutive games (through the 1996 season).

	Player	Team	Games	Career
1.	Cal Ripken Jr.	Baltimore	2,315	05/30/82 to present
2.	Lou Gehrig	New York	2,131	06/01/25 to 04/30/39
3.	Everett Scott	Boston/NY	1,307	06/20/16 to 05/05/25
4.	Steve Garvey	LA/San Diego	1,207	09/03/75 to 07/29/83
5.	Billy Williams	Chicago Cubs	1,117	09/02/70 to 09/22/93

SOURCE: *The World Almanac and Book of Facts 1997,* World Almanac Books, 1996

The Players Running the Most

REALLY, if you think about it, the object in baseball is the same as in track. That is, to run. Sound odd? Think about it. In baseball you're hitting the ball only to buy enough time to get around that diamond. The farther you hit it, the farther you get to run. And if you don't hit it—if you whiff away until you strike out, you simply don't get to run. It's that easy. So keep your eye on the ball. You're going to need to if you intend to get in any exercise at all.

So who's running the **most**? The following are. They are the players who have had the **most** career runs during regular season games.

	Player	Runs
1.	Ty Cobb	2,245
2.	Babe Ruth	2,174
	Hank Aaron	2,174

4.	Pete Rose	2,165
5.	Willie Mays	2,062
6.	Stan Musial	1,949
7.	Lou Gehrig	1,888
8.	Tris Speaker	1,882
9.	Mel Ott	1,859
10.	Frank Robinson	1,829

SOURCE: *The 1997 Information Please Sports Almanac,* Houghton Mifflin, 1996

Hitting the Most Home Runs

DURING the 1961 baseball season Roger Maris, playing for the New York Yankees, set a major league record for the **most** home runs in a single season. Maris hit 61 home runs in 162 games and 590 turns at bat, beating the previous single-season record of 60 home runs, set by Babe Ruth while playing for the Yanks during the 1927 season. Ruth played in 151 games that year and was at bat 540 times. Ruth's 1921 season total of 59 home runs in 152 games with 540 times at bat still stands as the third-highest number of home runs in a single season.

Below are the players who have hit the **most** career home runs during the regular season.

	Player	Years	At-Bats	Home Runs	AB/HR
1.	Hank Aaron	23	12,364	755	16.4
2.	Babe Ruth	22	8,399	714	11.8
3.	Willie Mays	22	10,881	660	16.5
4.	Frank Robinson	21	10,006	586	17.1
5.	Harmon Killebrew	22	8,147	573	14.2
6.	Reggie Jackson	21	9,864	563	17.5
7.	Mike Schmidt	18	8,352	548	15.2
8.	Mickey Mantle	18	8,102	536	15.1
9.	Jimmie Foxx	20	8,134	534	15.2
10.	Ted Williams	19	7,706	521	14.8
	Willie McCovey	22	8,197	521	15.7

SOURCES: *The Guinness Book of Records, 1996,* Bantam, 1996;
The 1997 Information Please Sports Almanac, Houghton Mifflin, 1996

The Most Steals and Still No Police Interference

RICKEY Henderson holds the major league record for stolen bases with 1,186, followed by Lou Brock (938), Billy Hamilton (915), and Ty Cobb (892).

SOURCE: *The 1997 Information Please Sports Almanac,* Houghton Mifflin, 1996

The Most World Series Wins

MAJOR league baseball started in the U.S. with the formation of the National League in 1876. The rival American League was started in 1901, and two years later Pittsburgh, champions of the National League, invited American League champions Boston to participate in a best-of-nine-games series to establish the "real" champions. Boston won 5–3. The next year the National League champions, New York, refused to play Boston, and there was no World Series. It was resumed in 1905 and has been held every year since, except 1994. It has been a best-of-seven-games series since 1905, with the exception of 1919–1921, when it reverted to a nine-game series.

Can you guess which team has won the World Series the **most** (through the 1996 season)? If not, we'll tell you.

1.	New York Yankees	23
2.	Philadelphia–Kansas City–Oakland Athletics	9
	St. Louis Cardinals	9
4.	Brooklyn–Los Angeles Dodgers	6
5.	Boston Red Sox	5
	Cincinnati Reds	5
	New York–San Francisco Giants	5
	Pittsburgh Pirates	5
9.	Detroit Tigers	4
10.	St. Louis–Baltimore Orioles	3
	Washington Senators–Minnesota Twins	3

SOURCE: *The 1997 Information Please Sports Almanac,* Houghton Mifflin, 1996

Walking the Most

WHEN one team feels a bit intimidated by a batter for the opposing team, they can do something about it. No, they can't complain or make a scene, but they can intentionally keep the batter from hitting the ball by walking him or her. Unfortunately, this does send the batter straight to first base, but it does stop the looming threat of a big hit.

The players who have been walked the **most** over their careers are:

	Player	Walks
1.	Babe Ruth	2,056
2.	Ted Williams	2,019
3.	Joe Morgan	1,865
4.	Carl Yastrzemski	1,845
5.	Mickey Mantle	1,734
6.	Mel Ott	1,708
7.	Rickey Henderson*	1,675
8.	Eddie Yost	1,614
9.	Darrell Evans	1,605
10.	Stan Musial	1,599
11.	Pete Rose	1,566

*Still active through the 1996 season.

SOURCE: *The 1997 Information Please Sports Almanac,* Houghton Mifflin, 1996

Striking Out the Most

ON the other hand, there are those batters who step up to the plate and don't exactly deliver, sending glee into the heart of the ball's deliverer—the opposing team. Following are the players who have struck out the **most**.

	Player	Strikeouts
1.	Reggie Jackson	2,597
2.	Willie Stargell	1,936
3.	Mike Schmidt	1,883
4.	Tony Perez	1,867
5.	Dave Kingman	1,816
6.	Bobby Bonds	1,757
7.	Dale Murphy	1,748
8.	Lou Brock	1,730
9.	Mickey Mantle	1,710
10.	Harmon Killebrew	1,699

SOURCE: *The 1997 Information Please Sports Almanac,* Houghton Mifflin, 1996

Pitching the Most Innings

SOME guys are born with an arm and there's just no doubt about it, and the following pitchers have some pretty good arms. They are the pitchers who have pitched the **most** career innings.

	Pitcher	Innings
1.	Cy Young	7,356
2.	Pud Galvin	5,941⅓
3.	Walter Johnson	5,923⅔
4.	Phil Niekro	5,403⅓
5.	Nolan Ryan	5,387
6.	Gaylord Perry	5,350⅓
7.	Don Sutton	5,280⅓
8.	Warren Spahn	5,243⅔
9.	Steve Carlton	5,217⅓
10.	Grover Alexander	5,189⅔

SOURCE: *The 1997 Information Please Sports Almanac,* Houghton Mifflin, 1996

Pitchers Winning the Most

SOME of the same pitchers who have pitched the **most** innings have also racked up the **most** wins. Have a look and compare their records.

	Pitcher	Years	Games Started	Wins	Losses	Pct.
1.	Cy Young	22	815	511	316	.618
2.	Walter Johnson	21	666	416	279	.599
3.	Christy Mathewson	17	551	373	188	.665
	Grover Alexander	20	598	373	208	.642
5.	Warren Spahn	21	665	363	245	.587
6.	Kid Nichols	15	561	361	208	.634
	Pud Galvin	14	682	361	308	.540
8.	Tim Keefe	14	594	342	225	.603
9.	Steve Carlton	24	709	329	244	.574
10.	Eddie Plank	17	527	327	193	.629

SOURCE: *The 1997 Information Please Sports Almanac,* Houghton Mifflin, 1996

Batting Average Mosts

PETE Rose holds the record for the **most** career hits in major league Baseball, an incredible 4,256 in 14,053 turns at bat over 24 years. Ty Cobb, who also played for 24 years, hit 4,191 in 11,429 turns at bat, the second-highest number of career hits. However, Cobb's batting average of .367 is the **most** hits per turn at bat of any player in major league baseball.

The players whose hits per time at bat ("batting average") puts them in the league of **mosts** are:

	Player	At Bats	Hits	Average
1.	Ty Cobb	11,429	4,191	.367
2.	Rogers Hornsby	8,137	2,930	.358
3.	Joe Jackson	4,981	1,774	.356
4.	Ed Delahanty	7,509	2,597	.346
5.	Tris Speaker	10,197	3,514	.345
6.	Ted Williams	7,706	2,654	.344
7.	Billy Hamilton	6,284	2,163	.344
8.	Willie Keeler	8,585	2,947	.343
9.	Dan Brouthers	6,711	2,296	.342
10.	Babe Ruth	8,399	2,873	.342
11.	Harry Heilmann	7,787	2,660	.342

SOURCE: *The 1997 Information Please Sports Almanac,* Houghton Mifflin, 1996

The Players Playing for the Most

LATELY, the sports pages have been as much about who's winning and losing in salary arbitration as who's winning and losing on the field or in the arena. Though from the numbers we're all reading, it seems that everyone is winning.

Below are the athletes who made the **most** money in salaries and endorsements during 1996 as estimated by *Forbes* magazine.

	Athlete	Sport	Salary/Winnings	Endorsements	Total ($)
1.	Mike Tyson	Boxing	75,000,000	0	75,000,000
2.	Michael Jordan	Basketball	12,600,000	40,000,000	52,600,000
3.	Michael Schumacher	Auto Racing	25,000,000	8,000,000	33,000,000
4.	Shaquille O'Neil	Basketball	7,400,000	17,000,000	24,400,000
5.	Emmitt Smith	Football	13,000,000	3,500,000	16,500,000
6.	Evander Holyfield	Boxing	15,000,000	500,000	15,500,000

	Athlete	Sport	Salary/Winnings	Endorsements	Total ($)
7.	Andre Agassi	Tennis	2,200,000	13,000,000	15,200,000
8.	Arnold Palmer	Golf	100,000	15,000,000	15,100,000
9.	Dennis Rodman	Basketball	3,900,000	9,000,000	12,900,000
10.	Patrick Ewing	Basketball	11,900,000	1,000,000	12,900,000

SOURCE: *Forbes* Magazine, Dec. 16, 1996

Making the Most Calls

BEGINNING in 1905, Bill Klem served as a National League umpire for over thirty-seven years, the **most** seasons of any major league umpire. His career included officiating in eighteen World Series, the last in 1940.

SOURCE: Association of National Baseball League Umpires

The Super Super Bowl Winners

WHO'S won it the **most** times?

	Team	Wins	Year	Coach
1.	Dallas Cowboys	5	1972	Tom Landry
			1978	Tom Landry
			1993	Jimmy Johnson
			1994	Jimmy Johnson
			1996	Barry Switzer
	San Francisco 49ers	5	1982	Bill Walsh
			1985	Bill Walsh
			1989	Bill Walsh
			1990	George Seifert
			1995	George Seifert
2.	Pittsburgh Steelers	4	1975	Chuck Noll
			1976	Chuck Noll
			1979	Chuck Noll
			1980	Chuck Noll
3.	Green Bay Packers	3	1967	Vince Lombardi
			1968	Vince Lombardi
			1997	Mike Holmgren

Oakland-LA-Oakland Raiders	3	1977	John Madden
		1981	Tom Flores
		1984	Tom Flores
Washington Redskins	3	1983	Joe Gibbs
		1988	Joe Gibbs
		1992	Joe Gibbs
4. Miami Dolphins	2	1973	Don Shula
		1974	Don Shula
New York Giants	2	1987	Bill Parcels
		1991	Bill Parcels

The **most** Super Bowl appearances by a team is 8, by the Dallas Cowboys.

SOURCE: National Football League

The Coach with the Most

THE **most** wins by an NFL coach as of the start of the 1996 season are listed below (including post-season games).

	Coach	Years	Team(s)	Wins	Winning Percentage
1.	Don Shula	33	Colts, Dolphins	347	.665
2.	George Halas	40	Bears	324	.671
3.	Tom Landry	29	Cowboys	270	.601
4.	Curly Lambeau	33	Packers, Cardinals, Redskins	229	.623
5.	Chuck Noll	23	Steelers	209	.572
6.	Chuck Knox	22	Rams, Bills, Seahawks	193	.550
7.	Paul Brown	21	Browns, Bengals	170	.607
8.	Bud Grant	18	Vikings	168	.605
9.	Steve Owen	23	Giants	154	.582
10.	Joe Gibbs	12	Redskins	140	.683

SOURCE: *The World Almanac and Book of Facts 1997*, World Almanac Books, New Jersey, 1996

The Most MVPs

Most Valuable Player, and you can take that to the bank! The following are the players who have won such honors the **most** times.

	Player	MVP	Years	Team(s)
1.	Jim Brown	3	1958 1963 1965	Cleveland Browns
2.	Earl Campbell	3	1978 1979 1980	Houston Oilers
	Johnny Unitas	2	1957 1967	Baltimore Colts
4.	Y. A. Tittle	2	1961 1963	New York Giants
	Brett Favre	2	1995 1996	Green Bay Packers
	Walter Payton	2	1977 1985	Chicago Bears
	Steve Young	2	1992 1994	San Francisco 49ers

SOURCE: *The World Almanac and Book of Facts 1997,* World Almanac Books, New Jersey, 1996

The Most Concrete and People

EVER been to a pro football game? You stepped into the stadium and your eyes just about bugged out. Those places are huge. But which are the biggest and have the **most** capacity?

	Team	Stadium	Turf	Year Built	Capacity
1.	Detroit Lions	Pontiac Silverdome	A	1975	80,368
2.	Buffalo Bills	Rich Stadium	A	1973	80,024
3.	Kansas City Chiefs	Arrowhead Stadium	G	1972	79,101
4.	New York Giants	Giants Stadium (NJ)	A	1976	78,148
5.	New York Jets	Giants Stadium (NJ)	A	1976	77,803
6.	Denver Broncos	Mile High Stadium	G	1948	76,273
7.	Miami Dolphins	Pro Player Stadium	G	1987	74,916

8.	Tampa Bay Buccaneers	Tampa Stadium	G	1967	74,301
9.	Phoenix Cardinals	Sun Devil Stadium	G	1958	73,273
10.	Jacksonville Jaguars	Jacksonville Municipal Stadium	G	1995	73,000
11.	Carolina Panthers	Ericsson Stadium	G	1996	72,520
12.	Atlanta Falcons	Georgia Dome	A	1992	71,228
13.	San Francisco 49ers	3Com Park	G	1960	70,207
14.	New Orleans Saints	Louisiana Superdome	A	1975	69,056
15.	Chicago Bears	Soldier Field	G	1924	66,944

SOURCE: *The World Almanac and Book of Facts 1997*, World Almanac Books, New Jersey, 1996

The Most National College Football Titles

PRIOR to the media's picking the national champions in college football, it used to be done by a variety of methods. During these years, 1869 to 1935, Yale had the **most** national championships with 18, Princeton was next with 17, Harvard with 9, Michigan and Notre Dame with 7. Even Penn State, a perennial powerhouse in a more recent era, won two national championships back then. Since 1936, the media have been picking our champions, and over the years the following schools have won the college football national championship the **most**.

	School	Wins	Year	Coach
1.	Notre Dame	9	1943	Frank Leahy
			1946	Frank Leahy
			1947	Frank Leahy
			1949	Frank Leahy
			1964	Ara Parseghian
			1966	Ara Parseghian
			1973	Ara Parseghian
			1977	Dan Devine
			1988	Lou Holtz
2.	Alabama	7	1961	Bear Bryant
			1964	Bear Bryant
			1965	Bear Bryant
			1973	Bear Bryant
			1978	Bear Bryant
			1979	Bear Bryant
			1992	Gene Stallings

	School	Wins	Year	Coach
3.	Ohio State	6	1942	Paul Brown
			1954	Woody Hayes
			1957	Woody Hayes
			1961	Woody Hayes
			1968	Woody Hayes
			1970	Woody Hayes
	Oklahoma	6	1950	Bud Wilkinson
			1955	Bud Wilkinson
			1956	Bud Wilkinson
			1974	Barry Switzer
			1975	Barry Switzer
			1985	Barry Switzer
5.	USC	5	1962	John McKay
			1967	John McKay
			1972	John McKay
			1974	John McKay
			1978	John Robinson

Other notable champions with the **most** wins include Florida, Minnesota, and Nebraska as 4-time winners; Michigan State and Texas with 3 wins; and Army, Georgia Tech, Penn State, and Pittsburgh with 2 wins each.

Bear Bryant won the championship 6 times, the **most** of any present-day coach.

SOURCE: *The 1996 Information Please Sports Almanac,* Houghton Mifflin, 1996

The Most Coaching Wins

WHO'S **most** used to winning? The answer to that would be coaches that win the **most**, and following is a list of all-time Division 1-A win leaders.

	Coach	Wins
1.	Paul "Bear" Bryant	323
2.	Glenn "Pop" Warner	319
3.	Amos Alonzo Stagg	314
4.	Joe Paterno	278
5.	Bobby Bowden	259

6.	Woody Hayes	238
7.	Bo Schembechler	234
8.	Tom Osborne	231
9.	LaVell Edwards	214
10.	Hayden Fry	213
11.	Jess Neely	207
12.	Lou Holtz	208
13.	Warren Woodson	203
14.	Eddie Anderson	201
	Vince Dooley	201

Note that Joe Paterno, Bobby Bowden, Tom Osborne, LaVell Edwards, Hayden Fry, and Lou Holtz are still coaching today. Eddie Robinson of Grambling State (not ranked above because Grambling is not a Division 1-A school) has over 400 wins to date.

Figures based on wins accumulated up until the start of the 1996 season.

SOURCE: *The 1997 World Almanac and Book of Facts,* World Almanac Books, New Jersey, 1996

The Most Wins in a Row

SINCE 1936, can you guess which teams have gone on a streak and won the **most** games in a row? Below are the answers.

	Team	Win Streak	Years
1.	Oklahoma	47	1953–57
2.	Toledo	35	1969–71
3.	Oklahoma	31	1948–50
4.	Texas	30	1968–70
5.	Miami—Florida	29	1990–93
6.	Alabama	28	1991–93
	Alabama	28	1978–80
	Oklahoma	28	1973–75
	Michigan State	28	1950–53

SOURCE: *The 1996 World Almanac and Book of Facts*

Not Enough Hot Dogs!

SINCE the NCAA has been keeping records, beginning in 1948, the **most** fans to attend a football game was 106,255, at Michigan Football Stadium, on October 23, 1983. Michigan lost that day to Ohio State and, amazingly, the stadium made it through the day.

The Rose Bowl attracted the **most** fans for a college bowl game. Ohio State lost that game to USC, 42 to 17.

SOURCE: National Collegiate Athletic Association (NCAA)

The Most Wins over the Century

BELIEVE it or not, college football has been around for more than one hundred years. Hard to believe, isn't it?

Think of some of the Division 1-A teams winning the **most** games today and you'll be pretty close to those that have won the **most** games on a percentage basis over the last hundred years or so. Figures run through the 1995 season and include bowl games.

	School	Years	Games	Wins	Percentage
1.	Notre Dame	107	990	738	.760
2.	Michigan	116	1,042	756	.743
3.	Alabama	101	996	703	.727
4.	Oklahoma	101	974	670	.715
5.	Texas	103	1,017	705	.709
6.	Ohio State	106	1,003	679	.703
7.	USC	103	960	647	.702
8.	Nebraska	106	1,028	698	.698
9.	Penn State	109	1,030	695	.695
10.	Tennessee	99	989	656	.690

SOURCE: *The 1997 Information Please Sports Almanac,* Houghton Mifflin, 1996

Basketball Mosts

IT'S snowing outside. What do you do? Do what **most** others do. Turn on the TV set. What's going to be on? **Most** likely a basketball game. Before you sink too deep into the couch, though, have a glance to see what teams and players have done the **most** for the great game of basketball over the years.

And that begins with what team has won the NBA championship the **most**.

	Team	Total Number of Championships Won	Year	Coach
1.	Boston Celtics	16	1957	Red Auerbach
			1959	Red Auerbach
			1960	Red Auerbach
			1961	Red Auerbach
			1962	Red Auerbach
			1963	Red Auerbach
			1964	Red Auerbach
			1965	Red Auerbach
			1966	Red Auerbach
			1968	Bill Russell
			1969	Bill Russell
			1974	Tommy Heinsohn
			1976	Tommy Heinsohn
			1981	Bill Fitch
			1984	K. C. Jones
			1986	K. C. Jones
2.	Minneapolis–Los Angeles Lakers	11	1949	John Kundla
			1950	John Kundla
			1952	John Kundla
			1953	John Kundla
			1954	John Kundla
			1972	Bill Sharman
			1980	Paul Westhead
			1982	Pat Riley
			1985	Pat Riley
			1987	Pat Riley
			1988	Pat Riley
3.	Chicago Bulls	4	1991	Phil Jackson
			1992	Phil Jackson
			1993	Phil Jackson
			1996	Phil Jackson

SOURCE: National Basketball Association

NBA Arenas Holding the Most

So you don't feel like staying inside? Then go out for a basketball game. Be prepared to do a little more mixing and mingling than you would in your living room, though, because the following NBA arenas hold the **most** spectators.

	Arena	Year Built	City	Team	Capacity
1.	SkyDome	1989	Toronto, Ont.	Raptors	25,356
2.	Charlotte Coliseum	1988	Charlotte, NC	Hornets	24,042
3.	United Center	1994	Chicago, IL	Bulls	21,711
4.	The Palace of Auburn Hills	1988	Auburn Hills, MI	Pistons	21,454
5.	Rose Garden	1995	Portland, OR	Trailblazers	21,401
6.	CoreStates Center	1996	Philadelphia, PA	76ers	21,000
7.	The Alamodome	1993	San Antonio, TX	Spurs	20,662
8.	Gund Arena	1994	Cleveland, OH	Cavaliers	20,562
9.	Continental Airlines Arena	1981	East Rutherford, NJ	Nets	20,039
10.	Delta Center	1991	Salt Lake City, UT	Jazz	19,911

SOURCE: *The World Almanac and Book of Facts 1997,* World Almanac Books, New Jersey, 1996

The NBA Coaches with the Most Wins per Games

WHAT coaches lead the NBA with the **most** games won based on the total games played? You might be surprised to find out that a lot of these guys are still around and still winning their share of games today.

Requirements to make the following list include *(a)* being a very good coach and *(b)* having coached in the NBA for either at least 6 seasons or for at least 350 games. Figures are good through the 1995–1996 basketball season.

	Coach	Years	Wins	Percentage
1.	Phil Jackson	7	495	.722
2.	Pat Riley	14	935	.692
3.	Billy Cunningham	8	520	.689
4.	K. C. Jones	10	603	.661
5.	Red Auerbach	20	1,037	.654
6.	Tommy Heinson	9	474	.616

7.	Rick Adelman	7	363	.609
8.	Chuck Daly	12	638	.599
9.	Larry Costello	10	467	.591
10.	John Kundla	11	485	.589
	Jerry Sloan	11	552	.589

SOURCE: *The 1997 Information Please Sports Almanac,* Houghton Mifflin, 1996

Winning the Most Basketball Games

THOUGH Phil Jackson, now of the Chicago Bulls, has won the **most** games by percentage of games played, you can see that the coach who has flat out won the **most** games is Lenny Wilkins, coach of the Atlanta Hawks, who has now won the **most** regular season games in the NBA, having passed even Red Auerbach's once seemingly untouchable record of **most** wins.

Below are the **most** successful NBA coaches when measured by the career games their teams have won (regular season and playoffs).

	Coach	Yrs	W	L	Pct.	Titles
1.	Lenny Wilkens*	23	1,078	920	.540	1
2.	Red Auerbach	20	1,037	548	.654	9
3.	Dick Motta*	24	974	1,035	.485	1
4.	Bill Fitch*	23	946	1,046	.475	1
5.	Pat Riley*	14	935	417	.692	4
6.	Jack Ramsay	21	908	841	.519	1
7.	Don Nelson*	19	902	690	.567	0
8.	Cotton Fitzsimmons	20	867	816	.515	0
9.	Gene Shue	22	814	908	.473	0
10.	Red Holzman	18	754	652	.536	2
	John MacLeod	18	754	711	.515	0

*Coaches active during the 1995–1996 season

SOURCE: *The 1997 Information Please Sports Almanac,* Houghton Mifflin, 1996

The Most Valuable Player

VOTED on by the players from 1956 to 1980, then by a panel of sports writers since 1981, the NBA **Most** Valuable Players that have won the **most** coveted award the **most** are:

Player (position)	Times Won	Year	Team
1. Kareem Abdul-Jabbar (C)	6	1971	Milwaukee
		1972	Milwaukee
		1974	Los Angeles
		1976	Los Angeles
		1977	Los Angeles
		1980	Los Angeles
2. Bill Russell (C)	5	1958	Boston
		1961	Boston
		1962	Boston
		1963	Boston
3. Wilt Chamberlain (C)	4	1960	Philadelphia
		1966	Philadelphia
		1967	Philadelphia
		1968	Philadelphia
Michael Jordan (G)	4	1988	Chicago
		1991	Chicago
		1992	Chicago
		1996	Chicago
5. Larry Bird (F)	3	1984	Boston
		1985	Boston
		1986	Boston
Magic Johnson (G)	3	1987	Los Angeles
		1989	Los Angeles
		1990	Los Angeles
Moses Malone (C)		1979	Houston
		1982	Houston
		1983	Philadelphia

SOURCE: National Basketball Association

The Most Baskets, on Average

IF we look at who scored the **most** points over a lifetime, Kareem Abdul-Jabbar would hold the record, with 38,387 points during a 20-year career. Wilt Chamberlain and Moses Malone would follow, with totals of 31,419 and 27,409 points, respectively. But in this section, we're going to see who has scored the **most** points with respect to the number of games played.

Figures are good through the 1995–1996 season and include only those players with at least 400 games or 10,000 points under their belts.

	Player	Years Played	Games	Points	Avg.
1.	Michael Jordan	11	766	24,489	32.0
2.	Wilt Chamberlain	14	1,045	31,419	30.1
3.	Elgin Baylor	14	846	23,149	27.4
4.	Jerry West	14	932	25,192	27.0
5.	Bob Pettit	11	792	20,880	26.4
6.	George Gervin	10	791	20,708	26.2
7.	Karl Malone	11	898	23,343	26.0
8.	Dominique Wilkins	13	984	25,309	25.8
9.	Oscar Robertson	14	1,040	26,710	25.7
10.	David Robinson	7	557	14,260	25.6
11.	Kareem Abdul-Jabbar	20	1,560	38,387	24.6
12.	Larry Bird	13	897	21,791	24.3
13.	Hakeem Olajuwon	12	900	21,840	24.3
14.	Adrian Dantley	15	955	23,177	24.3
15.	Pete Maravich	10	658	15,948	24.2
16.	Patrick Ewing	11	835	19,788	23.7
17.	Charles Barkley	11	819	19,091	23.3
18.	Rick Barry	10	794	18,395	23.2
19.	Paul Arizin	10	713	16,266	22.8
20.	Mitch Richmond	8	600	13,653	22.8

Still active today are Michael Jordan, Karl Malone, David Robinson, Hakeem Olajuwon, Patrick Ewing, Charles Barkley, and Mitch Richmond.

SOURCE: *The 1996 Information Please Sports Almanac*

Scoring the Most

BELOW are the players who have scored the **most** points in a career, for combined NBA-ABA regular season games (through the 1995–96 season).

	Player	Total Years	Total Points
1.	Kareem Abdul-Jabbar	20	38,387
2.	Wilt Chamberlain	14	31,419
3.	Moses Malone	19	27,409
4.	Elvin Hayes	16	27,313

Player	Total Years	Total Points
5. Oscar Robertson	14	26,710
6. John Havlicek	16	26,395
7. Alex English	15	25,613
8. Dominique Wilkins	13	25,389
9. Jerry West	14	25,192
10. Michael Jordan	11	24,489

Michael Jordan is the only player active through the 1995–96 season.

The Most Points Scored in a Game

MICHAEL Jordan's game scores of 30, 40, and even 50 points always grab headlines. But think of the headlines for the following **most** scores per game.

Player	Game	Year	Points
1. Wilt Chamberlain	Phi vs NY	1962	100
2. Wilt Chamberlain	Phi vs LA	1961	78
3. Wilt Chamberlain	Phi vs Chi	1962	73
4. Wilt Chamberlain	SF at NY	1962	73
5. David Thompson	Den at Det	1978	73
6. Wilt Chamberlain	SF at LA	1962	72
7. Elgin Baylor	LA at NY	1960	71
8. David Robinson	SA at LAC	1994	71
9. Wilt Chamberlain	SF at Syr.	1963	70
10. Michael Jordan	Chi at Cle	1990	69

SOURCE: National Basketball Association

The Most Games Played

YOU can't get these guys off the court. They also happen to be some of the best basketball players in the history of the game. Figures are for combined NBA and ABA games played through the 1994–95 season.

Player	Years	Dates	Games
1. Robert Parish*	20	1976–	1,568
2. Kareem Abdul-Jabbar	20	1969–89	1,560

3.	Moses Malone	19	1976–95	1,455
4.	Artis Gilmore	17	1971–88	1,329
5.	Elvin Hays	16	1969–84	1,303
6.	Caldwell Jones	17	1973–90	1,299
7.	John Havlicek	16	1963–78	1,270
8.	Julius Erving	16	1971–87	1,243
9.	Dan Issel	15	1970–85	1,218
10.	Billy Paultz	15	1950–85	1,124

*Still active

SOURCE: *The 1997 Information Please Sports Almanac,* Houghton Mifflin, 1996

Most Feet and Inches

THE player rising the **most** above the other players is seven-foot seven-inch Gheroge Muresan. He made his pro debut playing for the Washington Bullets in 1994 and is the tallest player in professional basketball history.

SOURCE: National Basketball Association

College Basketball Championships

WHO has won the **most** men's championships since 1938 (through the 1996 season)?

	College Team	Wins	Years	Coach
1.	UCLA	11	1964	John Wooden
			1965	John Wooden
			1967	John Wooden
			1968	John Wooden
			1969	John Wooden
			1970	John Wooden
			1971	John Wooden
			1972	John Wooden
			1973	John Wooden
			1975	John Wooden
			1995	Jim Harrick
2.	Kentucky	6	1948	Adolph Rupp
			1949	Adolph Rupp

	College Team	Wins	Years	Coach
			1951	Adolph Rupp
			1958	Adolph Rupp
			1978	Joe B. Hall
			1996	Rick Pitino
3.	Indiana	5	1940	Branch McCracken
			1953	Branch McCracken
			1976	Bob Knight
			1981	Bob Knight
			1987	Bob Knight

SOURCE: NCAA

The Most Tournament Appearances

THROUGH 1996, the following men's teams have shown up and played at the NCAA Tournament the **most**.

	College Team	Appearances	W–L	Final 4	Wins
1.	Kentucky	38	72–34	11	6
2.	UCLA	32	74–25	15	11
3.	North Carolina	30	68–30	12	3
4.	Louisville	26	45–28	7	2
5.	Indiana	25	50–20	7	5
6.	Kansas	25	54–25	10	2
7.	Notre Dame	24	25–28	1	—
8.	St. John's	23	23–25	2	—
	Villanova	23	36–23	3	1
	Syracuse	23	35–24	3	—

SOURCE: *The 1997 Information Please Sports Almanac,* Houghton Mifflin, 1996

The NCAA Coaches Winning the Most Title Tournament

THE following NCAA Division 1 mens basketball coaches have the **most** wins in the NCAA Tournament through 1996.

	Coach	School Team	Years	Wins	Tournaments
1.	Dean Smith	North Carolina	1967–96	61	26
2.	John Wooden	UCLA	1950–75	47	16

3.	Bob Knight	Indiana	1973–96	40	20
4.	Denny Crum	Louisville	1972–96	39	20
5.	Mike Krzyzewski	Duke	1984–96	39	12
6.	John Thompson	Georgetown	1975–96	34	19
7.	Jerry Tarkanian	Long Beach State,			
		UNLV	1970–91	31	13
8.	Adolph Rupp	Kentucky	1942–72	30	20
9.	Jim Boeheim	Syracuse	1977–96	27	17
10.	Guy Lewis	Houston	1961–84	26	14

SOURCE: NCAA

The Most Highly Regarded Teams of All Time

WHAT teams do **most** consider to be the greatest college basketball teams of all times? Several **mosts** went into this category, including victories, player performance, schedules, and so on, but with a panel including the likes of Vic Bubas, Denny Crum, Wayne Duke, Dave Gavitt, Joe B. Hall, Jud Heathcote, Hank Iba, Pete Newell, Dean Smith, John Thompson, and John Wooden, you can be sure **most** others would agree that these teams are the best of all time.

School Team	Standout Player	Years
UCLA	Lew Alcindor (Kareem Abdul-Jabbar)	1967–1969
Indiana State	Larry Bird	1979
Kansas	Wilt Chamberlain	1957
Michigan State	Magic Johnson	1979
North Carolina	Michael Jordan	1982

SOURCE: *The 1996 Information Please Sports Almanac*

The Most Women's College Basketball Championships

TENNESSEE has been in the **most** women's finals games since the inception of the tournament in 1982. The record it holds is five, with three wins. It might have been four wins if the team had beaten the University of Connecticut in the 1995 finals, but it lost, and UConn went on to win the title and the **most** games in a row in NCAA Division 1 competition, men or women. Read on to see who else has the **most** wins.

College Team	Wins	Year	Coach
1. Tennessee	4	1987 1989 1991 1996	Pat Summitt
2. Louisiana Tech	2	1982 1988	Sonja Hogg Leon Barmore
Stanford	2	1990 1992	Tara VanDerveer
USC	2	1983 1984	Linda Sharp

SOURCE: *The 1997 Information Please Sports Almanac*, Houghton Mifflin, 1996

The Most Times in Possession of Lord Stanley's Cup

THAT would be the Stanley Cup, and Lord Stanley is the namesake of hockey's **most** famous trophy. So in case you live amongst palms and orange trees, and the closest you've ever gotten to ice is the freezer in your kitchen, what we're talking about here is hockey! And below we take a look at who has won the NHL championship, also known as the Stanley Cup, the **most** times through the 1995–1996 season.

Team	Wins	Last Win	Coach
1. Montreal Canadiens	23	1993	Jacques Demers
2. Toronto Arenas/St. Pat's Maple Leafs	13	1967	Punch Imlach
3. Detroit Red Wings	7	1955	Jimmy Skinner
4. Boston Bruins	5	1972	Tom Johnson
5. Edmonton Oilers	5	1990	John Muckler
6. New York Islanders	4	1983	Al Arbour
7. New York Rangers	4	1994	Mike Keenan
8. Ottawa Senators	4	1927	Dave Gill
9. Chicago Blackhawks	3	1961	Rudy Pilous

SOURCE: National Hockey League

All-Time NHL Mosts

WHO has the **most** goals and the **most** assists and **most** points in the game of hockey? The following do (through the 1995–1996 regular season). Not surprisingly, the Great One's name is at the top of the list.

	Player	Years	Games	Goals	Assists	Points
1.	Wayne Gretzky	17	1,253	837	1,771	2,608
2.	Gordie Howe	26	1,767	801	1,049	1,850
3.	Marcel Dionne	18	1,348	731	1,040	1,771
4.	Phil Esposito	18	1,282	717	873	1,590
5.	Mark Messier	17	1,201	539	929	1,468
6.	Stan Mikita	22	1,394	541	926	1,467
7.	Bryan Trottier	18	1,279	524	901	1,425
8.	Paul Coffey	16	1,154	372	1,038	1,410
9.	Dale Hawerchuk	15	1,137	506	869	1,375
10.	Mario Lemieux	11	669	563	809	1,372

Keep in mind that Wayne Gretzky, Mark Messier, Paul Coffey, and Mario Lemieux are still playing today.

SOURCE: *The 1997 Information Please Sports Almanac.* Houghton Mifflin, 1996

Raising the Most Cane

WHO in the NHL has been given the **most** penalty minutes over the years?

	Player	Years	Games	Minutes
1.	Tiger Williams	14	962	3,966
2.	Dale Hunter	16	1,181	3,218
3.	Chris Nilan	13	688	3,043
4.	Tim Hunter	15	769	3,011
5.	Marty McSorley	13	775	2,892
6.	Willi Plett	12	834	2,572
7.	Basil McRae	15	563	2,445
8.	Rick Tocchet	12	788	2,371
9.	Jay Wells	17	1,077	2,346
10.	Bob Probert	10	552	2,327

Dale Hunter, Tim Hunter, Marty McSorley, Basil McRae, Rick Tocchet, Jay Wells, and Bob Probert are still playing—still out there raising hell on ice.

SOURCE: *The 1997 Information Please Sports Almanac,* Houghton Mifflin, 1996

Tennis Anyone?

Most of us have probably picked up a racket at some point in our lives. Some of us kept hold of them. Others threw them right back down. But whether you're a player or not, you surely can appreciate the talents of the following women. They have been ranked number one in women's tennis the **most** times through 1996.

	Player	Times Number One	Years
1.	Helen Wills Moody	9	1927–33, 1935, 1938
2.	Steffi Graf	8	1987–90, 1993–96
3.	Margaret Smith Court	7	1962–65, 1969–70, 1973
	Martina Navratilova	7	1978–79, 1982–86
5.	Chris Evert Lloyd	5	1975–77, 1980–81
6.	Margaret Osborne duPont	4	1947–50
	Billie Jean King	4	1966–68, 1972
8.	Monica Seles	3	1991–92, 1995
	Maureen Connolly	3	1952–54
10.	Maria Bueno	2	1959–60
	Althea Gibson	2	1957–58
	Suzanne Lenglen	2	1925–26

Steffi Graf and Monica Seles are still active and winning in women's singles tennis.

SOURCE: Women's Tennis Association Tour

Men's Tennis and Most Number One Rankings

WHO has been ranked number one in men's tennis the **most**? Rankings are compiled through the 1995 season.

	Player	Times Number One	Years
1.	Bill Tilden	6	1920–25
2.	Jimmy Connors	5	1974–78
3.	Henri Cochet	4	1928–31
	Rod Laver	4	1961–62, 1968–69
	Ivan Lendl	4	1985–87, 1989
	John McEnroe	4	1981–84
7.	John Newcombe	3	1967, 1970–71
	Fred Perry	3	1934–36
	Pete Sampras	3	1993–95

SOURCE: *The 1997 Information Please Sports Almanac,* Houghton Mifflin, 1996

The Most Grand Slam Titles—Women

SOMETIMES the number of Grand Slam titles won is as important a marker as the number one ranking. Rankings are compiled through the 1995 tennis season and include all the Grand Slam tournaments. They are the Australian Open, the French Open, Wimbledon, and the U.S. Open.

	Player	Aus	Fre	Wim	U.S.	Total
1.	Margaret Smith Court	11	5	3	5	24
2.	Steffi Graf	4	5	7	5	21
3.	Helen Wills Moody	n/a	4	8	7	19
4.	Chris Evert Lloyd	2	7	3	6	18
	Martina Navratilova	3	2	9	4	18
6.	Billie Jean King	1	1	6	4	12
	Suzanne Lenglen	n/a	6	6	0	12
8.	Maureen Connolly	1	2	3	3	9
	Monica Seles	4	3	0	2	9
10.	Molla Bjurstedt Mallory	n/a	n/a	0	8	8

n/a = not applicable

SOURCE: *The 1997 Information Please Sports Almanac.* Houghton Mifflin, 1996

The Most Grand Slam Titles—Men

WHAT men have won the **most** Grand Slam tournaments through 1996?

	Player	Aus	Fre	Wim	U.S.	Total
1.	Roy Emerson	5	2	2	2	12
2.	Bjorn Borg	0	6	5	0	11
	Rod Laver	3	2	4	2	11
4.	Bill Tilden	n/a	0	3	7	10
5.	Jimmy Connors	1	0	2	5	8
	Ivan Lendl	2	3	0	3	8
	Fred Perry	1	1	3	3	8
	Ken Rosewall	4	2	0	2	8
	Pete Sampras	1	0	3	4	8

n/a = not applicable

SOURCE: Association of Tennis Professionals Tour

The Most Grand Slam Titles Period!

WHO has won the **most** titles without regard to gender? Margaret Smith Court, who played from 1960 to 1975. She owns 62 titles, having won 24 singles, 19 doubles, and 19 mixed doubles titles. The great Martina Navratilova is second, with 56 wins, 18 coming in singles, 31 in doubles, and 7 in mixed doubles. Billie Jean King is third, with 39 total titles. The title king on the men's tour remains Roy Emerson, with 28 titles between 1959 and 1971.

SOURCE: Women's Tennis Association Tour, Association of Tennis Professionals Tour

The Women Making the Most in Tennis

FOLLOWING are the players who have made the **most** money from tournaments over their playing years. These figures do not include endorsement money and are for the years 1968 through Oct. 14, 1996. Earnings from doubles and mixed doubles play are included.

	Player	Earnings (dollars)
1.	Martina Navratilova	20,283,727
2.	Steffi Graf	16,769,196

3.	A. Sanchez Vicario	9,762,460
4.	Chris Evert	8,896,195
5.	Monica Seles	8,475,730
6.	Gabriela Sabatini	7,888,822
7.	Helena Sukova	5,651,662
8.	Pam Shriver	5,286,382
9.	Jana Novotna	5,079,274
10.	Conchita Martinez	4,733,408

Keep in mind that purses are occasionally raised, thus favoring the younger players.

SOURCES: Women's Tennis Association Tour;
The 1997 Information Please Sports Almanac, Houghton Mifflin, 1996

The Men Making the Most in Tennis

LIKE the women, men are also making their fair share of winnings money on the courts. Read on to see which men have made the **most** over the years, and keep in mind that the figures below do not include endorsements earned by players. Increasingly over the years, and especially in popular sports (other than boxing), endorsement money often exceeds earnings on the court—as if any of the following need it!

	Player	Earnings (dollars)
1.	Ivan Lendl	20,512,417
2.	Stefan Edberg	18,137,745
3.	Boris Becker	16,306,864
4.	Pete Sampras	13,568,034
5.	John McEnroe	12,239,622
6.	Jim Courier	10,352,364
7.	Andre Agassi	8,746,365
8.	Jimmy Connors	8,513,840
9.	Goran Ivanisevic	8,202,988
10.	Michael Stich	8,005,092

Figures are from 1968 through Oct. 14, 1996, and include doubles and mixed doubles earnings. Not on the list is the leading 1996 money winner Yevgeny Kafelnikov, who made an astounding $1,863,713.

SOURCE: Association of Tennis Professionals Tour;
The 1997 Information Please Sports Almanac, Houghton Mifflin, 1996

The Most PGA Player of the Year Awards

WE'RE off tennis and onto golf, another game played by individuals for a great deal of money. But who is the best of all time and who has won the **most** PGA Player of the Year Awards—golfing's equivalent to the NFL's or NBA's MVP? The following have, and though we can't make the call as to who is the best golfer ever, you can look at who has won this coveted award the **most** and decide for yourself.

	Golfer	Times Won	Years Won
1.	Tom Watson	6	1977
			1978
			1979
			1980
			1982
			1984
2.	Jack Nicklaus	5	1967
			1972
			1973
			1975
			1976
3.	Ben Hogan	4	1948
			1950
			1951
			1953
4.	Julius Boros	2	1952
			1963
	Billy Casper	2	1966
			1970
	Arnold Palmer	2	1960
			1962
	Nick Price	2	1993
			1994

The PGA of America Player of the Year Award has only been given out since 1948. The above results are good through the 1995–96 season. Any bets on Tiger Woods for the 1996–97 season?

SOURCE: Professional Golfers' Association

Men's Golf Major Championship Leaders

IN golf, major championships include only the **most** prestigious of all golf tournaments. They are the U.S. Open, the British Open, the PGA Championship, the Masters, the U.S. Amateur, and the British Amateur tournaments.

The following players have the highest totals as a result of having won such tournaments the **most** times.

	Player	Wins
1.	Jack Nicklaus	20
2.	Bobby Jones	13
3.	Walter Hagen	11
4.	Ben Hogan	9
	Gary Player	9
	John Ball	9
7.	Arnold Palmer	8
	Tom Watson	8
9.	Harold Hilton	7
	Gene Sarazen	7
	Sam Snead	7
	Harry Varden	7
	Lee Trevino	6
14.	Nick Faldo	6

Figures are through 1996.

SOURCE: Professional Golfers' Association;
The 1997 Information Please Sports Almanac, Houghton Mifflin, 1996

Women's Golf Major Championship Leaders

LIKE men's golf, women's golf also has a handful of prestigious tournaments that are collectively called Major Championships. These include the U.S. Open, the LPGA Championship, the du Mourier Classic, the Nabisco–Dinah Shore, Titleholders (1937–72), the Western Open (1937–67), the U.S. Amateur, and the British Amateur tournaments.

Following are the LPGA golfers who have won the **most** titles collectively.

	Player	Wins
1.	Patty Berg	16
2.	Mickey Wright	13
	Louise Suggs	13
4.	Babe Zaharias	12
5.	Betsy Rawls	8
6.	JoAnne Carner	7
7.	Kathy Whitworth	6
	Pat Bradley	6
	Juli Inkster	6
	Patty Sheehan	6
	Glenna C. Vare	6

Results are through the 1996 LPGA season. Keep in mind that Joanne Carner, Pat Bradley, Juli Inkster, and Patty Sheehan are still actively playing.

SOURCE: Ladies Professional Golf Association;
The 1997 Information Please Sports Almanac, Houghton Mifflin, 1996

The Most Money for the Fewest Strokes

WE'RE about to take a look at which professional golfers have made the **most** in earnings from their sport for all time. You should recognize some of their names, as their enormous skills have made **most** of those at the top household words.

	Player	Earnings (dollars)
1.	Lee Trevino	9,531,346
2.	Ray Floyd	9,146,509
3.	Jack Nicklaus	7,222,744
4.	George Archer	6,986,414
5.	Hale Irwin	6,644,199
6.	Jim Colbert	6,496,042
7.	Bob Charles	6,400,146
8.	Chi Chi Rodriguez	6,342,749
9.	Dave Stockton	5,946,153
10.	Mike Hill	5,703,859
11.	Gary Player	5,598,163
12.	Miller Barber	5,126,418

13.	Bruce Crampton	5,054,861
14.	Dale Douglass	5,033,273
15.	J. C. Snead	5,003,511

The above figures are for PGA and Senior PGA earnings combined through 1995. If we chose to look at PGA players only with the **most** in tournament money, the top five would be (1) Greg Norman, with $9,592,829, (2) Tom Kites, with $9,337,998, (3) Payne Stewart, with $7,389,479, (4) Nick Price, with $7,338,119, (5) Fred Couples, with $7,188,408. Emphasis was given to Senior PGA players as, again, they were playing before the recent, big increases in tournament money.

SOURCE: *The 1997 Information Please Sports Almanac,* Houghton Mifflin, 1996

The Most Money for the Women Golfers

LIKE the men, the women are out there swinging their way around the golf course, too, all in the name of sport and for a few dollars to boot! For a long time, women's professional sports suffered when it came to earnings, but as you can see by the following numbers, the LPGA has come into its own.

Read on to see who has won the **most** money with their clubs in the LPGA through 1995.

	Golfer	Earnings (dollars)
1.	Betsy King	5,374,023
2.	Pat Bradley	5,141,019
3.	Beth Daniel	4,972,216
4.	Patty Sheehan	4,788,546
5.	Nancy Lopez	4,275,685
6.	Amy Alcott	3,135,772
7.	Dottie Mochrie	3,095,716
8.	JoAnne Carner	2,878,105
9.	Ayako Okamoto	2,735,630
10.	Rosie Jones	2,620,006
11.	Jane Geddes	2,601,295
12.	Jan Stephenson	2,347,897
13.	Meg Mallon	2,297,045
14.	Juli Inkster	2,266,157
15.	Colleen Walker	2,265,000

SOURCE: *The 1997 Information Please Sports Almanac,* Houghton Mifflin, 1996

The Most World Cups in the Wide World of Soccer

EVERY four years since 1930, the countries of the world have been facing off in the universal game of soccer, in a competition called the World Cup. The national teams of virtually all countries compete in preliminary rounds; then twenty (originally sixteen) finalists gather in one country and play the final rounds. The national teams that have won the World Cup the **most** are listed below.

	Team	Times Won	Years Won
1.	Brazil	4	1958
			1962
			1970
			1994
2.	Italy	3	1934
			1938
			1982
	West Germany	3	1954
			1974
			1990
4.	Argentina	2	1978
			1986
	Uruguay	2	1930
			1950

Neither the U.S. nor Canada has ever won the World Cup, though the U.S. did host the final rounds in 1994, during which time **most** attendance records were shattered. England won the World Cup once, in 1966.

One hundred thirty-eight countries participated in the 1994 World Cup from qualifiers on.

SOURCE: Fédération Internationale de Football Associations

NASCAR Winners

IF you're not sure what NASCAR is, you haven't been watching much television, have you? In recent years the sport has caught the public's eye and has become a contender with other mainstream sporting events. Maybe now you're remembering. You know, those cars that look like everyday cars except for all the wild paint schemes and decals? Oh, and there's one other difference, NASCAR circuit race cars are capable of exceeding two hundred miles per hour for sustained periods of time.

Following are NASCAR's **most** successful drivers through 1995.

	Driver	Wins
1.	Richard Petty	200
2.	David Pearson	105
3.	Bobby Allison	84
	Darrell Waltrip	84
5.	Cale Yarborough	83
6.	Dale Earnhardt	68
7.	Lee Petty	54
8.	Ned Jarrett	50
	Junior Johnson	50
10.	Herb Thomas	48
11.	Buck Baker	46
12.	Rusty Wallace	41
13.	Bill Elliott	40
	Tim Flock	40
15.	Bobby Isaac	37
16.	Fireball Roberts	34
17.	Rex White	28
18.	Fred Lorenzen	26
19.	Jim Paschal	25
20.	Joe Weatherly	24

Any wonder why Richard Petty is referred to as "King Richard"? Besides the **most** victories, he has also won the pole position for starting races the **most** times, with 127 claims.

Darrell Waltrip, Dale Earnhardt, Bill Elliott, and Rusty Wallace are still actively racing.

SOURCE: National Association for Stock Car Auto Racing;
The 1997 Information Please Sports Almanac, Houghton Mifflin, 1996

The Most NASCAR Earnings

THESE boys are out there driving fast and risking their lives, and some of them are making a lot of money for it! Read on to see who has won the **most** money on the NASCAR circuit.

Records are through the 1995 season.

	Driver	Earnings (dollars)
1.	Dale Earnhardt	25,948,545
2.	Bill Elliott	15,540,479
3.	Darrell Waltrip	14,441,866
4.	Rusty Wallace	12,754,720
5.	Terry Labonte	10,454,755
6.	Mark Martin	10,030,812
7.	Ricky Rudd	10,023,314
8.	Geoff Bodine	9,412,788
9.	Harry Gant	8,438,104
10.	Richard Petty	7,755,409
11.	Ken Schrader	7,703,183
12.	Sterling Martin	7,354,232
13.	Kyle Petty	7,187,699
14.	Bobby Allison	7,102,233
15.	Jeff Gordon	6,898,319
16.	Davey Allison	6,726,974
17.	Morgan Shepherd	6,682,190
18.	Ernie Irvan	5,653,996
19.	Dale Jarrett	5,067,402
20.	Alan Kulwicki	5,061,202

Keep in mind that NASCAR purses have increased dramatically over the years, thus younger drivers get a disproportionate boost over the older drivers such as Richard Petty (twice as many wins as the nearest racer).

About half of the above drivers are still racing today.

SOURCE: *The 1997 Information Please Sports Almanac,* Houghton Mifflin, 1996

The Most Indy Car Wins

WHEN you think of race cars, you're likely thinking of the sleek, wing-like Indy car designs. These cars are beyond fast. The 1996 winner of the pole position in the Indianapolis 500 maintained an average speed of 233.718 miles per hour around the famous oval track. Now that's fast! Read on and see who has won the **most** races through the 1995 season. And even if you don't know racing, you surely know some of these names.

	Driver	Career Wins
1.	A. J. Foyt	67
2.	Mario Andretti	52
3.	Al Unser	39
4.	Bobby Unser	35
5.	Al Unser Jr.	31
6.	Michael Andretti	30
7.	Rick Mears	29
8.	Johnny Rutherford	27
9.	Roger Ward	26
10.	Gordon Johncock	25
11.	Ralph DePalma	24
	Bobby Rahal	24
13.	Tommy Milton	23
14.	Tony Bettenhausen	22
	Emerson Fittipaldi	22
16.	Earl Cooper	20
17.	Jimmy Bryan	19
	Jimmy Murphy	19
19.	Ralph Mulford	17
	Danny Sullivan	17

Al Unser Jr., Michael Andretti, Bobby Rahal, Emerson Fittipaldi, and Danny Sullivan are still actively racing today.

SOURCE: *The 1997 Information Please Sports Almanac,* Houghton Mifflin, 1996

The Most Indy Money

LIKE NASCAR drivers, Indy drivers are also out there risking life and limb, but a number of them are also being nicely compensated for it. Read on to see which drivers have made the **most** money in Indy earnings over their racing careers.

	Driver	Earnings (in dollars)
1.	Al Unser Jr.	16,738,906
2.	Bobby Rahal	14,349,710
3.	Emerson Fittipaldi	13,863,625

	Driver	Earnings (in dollars)
4.	Mario Andretti	11,552,154
	Michael Andretti	12,277,869
6.	Rick Mears	11,050,807
7.	Danny Sullivan	8,844,129
8.	Arie Luyendyk	7,372,188
9.	Al Unser	6,740,843
10.	Raul Boesel	5,997,887
11.	A. J. Foyt	5,357,589
12.	Scott Brayton	4,807,214
13.	Roberto Guerrero	4,468,116
14.	Scott Goodyear	4,460,711
15.	Paul Tracy	4,402,770
16.	Tom Sneva	4,392,993
17.	Teo Fabi	4,367,117
18.	Johnny Rutherford	4,209,232
19.	Jacques Villeneuve	4,097,732
20.	Gordon Johncock	3,431,414

Figures are through the 1995 racing season.

More than half of the above drivers are still actively racing. Note too that purses have gone up and that is why all-time victory leaders aren't scoring as high in terms of the **most** money won.

SOURCE: *The 1997 Information Please Sports Almanac,* Houghton Mifflin, 1996

The Most World Cups in Women's Skiing

DOWNHILL skiing. Many of us have tried it. Some have liked it, and others haven't walked away from it fully intact. Good thing it's also a great spectator sport.

World Cup skiing is made up of the slalom, the giant slalom, the super giant slalom, and the all-out downhill racing disciplines. Each year, a tally of a ski racer's performance is made, and the skier scoring the **most** points wins. Following are those who have won the World Cup the **most** times since its inception in 1967, through the 1995–96 season.

	Skier	Times Won	Country	Years Won
1.	Annemarie Proell	6	Austria	1971
				1972

			1973
			1974
			1975
			1979
2.	Petra Kronberger	3	Austria	1990
			1991
			1992
	Vreni Schneider	3	Switzerland	1989
			1994
			1995

SOURCE: *The 1997 Information Please Sports Almanac,* Houghton Mifflin, 1996

The Most World Cups in Men's Skiing

MEN'S World Cup winners are computed in the same manner as women's. Following are the men's ski racers that have won the World Cup the **most** times through the 1995–96 season.

	Skier	Times Won	Country	Years Won
1.	Marc Girardelli	5	Luxembourg	1985
				1986
				1989
				1991
				1993
2.	Gustavo Thoeni	4	Italy	1971
				1972
				1973
				1975
	Pirmin Zurbriggen	4	Switzerland	1984
				1987
				1988
				1990
4.	Phil Mahre	3	U.S.	1981
				1982
				1983
	Ingemar Stenmark	3	Sweden	1976
				1977
				1978

It is generally accepted that the skier who is best at all events rather than just one discipline (slalom–giant slalom–super giant slalom–downhill) will do the best in terms of racking up the **most** World Cup points. Whereas slalom specialists like Ingemar Stenmark had to win a disproportionate number of slalom races just to keep up in the World Cup's all-around standings.

SOURCE: *The World Almanac and Book of Facts 1997,* World Almanac Books, 1996

The Most Fights Without a Loss

WE'RE talking boxing now and no, it's not Tyson or Foreman or Ali or Frazier or either of the Sugar Rays. Pedro Carrasco won the **most** fights, with 83 consecutive wins from April 22, 1964, to September 3, 1970.

SOURCE: World Boxing Council

The Most Boxing Titles

THOMAS "Hit Man" Hearns and Sugar Ray Leonard are at a draw. Each man has held the **most** world boxing titles, and in each case that is five. Hearns collected his between 1980 and 1991; Leonard between 1979 and 1988.

SOURCE: World Boxing Council

Big Saltwater Fish

IN the mood for a little of the outdoor sporting life? Why step out, we'll catch the **most** fish for you right here.

Wondering what the world records are and which record-holding fish weighed the **most**? Below we tell you, but remember that these fish were caught on rod and reel only and do not include commercial-fishing harvests. Records are good to October 1996.

	Species	Weight	Location
1.	Great Barracuda	85 lbs	Bermuda
2.	Bluefish	31 lbs 12 oz	North Carolina
3.	Bonefish	19 lbs	South Africa
4.	Cobia	135 lbs 9 oz	Australia

5.	Atlantic Cod	98 lbs 12 oz	New Hampshire
6.	Dolphin Fish	87 lbs	Costa Rica
7.	Grouper (Warsaw)	436 lbs 12 oz	Florida
8.	Halibut (Atlantic)	255 lbs 4 oz	Massachusetts
9.	King Mackerel	90 lbs	Key West
10.	Atlantic Blue Marlin	1,402 lbs 2 oz	Brazil
11.	Pacific Blue Marlin	1,376 lbs	Hawaii
12.	Black Marlin	1,560 lbs	Peru
13.	Striped Marlin	494 lbs	New Zealand
14.	White Marlin	181 lbs 14 oz	Brazil
15.	Atlantic Sailfish	141 lbs 1 oz	Angola
16.	Pacific Sailfish	221 lbs	Ecuador
17.	Hammerhead Shark	991 lbs	Florida
18.	Great White Shark	2,664 lbs	Australia
19.	Mako Shark	1,115 lbs	Mauritius
20.	Tiger Shark	1,780 lbs	South Carolina
21.	Swordfish	1,182 lbs	Chile
22.	Tarpon	283 lbs 4 oz	Sierra Leone
23.	Bluefin Tuna	1,496 lbs	Nova Scotia
24.	Wahoo	155 lbs 8 oz	Bahamas
25.	Southern Yellowtail	114 lbs 10 oz	New Zealand

A 3,388-pound great white shark (724 pounds heavier than the above world record holder) was caught in Australia but was disqualified as the angler used whale meat as bait.

SOURCE: International Game Fish Association

Freshwater-Fish Mosts

So the ocean's a little too deep or too far away or too rough for you. Then how about a freshwater inland lake for a bit of fishing? The fish won't bite you, and you'll never go thirsty. So read on for a look at the world record fish that weigh the **most** in their particular category (to October 1996).

	Species	Weight	Location
1.	Largemouth Bass	22 lbs 4 oz	Georgia
2.	Peacock Bass	27 lbs	Brazil
3.	Smallmouth Bass	10 lbs 14 oz	Kentucky
4.	Bluegill	4 lbs 12 oz	Alabama

	Species	Weight	Location
5.	Carp	75 lbs 11 oz	France
6.	Blue Catfish	109 lbs 4 oz	South Carolina
7.	Channel Catfish	58 lbs	South Carolina
8.	Flathead Catfish	91 lbs 4 oz	Texas
9.	White Crappie	5 lbs 3 oz	Mississippi
10.	Alligator Gar	279 lbs	Texas
11.	Arctic Grayling	5 lbs 15 oz	Northwest Territory
12.	Muskellunge	67 lbs 8 oz	Wisconsin
13.	Nile Perch	191 lbs 8 oz	Kenya
14.	Yellow Perch	4 lbs 3 oz	New Jersey
15.	Northern Pike	55 lbs 1 oz	West Germany
16.	Atlantic Salmon	79 lbs 2 oz	Norway
17.	Chinook	97 lbs 4 oz	Alaska
18.	Coho Salmon	33 lbs 4 oz	New York
19.	Sockeye Salmon	15 lbs 3 oz	Alaska
20.	White Sturgeon	468 lbs	California
21.	Brook Trout	14 lbs 8 oz	Ontario
22.	Brown Trout	40 lbs 4 oz	Arkansas
23.	Lake Trout	66 lbs 8 oz	Northwest Territory
24.	Rainbow Trout	42 lbs 2 oz	Alaska
25.	Walleye	25 lbs	Tennessee

SOURCE: International Game Fish Association

Mosts
from the World of
Vacations

READY FOR A little time off, but can't think of where to go or what to do? Well, have a look and see what **most** other people are doing with their leisure time.

Spending the Most to Attract the Most

WHAT country wants your vacation dollars the **most**? Well, it's likely to be the one that spends the **most** money to attract you. Following are countries that have allotted the **most** money to their tourism offices.

	Country	Tourism Budget (in U.S. dollars)
1.	Spain	$139,500,000
2.	Greece	134,700,000
3.	France	85,600,000
4.	United Kingdom	79,500,000
5.	South Korea	76,900,000
6.	Mexico	73,800,000
7.	Turkey	68,000,000
8.	Australia	62,800,000
9.	Italy	50,900,000
10.	Austria	62,800,000
11.	Poland	45,000,000
12.	Netherlands	43,000,000
13.	Malaysia	38,900,000
14.	Brazil	37,100,000
15.	Ireland	36,700,000

The U.S. federal government spent only $17,500,000 in 1992, though individual states, and often cities, too, have their own bureaus of tourism, whose budgets are not included in this total. The same is true of Canada ($20,900,000 spent by the federal government) and its provinces and cities.

SOURCE: "Total Budgets of National Tourism Offices, 1991–1993," *Hotel and Motel Management,* Apr. 1994

The Most Visited Countries

EVER wonder where everybody's going on their vacation? Well, if they're going abroad, **most** are going to the following countries. At least this is where U.S. travelers went the **most** in 1993.

	Country	U.S. Travelers
1.	Mexico	1,088,000
2.	Germany	1,060,000
3.	Canada	495,000
4.	United Kingdom	377,000
5.	Spain	155,000
6.	Italy	105,000
7.	France	89,000
8.	Ireland	86,000
9.	Israel	61,000
10.	Greece	60,000
11.	Australia	56,000
12.	Dominican Republic	36,000
13.	Switzerland	29,000
14.	Portugal	28,000
15.	Hong Kong	23,000
16.	Costa Rica	21,000
17.	Jerusalem	20,000
18.	Netherlands	11,000
	Argentina	11,000
	Egypt	11,000

SOURCE: *1993 Statistical Abstract of the United States*

The Most Visitors to the United States

WE know where Americans are going on vacations abroad, but who is that they're passing on their way there? Following are citizens from other countries who traveled to the U.S. the **most** during 1994.

	Country	No. of Visits
1.	Japan	3,652,000
2.	United Kingdom	3,238,000
3.	Germany	1,896,000
4.	France	894,000
5.	Brazil	611,000
6.	Italy	601,000
7.	Venezuela	523,000
8.	South Korea	482,000
9.	Argentina	453,000
10.	Australia	452,000

SOURCE: Cathy Lynn Grossman, "More Foreign Visitors Destined for the U.S.", *USA Today,*
May 23, 1994

Spending the Most on Hotels in Europe

YOU'VE finally decided to take that trip to Europe that you've only been able to dream about for years. But where will your money count for the **most?** In terms of hotels, it won't count for as much as you'd like in any of the following, where the average room rates rank among the **most** in all of Europe.

Figures are based on 1992 data.

	City, Country	Room Rates (in U.S. dollars)
1.	Paris, France	$245.64
2.	Geneva, Switzerland	202.18
3.	Madrid, Spain	177.83
4.	London, England	175.45
5.	Zurich, Switzerland	173.82
6.	Milan, Italy	172.96
7.	Rome, Italy	165.64
8.	Prague, Czech Republic	163.96
9.	Berlin, Germany	163.13
10.	Warsaw, Poland	151.97

Remember that these are 1992 rates and that they have likely gone up since, at least keeping pace with the rate of inflation.

SOURCE: "Paris Holds No. 1 European Spot in Room Rate," *Hotels,* Oct. 1993

The Top 20 Cities Worldwide

You've seen which world cities are the **most** expensive, but how about the cities that are the **most** worthwhile? According to the November 1995 issue of *Conde Nast Traveler*, the following are the world's **most** perfect vacation cities.

City
1. Sydney, Australia
2. San Francisco, California
3. Florence, Italy
4. Rome, Italy
5. Vienna, Austria
6. Salzburg, Austria
7. Paris, France
8. London, England
9. Kyoto, Japan
10. Vancouver, British Columbia
11. Santa Fe, New Mexico
12. Venice, Italy
13. Victoria, British Columbia
14. Amsterdam, Netherlands
15. Melbourne, Australia
16. Quebec City, Quebec
17. New Orleans, Louisiana
18. Charleston, South Carolina
19. Boston, Massachusetts
20. Toronto, Ontario

Criteria for selection was that **most** of *Conde Nast Traveler*'s readers said so. And that's good enough for us!

SOURCE: Conde Nast *Traveler,* November 1995

The Top U.S. Cities

The same readers of *Conde Nast Traveler* (November 1995) also sent in their opinions on just U.S. cities. Thousands responded and **most** said that the following cities offered the **most** as vacation spots.

	City, State
1.	San Francisco, California
2.	Santa Fe, New Mexico
3.	New Orleans, Louisiana
4.	Charleston, South Carolina
5.	Boston, Massachusetts
6.	Seattle, Washington
7.	San Antonio, Texas
8.	Washington, D.C.
9.	Savannah, Georgia
10.	New York, New York

Most Agree, They're the Top U.S. Hotels

So you've decided to stay in or go to the U.S. for your vacation. Being a discriminating person with finicky tastes, you've also decided that only the best will do for you on this much-needed vacation. May we suggest you start with the very finest in hotels? Following are the **most** highly regarded hotels in the U.S.

	Hotel	City
1.	Windsor Court	New Orleans
2.	Mansion on Turtle Creek	Dallas
3.	Ritz-Carlton	Chicago
4.	Four Seasons	Chicago
5.	Four Seasons	Washington, D.C.
6.	Pierre Four Seasons	New York City
7.	Four Seasons	Boston
8.	Ritz-Carlton	Philadelphia
9.	Ritz-Carlton, Buckhead	Atlanta
10.	Ritz-Carlton	Boston
11.	Harbor Court	Baltimore
12.	Willard Inter-Continental	Washington, D.C.
13.	Ritz-Carlton	San Francisco
14.	Four Seasons	Philadelphia
15.	Peninsula	Beverly Hills
16.	Peninsula	New York
17.	Four Seasons Olympic	Seattle
18.	Omni Hotel at Charleston Place	Charleston

Hotel	City
19. Hotel Bel-Air	Los Angeles
20. Hay-Adams Hotel	Washington, D.C.

SOURCE: *Conde Nast Traveler,* Nov. 1995

The Most-Visited National Parks

THINKING of taking the family to a national park this summer? Well, you might think about getting there earlier in the day than the rest: those lines at the toll gates can be killers, yet the wait is always worth it.

Following were the **most**-visited sites in the National Park System during 1994.

	Park	State(s)	Attendance
1.	Blue Ridge Parkway	NC, VA	16,928,639
2.	Golden Gate National Recreation Area	CA	14,695,711
3.	Lake Mead National Recreation Area	AZ, NV	9,566,725
4.	Great Smokey Mountains National Park	TN, NC	8,628,174
5.	George Washington Memorial National Parkway	VA, MD	5,619,821
6.	National Capital Parks	DC	5,435,837
7.	Natchez Trace National Parkway	MS, AL, TN	5,287,801
8.	Cape Cod National Seashore	MA	5,228,594
9.	Gulf Islands National Seashore	FL, MS	5,069,495
10.	Delaware Water Gap National Recreation Area	PA, NJ	4,773,659
11.	Grand Canyon National Park	AZ	4,364,319
12.	Statue of Liberty National Monument	NY, NJ	4,252,823
13.	Gateway National Recreation Area	NY, NJ	4,192,280
14.	Yosemite National Park	CA	3,962,117
15.	San Francisco Maritime National Historical Park	CA	3,733,911
16.	Castle Clinton National Monument	NY	3,481,327

17.	Chattahoochee River National Recreation Area	GA	3,472,026
18.	Olympic National Park	WA	3,381,573
19.	Colonial National Historical Park	VA	3,296,242
20.	Cuyahoga Valley National Recreation Area	OH	3,266,401

Yellowstone is number 22 on the list, with 3,046,145 visitors. Remember that it and some of America's other better known parks are in remote areas and get fewer visits in bad weather.

The total attendance in 1994 of all sites in the U.S. National Park System was 268,636,169, approximately the entire population of the U.S.

SOURCE: National Park Service, Department of the Interior

Getting Away From It All?

IF so, then consider one of the following sites administered by the National Parks System. They are ranked according to the **most** acreage within their boundaries.

	Site	State	Acres
1.	Wrangell–St. Elias	Alaska	8,331,604
2.	Gates of the Arctic	Alaska	7,523,888
3.	Denali	Alaska	5,000,000
4.	Katmai	Alaska	3,716,000
5.	Death Valley	California	3,367,628
6.	Glacier Bay	Alaska	3,225,284
7.	Lake Clark	Alaska	2,636,839
8.	Yellowstone	Wyoming	2,219,790
9.	Kobuk Valley	Alaska	1,750,421
10.	Everglades	Florida	1,506,499
11.	Grand Canyon	Arizona	1,217,158
12.	Glacier	Montana	1,013,572
13.	Olympic	Washington	922,163
14.	Big Bend	Texas	801,163
15.	Joshua Tree	California	793,954

Pretty big, aren't they? Here's something to try on for size. The state of Connecticut consists of 3,118,080 acres. It would rank number 7 on the above list.

SOURCE: *Backpacker Magazine*, Dec. 1994

The Most Beautiful Vacation Spots

BELIEVE it or not, there really is a ranking for the **most** beautiful spots in North America. Rand McNally and Company has come up with a rating system that includes terrain, open space, forests, inland water, rivers, wildlife preservation, and any natural attractions that might be judged as spectacular.

It rates the following as the vacation spots **most** blessed by nature.

	Place	State
1.	Redwoods-Shasta-Lassen	California
2.	Anchorage–Kenai Peninsula	Alaska
3.	Olympic Peninsula	Washington
	Seattle–Mt. Rainier–North Cascades	Washington
5.	Hawaii	Hawaii
6.	Crater Lake–Klamath Falls	Oregon
7.	Yosemite–Sequoia–Death Valley	California
8.	Bar Harbor–Acadia	Maine
9.	Zion–Bryce Canyon	Utah
10.	Yellowstone-Jackson-Tetons	Wyoming, Idaho, Montana
11.	Grand Canyon Country	Arizona
12.	Glacier National Park–Flathead Lake	Montana
13.	Lake Powell–Glen Canyon	Arizona, Utah
14.	Outer Banks	North Carolina
15.	Portland–Columbia River	Oregon
16.	Wine Country	California
17.	Coos Bay–South Coast	Oregon
18.	Rangeley Lakes	Maine
19.	Aspen-Vail	Colorado
20.	Salt Lake City	Utah

SOURCE: Rand McNally, *Vacation Places Rated*

The Best Vacation Spots

RAND McNally rates the following as America's **most** desirable vacation spots. Criteria include natural beauty, sporting fun, necessities, historical value, education, and entertainment.

Vacation Spot
1. Seattle–Mt. Rainier–North Cascades, Washington
2. Los Angeles, California
3. Hawaii
4. Miami–Gold Coast–Keys, Florida
5. San Francisco, California
6. Boston, Massachusetts
7. Chicago, Illinois
8. Denver–Rocky Mountains National Park, Colorado
9. New York City, New York
10. Tampa Bay–Southwest Coast, Florida

SOURCE: Rand McNally, *Vacation Places Rated*

The Cruise Ships with the Most

IF you really want to treat yourself to the **most,** then consider a cruise on one of the following liners. Rated by their sophisticated cuisine, excellent service, and creative itineraries, they'll provide you with the **most** luxurious of everything.

They are also known as "six-star" ships. In alphabetical order, they are as follows:

Ship	Company
Crystal Harmony	Crystal Cruises
Crystal Symphony	Crystal Cruises
Queen Odyssey	Royal Cruise Line
Radisson Diamond	Radisson Seven Seas Cruises
Royal Viking Sun	Cunard Line
Seabourn Pride	Seabourn Cruises
Seabourn Spirit	Seabourn Cruises
Sea Goddess I	Cunard Line
Sea Goddess II	Cunard Line
Silver Cloud	Silverseas Cruises

Ship	Company
Silver Wind	Silverseas Cruises
Song of Flower	Radisson Seven Seas Cruises

SOURCE: *Fielding's Guide to Worldwide Cruises,* 1996

The Most Romantic Cruises

YES, there is actually a ranking for the **most** romantic liners and their destinations. It's recommended that you take someone along with you though, as the cruises are meant for you to rekindle or launch a love affair—with someone you already know!

Here they are, in alphabetical order:

Ship	Company
CostaRomantica	Costa Cruises
Rotterdam	Holland America
Sea Goddess I	Cunard Line
Sea Goddess II	Cunard Line
Sea Cloud	Special Expeditions
Silver Cloud	Silversea Cruises
Silver Wind	Silversea Cruises
Wind Star	Windstar Cruises
Wind Song	Windstar Cruises
Wind Spirit	Windstar Cruises

SOURCE: *Fielding's Guide to Worldwide Cruises,* 1996

The Most Incredible Beaches!

THE **most** popular beach in America is Jones Beach on Long Island Sound. Over 10 million people visit it each year. But on our lists of beach **mosts,** it doesn't make it. We're only considering what one of the foremost authorities on beach rankings has to say, and that authority would be Dr. Stephen Leatherman of the University of Maryland. His rankings take fifty different factors into consideration when choosing the **most** desirable beaches in the U.S.

Following are the beaches in 1995 that have the **most** of everything, according to Leatherman.

	Beach	State
1.	St. Andrews	Florida
2.	Caladesi Island State Park	Florida
3.	Kailua	Hawaii
4.	St. George Island State Park	Florida
5.	St. Joseph Peninsula State Park	Florida
6.	Kaunaoa	Hawaii
7.	Wailea	Hawaii
8.	Hulopoe	Hawaii
9.	Cape Florida	Florida
10.	Fort Desoto Park	Florida
11.	Delnor-Wiggins Pass	Florida
12.	Perdido Key	Florida
13.	Ocracoke Island	North Carolina
14.	Sand Key Park	Florida
15.	Westhampton Beach	New York

SOURCE: Peter Bernstein and Christopher Ma, *The Practical Guide to Practically Everything*

Most Agree, It's All Downhill from Here!

MAYBE the beach isn't your thing, or maybe you have such a sunburn that all you can think of is something cool, even cold, and where you don't have to suck your gut in. May we suggest a skiing vacation? Though you can still get a sunburn in the high altitudes, you don't have to worry about that gut! It'll be safely hidden inside those layers of high-fashion outfits.

Following are the **most** popular ski resorts in North America in 1995, as told in *Ski Magazine*.

	Resort	Location
1.	Vail	Colorado
2.	Telluride	Colorado
3.	Aspen (Highlands)	Colorado
4.	Alta	Utah
5.	Whistler-Blackcomb	British Columbia
6.	Snowbird	Utah
7.	Snowmass	Colorado
8.	Taos Ski Valley	New Mexico
9.	Mammoth Mountain	California

	Resort	Location
10.	Steamboat	Colorado
11.	Park City	Utah
12.	Beaver Creek-Vail	Colorado
13.	Keystone	Colorado
14.	Squaw Valley	California
15.	Breckenridge	Colorado

Of course rankings vary from source to source, and so as not to show favoritism, we're including *Skiing Magazine*'s **most** popular ski resorts for 1995 (the top five) as well. They are: (1) Vail (Colorado), (2) Steamboat (Colorado), (3) Whistler-Blackcomb (British Columbia), (4) Sun Valley (Idaho), and (5) Alta (Utah).

Mosts
from the World of
Air Travel

COME FLY WITH US! We've distilled all those airline facts and figures floating about and laid them out in easy-to-read, simple-to-follow, ever-fascinating compilations of **mosts**. We know you'll be interested, too, because half a billion passengers boarded U.S. flights alone in 1994. That means there's a good chance that you too flew. And if you're like **most** of us, you'll want to know a little more about who's doing the **most** flying.

The U.S. Airlines Carrying the Most

AMERICAN business seems to have adopted the passenger airplane as its second office. Certainly, business travel accounts for the larger part of U.S. airline revenues, although anyone trying to book a flight over the holidays might question it.

In 1994, over 528 million passengers boarded U.S. airlines for both domestic and international flights. The following list shows which U.S. airlines carried the **most** passengers.

	Airline	Passengers
1.	Delta	86,909,000
2.	American	79,511,000
3.	United	78,664,000
4.	USAir	56,674,000
5.	Southwest	50,039,000
6.	Northwest	49,313,000
7.	Continental	35,013,000
8.	TWA	21,551,000
9.	America West	16,802,000
10.	Alaska	10,084,000

SOURCE: Air Transport Association of America, Washington, D.C.

The World Airlines Carrying the Most

THE world's airlines carried over 1.1 billion passengers in 1994, over half of them on U.S. airlines, and flew over 1.9 trillion passenger miles. That's an average of 1,727 miles per passenger! Multiplying the total distance traveled by the number of passengers on each airline tells us which airline flew the **most** passenger miles in 1994. Although American Airlines has the **most** aircraft of any passenger airline in the world, United Airlines actually carried more passengers and flew more passenger miles.

	Airline (Country)	Aircraft in Service	Passenger Miles (miles flown × total passengers)
1.	United Airlines (U.S.)	539	100,968,000,000
2.	American Airlines (U.S.)	672	97,039,900,000
3.	Delta Airlines (U.S.)	554	82,866,500,000
4.	Northwest Airlines (U.S.)	373	58,019,500,000
5.	British Airways (U.K.)	215	49,026,000,000
6.	Aeroflot (Russia)	n/a	47,499,500,000
7.	USAir (U.S.)	502	35,231,100,000
8.	JAL (Japan)	116	33,936,100,000
9.	Lufthansa (Germany)	219	32,722,500,000
10.	Air France (France)	144	27,049,100,000

n/a = not available

SOURCE: Air Transport Association of America, Washington, D.C.

The Countries Flying the Most

U.S. airlines like to stay busy. In 1994, they flew well over six times as many passenger miles than the airlines of any other nation. Below is a list of the ten countries whose airlines flew the **most** total passenger miles in 1994.

	Country	Passenger Miles (miles flown × total passengers)
1.	United States	480,513,000,000
2.	United Kingdom	74,533,000,000
3.	Japan	66,089,000,000

4.	Russian Federation	47,500,000,000
5.	France	36,786,000,000
6.	Australia	35,744,000,000
7.	Germany	32,896,000,000
8.	China	27,962,000,000
9.	Singapore	25,639,000,000
10.	Canada	25,120,000,000

SOURCE: Air Transport Association of America, Washington, D.C.

The U.S. Airports with the Most Air Traffic

OF the ten busiest airports in the world, seven are in the United States. With a capacity for serving the **most** passengers, nearly 75 million per year, Hartsfield Atlanta International Airport has the largest terminal in the world. However, Chicago's O'Hare Airport actually served the **most** passengers in 1995, with over 67 million travelers arriving and departing through its gates.

According to the Air Transport Association of America, these are the ten busiest airports in the U.S.:

	Airport	City	Passengers (millions)
1.	Chicago O'Hare International	Chicago, IL	67.3
2.	Hartsfeld International	Atlanta, GA	57.7
3.	DFW International	Dallas–Fort Worth, TX	54.3
4.	Los Angeles International	Los Angeles, CA	53.9
5.	San Francisco International	San Francisco, CA	36.3
6.	Miami International	Miami, FL	33.2
7.	Stapleton International	Denver, CO	31.0
8.	John F. Kennedy International	New York, NY	30.2
9.	DTW International	Detroit, MI	29.0
10.	McCarran International	Las Vegas, NV	28.0

SOURCE: Air Transport Association of America

The Global Airports with the Most Traffic

THOUGH Chicago's O'Hare International is the busiest airport in the U.S., its air traffic is primarily domestic. But if we're talking worldwide airports with the **most** international flights, then we're talking London's Heathrow Airport. In 1995, it hosted the **most** international flights, serving over 54 million passengers.

Here's a list of the world's busiest airports outside the U.S. as determined by the Airports Council International (for the year 1995).

	Airport	City, Country	Total Passengers (in millions)
1.	London Heathrow	London, U.K.	54.5
2.	Tokyo-Haneda International	Tokyo, Japan	45.8
3.	Frankfurt Main	Frankfurt, Germany	38.2
4.	Kimpo International	Seoul, South Korea	30.9
5.	Charles de Gaulle	Paris, France	28.4
6.	Hong Kong International	Hong Kong	28.0
7.	Paris Orly	Paris, France	26.7
8.	Amsterdam-Schiphol	Amsterdam, The Netherlands	25.4
9.	New Tokyo International	Tokyo, Japan	24.2
10.	Singapore-Changi	Singapore, China	23.2

SOURCE: Airports Council International

The Most-Traveled U.S. Airline Routes

WHERE are all these passengers going? According to the U.S. Department of Transportation, the **most** heavily traveled domestic route in 1993 was that between New York and Los Angeles. In fact, New York was the point of arrival or departure for seven of the ten busiest domestic routes in 1993.

	Route	Passengers
1.	New York–Los Angeles	2,735,140
2.	New York–Chicago	2,483,940
3.	New York–Boston	2,473,660
4.	Honolulu–Kahului, Maui	2,427,790
5.	New York–Miami	2,357,870
6.	New York–Washington	2,285,290
7.	Dallas–Fort Worth—Houston	2,186,940
8.	Los Angeles–San Francisco	2,037,710

| 9. | New York–San Francisco | 1,903,390 |
| 10. | New York–Orlando | 1,879,430 |

SOURCE: U.S. Dept. of Transportation

The Most-Traveled Airline Routes in the World

THE International Civil Aviation Organization reported in 1993 that the following flight routes carried the **most** passengers in the world. Remember, these figures are for international flights only.

	Route	Passengers
1.	London–Paris	3,402,000
2.	London–New York	2,276,000
3.	Hong Kong–Taipei	2,223,000
4.	Honolulu–Tokyo	2,131,000
5.	Kuala Lumpur–Singapore	2,109,000
6.	Seoul–Tokyo	2,023,000
7.	Hong Kong–Tokyo	2,019,000
8.	Amsterdam–London	1,775,000
9.	Dublin–London	1,770,000
10.	Bangkok–Hong Kong	1,649,000

SOURCE: International Civil Aviation Organization

What Passengers Complain About the Most

IN the United States, an average of 80.1 percent of airline flights arrive within fifteen minutes of their scheduled time, just 1 passenger in 7,883 gets bumped involuntarily from an overbooked flight, and 99.5 percent of passengers get their luggage when they arrive. Not bad, huh? But despite this level of service, in the first six months of 1995 the U.S. Department of Transportation received 3,313 complaints against U.S. and foreign passenger airlines, tour operators, travel agents, and cargo companies. Actually, this is down by 11 percent from the 3,723 complaints for the first six months of 1994.

So what is it that airline consumers complain about the **most?** Below is a list of complaint categories, ranked by number of complaints, from the Department of Transportation's *Air Travel Consumer Report* for the January through June 1995 travel period.

Complaint Description	Number of Complaints	Sub-Category
1. Flight problems	714	
Delays		(201)
Cancellations		(245)
Misconnections		(84)
2. Baggage	498	
3. Refunds	483	
4. Reservations, ticketing and boarding	402	
Disabled passengers		(108)
5. Customer service	390	
6. Other (cargo, security, etc.)	346	
Frequent flyer		(264)
7. Overbooking/bumping	190	
8. Fares (conditions, variations, etc.)	149	
9. Tours/tour packages	64	
10. Advertising (unfair or misleading)	56	
11. Smoking/no smoking	19	
12. Credit and billing	2	

SOURCE: *Air Travel Consumer Report,* Dept. of Transportation

The Airlines Receiving the Most Complaints

BEING bumped from a flight can be aggravating. *Really* aggravating. Who's the leading culprit, doing this to us the **most?** Southwest Airlines. During the first half of 1995, Southwest denied boarding to a total of 3,436 passengers, or 3.04 people per 10,000.

Baggage problems represented the second-highest category of consumer complaints during that same period, and TWA received the **most** mishandled baggage reports per passenger, a total of 60,095, or 6.33 reports per 1,000 consumers.

But which airlines actually received the **most** overall complaints? The Department of Transportation's report also ranks the ten largest air carriers by percentage of complaints per 100,000 passengers. Read on and see how many others share your grudge (if you have one) against a particular airline. Again, the period covered is the first half of 1995.

	U.S. Airline	Complaints	Passengers	Complaints per 100,000 Passengers
1.	TWA	155	10,262,241	1.51
2.	Continental	246	17,802,321	1.38
3.	America West	89	8,185,038	1.09
4.	United	324	38,172,937	0.85
5.	USAir	224	29,158,077	0.77
6.	American	282	39,627,201	0.71
7.	Delta	255	42,988,873	0.59
8.	Alaska	27	4,594,751	0.59
9.	Northwest	114	23,749,771	0.48
10.	Southwest	61	24,216,833	0.25

SOURCE: *Air Travel Consumer Report*, U.S. Dept. of Transportation

The Airlines with the Most On-Time Flights

FLIGHT delays resulted in over two hundred complaints in the first six months of 1995. But which airline gives you the best chance of being on time? Of the ten largest U.S. carriers, the U.S. Department of Transportation ranks the following as having the **most** on-time flight arrivals between July 1994 and June 1995. And please remember that "on-time arrivals" in the airline business means a flight arriving within fifteen minutes of its scheduled time.

	U.S. Airline	Percent of Arrivals On-Time
1.	Northwest	83.9
2.	Southwest	82.8
3.	United	81.9
4.	USAir	80.7
5.	Delta	79.9
	Alaska	79.9
7.	Continental	79.3
8.	American	78.6
9.	America West	77.9
10.	TWA	76.4

SOURCE: *Air Travel Consumer Report*, U.S. Dept. of Transportation

The Airports with the Most On-Time Flights

WHETHER or not your flight arrives on time may have as much to do with your destination as with your airline. Among U.S. airports, according to the U.S. Department of Transportation, Los Angeles has the worst on-time-arrival rate, just 69.2 percent, followed by San Francisco, with 69.8 percent.

But which cities have **most** on-time arrivals per scheduled landings? Read on, especially if you're the impatient sort.

	Airport	City	Percent of On-Time Arrivals
1.	Cincinnati–No. Kentucky International	Cincinnati, OH	83.9%
2.	Minneapolis–St. Paul International	St. Paul, MN	83.3
3.	Charlotte Douglas	Charlotte, NC	81.5
4.	Detroit Metro Wayne County	Detroit, MI	81.2
5.	Pittsburgh Greater International	Pittsburgh, PA	80.8
6.	New York La Guardia	New York, NY	80.3
7.	Chicago O'Hare International	Chicago, IL	80.2
8.	Stapleton International	Denver, CO	80.0
9.	Washington National	Washington, D.C.	79.9
10.	Salt Lake City International	Salt Lake City, UT	79.7

SOURCE: U.S. Dept. of Transportation

The Jumbo Jet Carrying the Most to Safety

THE Boeing 747 jumbo jet can carry the **most** passengers of any airplane used by scheduled passenger carriers. Although regularly scheduled 747 flights carry about 398 passengers, the plane's total capacity is 560. But on May 24, 1991, an El Al jumbo jet took off from Addis Ababa, Ethiopia, carrying 1,086 evacuating Jews to safety in Israel. But even that record of the **most** passengers carried was broken when two babies were born during the flight, bringing the total who arrived in Israel to 1,088, the **most** passengers ever flown in a commercial airliner. How do you accomplish such a feat? Well, you can start by removing the toilets, which El Al did. What makes this even more amazing is that this was just one of forty flights in a twenty-four-hour airlift code-named Operation Solomon, which carried a total of 14,200 evacuees to safety after the fall of the Marxist regime in Ethiopia.

SOURCE: El Al Airlines

Making the Most Crossings

THE **most** experienced transatlantic passenger is Flight Service Manager Charles M. Schimpf, who logged 2,880 Atlantic crossings between March 1948 and his retirement on September 1, 1984. That's an average of 6.4 trips across the ocean each month!

SOURCE: *The Guinness Book of Records 1996,* Bantam, 1996

Taking the Concorde the Most

WHEN your job requires you to commute regularly between London and New Jersey, it's understandable that you might want to make the trip as short as possible by flying aboard the Concorde. In March 1995, Fred Finn made his 707th supersonic transatlantic crossing, for a total of 11,023,000 miles, making him the **most** experienced supersonic passenger of all time.

SOURCE: Air France

The Most Lengthy Airline Ticket Ever

IN December 1984, Bruno Leunen of Brussels, Belgium, was issued an airline ticket costing $4,500 for a trip of 53,203 miles. The ticket, which measured 39 feet $4^{1}/_{2}$ inches had Leunen scheduled aboard 80 different airlines with 109 layovers, making this the **most** lengthy airline ticket ever sold.

SOURCE: *The Guinness Book of Records 1996,* Bantam, 1996

Longing to Fly the Most

BORN in 1915, John Long of the United States first tried to fly by strapping an ironing board to his shoulders and riding his bike as fast as he could down a hill. His desire to fly became a reality once technology caught up with him. Between May 1, 1933, and April, 1995, he logged 60,269 hours of flight time, making him the world's **most** experienced airplane pilot. Long spent over 12 percent of his 62 years piloting, amounting to more than 6 years of his life in a variety of aircraft.

SOURCE: *The Guinness Book of Records 1996,* Bantam, 1996

The Pilot Adapting to the Most

THE pilot to fly the **most** different and varied kinds of aircraft is James B. Taylor Jr. (1897–1942). As a test and demonstration pilot for the U.S. Navy and several aircraft manufacturers, Taylor flew 461 different kinds of planes during his twenty-five-year career.

SOURCE: *Guinness Book of Records 1996,* Bantam, 1996

Mosts
from the World of
Motor Vehicles

WHEN IT COMES to cars, we care for them, pamper them, maintain them, and covet them. You'd think we were talking about lovers.

Welcome to the world of motor vehicles and our absolute, undeniable love for them.

Flat Out, the Most Motor Vehicles

BY the end of 1993, worldwide registrations for passenger cars and other motor vehicles totaled 617,087,061. The number of registered passenger cars alone was an astounding 469,460,221. With the world's population at about 5.5 billion, that amounts to 1 motor vehicle for every 9 men, women, and children on the planet, and 1 passenger car for every 12.

The U.S. has the **most** motor vehicles—31.5 percent of the entire world's total in 1993 and more than three times that of Japan, which has the second-highest total. The tiny country of San Marino, which covers just 23.6 square miles inside Italy, just inland from the Adriatic Sea, has only about 24,000 people. But with 25,519 registered vehicles, of which 22,159 are passenger autos, San Marino has the **most** motor vehicles per capita of any country in the world—more than one vehicle and just under one passenger car for every citizen. At the other end of the spectrum are poorer countries like Ethiopia, with a per capita vehicle ratio of 1 to 869, and Bangladesh, at 1 to 915.

According to the American Automobile Manufacturers Association, the following are the countries where the **most** vehicles can be found (as of 1993).

	Country	Passenger Cars	Other Motor Vehicles	Total Registered	Percent of World Total
1.	U.S.	146,314,296	47,749,186	194,063,482	31.5
2.	Japan	40,772,325	22,590,209	63,362,534	10.3

	Country	Passenger Cars	Other Motor Vehicles	Total Registered	Percent of World Total
3.	Germany	39,202,066	2,787,225	41,989,291	6.8
4.	Italy	29,600,000	2,745,500	32,345,500	5.2
5.	France	24,385,000	5,065,000	29,450,000	4.8
6.	U.K.	23,402,347	3,603,518	27,005,865	4.4
7.	Commonwealth of Independent States	13,549,000	9,856,000	23,405,000	3.8
8.	Canada	13,477,896	3,712,486	17,190,382	2.8
9.	Spain	13,440,694	2,859,438	16,300,132	2.6
10.	Brazil	11,613,000	3,246,800	14,859,800	2.4
	World Total	469,460,221	147,626,840	617,087,061	100.0

The States with the Most Motor Vehicles

In the U.S., California has the **most** registered vehicles, with a combined total of 22.9 million cars, trucks, buses, and other vehicles. That's not too surprising, considering California also has the largest population. In fact, the top ten vehicle-owning states are also the top ten in population, with the only exception being North Carolina, which has more people than Georgia but fewer vehicles.

Overall, these ten states with the **most** motor vehicles have 54.7 percent of the U.S. population and about 51.6 percent of the nation's vehicles. The ten states, as of 1994, are listed in the table below. Note also that the table shows the 1994 nationwide totals. By comparing these totals to the totals in 1993 (see the previous article), you can see how much the total number of vehicles in the U.S. has increased.

	State	Passenger Cars	Other Motor Vehicles	Total Registered	Percent of U.S. Total
1.	California	17,414,000	5,548,000	22,962,000	11.7%
2.	Texas	8,902,000	4,253,000	13,155,000	6.7
3.	New York	8,813,000	1,420,000	10,233,000	5.2
4.	Florida	7,883,000	2,060,000	9,943,000	5.1
5.	Ohio	7,570,000	1,844,000	9,414,000	4.8
6.	Pennsylvania	6,674,000	1,711,000	8,385,000	4.3

7.	Illinois	6,704,000	1,426,000	8,130,000	4.2
8.	Michigan	5,774,000	1,688,000	7,462,000	3.8
9.	New Jersey	5,193,000	470,000	5,663,000	2.9
10.	Georgia	3,846,000	1,737,000	5,583,000	2.9
	1994 U.S. Totals	147,171,000	48,298,000	195,469,000	

SOURCES: Federal Highway Administration; U.S. Dept. of Transportation; U.S. Dept. of Commerce, Bureau of the Census

The States with the Most Motor Vehicles Per Capita

THE U.S. has about 751 motor vehicles per 1,000 residents. But in four states, motor vehicles actually outnumber people. Wyoming, the state with the **most** per capita motor vehicles, has a population of 475,981 and approximately 572,000 registered vehicles. Of course, this total includes vehicles used on farms and ranches as well as municipal vehicles like buses and snow plows. Still, that's 20 percent more vehicles than people, or a ratio of 1,202 motor vehicles per 1,000 residents. Wyoming also has the **most** trucks, buses, and other non-automobiles in relation to passenger cars in the country. With 290,000 passenger cars and 282,000 other vehicles, the numbers are nearly even.

Following are states where motor vehicles outnumber people, making for the **most** per capita vehicles in the country.

	State	Population	Registered Vehicles	Vehicles per 1,000 Residents
1.	Wyoming	475,981	572,000	1,202
2.	South Dakota	721,164	819,000	1,136
3.	Montana	856,047	946,000	1,105
4.	North Dakota	637,988	670,000	1,050

SOURCES: U.S. Dept. of Transportation; U.S. Dept. of Commerce, Bureau of the Census

Producing the Most Worldwide

THE U.S. produced 75.7 percent of the world's automobiles back in 1950. Thirty years later, in 1980, Japan auto manufacturers outproduced the U.S. for the first time, and that trend continued until 1994. Now, although Japan still produces the **most** passenger cars, the U.S. produces the **most** motor vehicles of other kinds, twice the number of Japan. This increase in U.S. non-passenger-car production of 15.7 percent over 1993 brought the U.S. ahead of Japan in overall motor vehicle production for the first time in fourteen years.

According to the American Automobile Manufacturers Association, the world's twenty-six motor-vehicle-producing countries manufactured an all-time high of 49.7 million vehicles in 1994, with the U.S. producing 24.7 percent of the total, its highest percentage since 1987.

The countries producing the **most** motor vehicles (as of 1994) are:

	Country	Passenger Cars	Other Motor Vehicles	Total Vehicles	Percent of World Production
1.	U.S.	6,613,970	5,648,767	12,262,737	24.7
2.	Japan	7,801,317	2,752,802	10,554,119	21.2
3.	Germany	4,093,685	262,453	4,356,138	8.8
4.	France	3,175,213	383,225	3,558,438	7.2
5.	Canada	1,215,830	1,105,981	2,321,811	4.7
6.	South Korea	1,805,895	505,768	2,311,663	4.7
7.	Spain	1,821,696	320,566	2,142,262	4.3
8.	U.K.	1,466,823	227,815	1,694,638	3.4
9.	Brazil	1,248,773	332,616	1,581,389	3.2
10.	Italy	1,340,878	193,591	1,534,469	3.1
	World Total	35,365,228	14,327,704	49,692,932	

SOURCE: American Automobile Manufacturers Association

Which States Produce the Most Motor Vehicles

WITH cars and trucks rolling off the production lines day after day in cities like Detroit (nicknamed "The Motor City"), Lansing, and Dearborn, the state of Michigan is where the **most** motor vehicles are manufactured in the U.S. However, Indiana is where the **most** recreational vehicles (travel trailers, folding camp trailers, motor homes, and van conversions) are produced each year. According to the Recreational Vehicle Industry Association, a total of 441,000 recreational vehicles were produced in the U.S. in 1994, and 261,028 of them, a full 59.2 percent, were manufactured in Indiana.

Following are the states where the **most** motor vehicles are produced (in 1994).

	State	Passenger Cars	Other Motor Vehicles	Total Vehicles	Percent of U.S. Prod.
1.	Michigan	2,153,386	1,280,236	3,433,622	28.1
2.	Ohio	959,856	894,244	1,854,100	15.2
3.	Missouri	187,748	732,346	920,094	7.5
4.	Kentucky	301,068	499,288	800,356	6.5
5.	Tennessee	592,656	142,926	735,582	6.0
6.	Illinois	690,421	0	690,421	5.6
7.	Delaware	451,832	0	451,832	3.7
8.	California	299,327	133,713	433,040	3.5
9.	Georgia	399,617	0	399,617	3.3
10.	Indiana	54,002	328,609	382,611	3.1
	U.S. Total	6,601,223	5,636,918	12,238,141	

SOURCES: American Automobile Manufacturers and Recreational Vehicle Industry Association

The Companies Manufacturing the Most

THE list of the world's top ten motor vehicle manufacturers is, not surprisingly, topped by corporate giant General Motors, which produced the **most** passenger cars in 1993. Ford Motor Company, however, produced the **most** non-passenger-car vehicles. And though Chrysler ranked just twelfth in passenger-car production, its other vehicle production, the world's third highest, helped it earn an overall production ranking of sixth. These totals, compiled by the American Automobile Manufacturers Association from published reports by vehicle associations in various countries, are for the production in all of the facilities owned by each of the companies worldwide.

Following are the manufacturers that produce the **most** motor vehicles worldwide (as of 1993).

	Company	Country	Passenger Cars	Other Motor Vehicles	Total Vehicles	Percent of World Production
1.	G.M.	U.S.	4,852,168	2,031,762	6,883,930	14.9
2.	Ford	U.S.	3,619,997	2,344,875	5,964,872	12.9
3.	Toyota	Japan	3,382,187	848,185	4,230,372	9.1
4.	Volkswagen	Germany	2,630,822	168,523	2,799,345	6.1
5.	Nissan	Japan	2,215,457	570,822	2,786,279	6.0

	Company	Country	Passenger Cars	Other Motor Vehicles	Total Vehicles	Percent of World Production
6.	Chrysler	U.S.	910,471	1,388,800	2,299,271	5.0
7.	PSA (Peugeot-Citroën)	France	1,937,017	132,455	2,069,472	4.5
8.	Renault	France	1,642,705	254,348	1,897,053	4.1
9.	Honda	Japan	1,526,297	129,035	1,655,332	3.6
10.	Mitsubishi	Japan	1,134,063	440,616	1,574,679	3.4
	World Total		33,767,928	12,538,935	46,306,863	

SOURCE: American Automobile Manufacturers Association

The Most Prolific Plant

THE automobile plant that produces the **most** vehicles in the world is the Volkswagenwerk, located in Wolfsburg, Germany. The plant employs over 60,000 people and has the capacity to manufacture 4,000 vehicles per week or 208,000 each year. The facility covers 1,878 acres, with buildings covering 371 acres, and includes 46 miles of rail sidings.

SOURCE: American Automobile Manufacturers Association

Midsize Cars Sell the Most

OVERALL U.S. sales of new motor vehicles in 1994 totaled 15,411,340. Of these, 8,990,483 were passenger cars (7,255,303 domestic, 1,735,180 imports) and 6,420,857 were trucks and other vehicles (5,995,227 domestic, 425,630 imports). Sales of domestic autos represented 86 percent of the U.S. total, with sales of imports representing just 14 percent. Midsize cars proved to be the **most** popular passenger cars in 1994, capturing 45.6 percent of the U.S. market. Next were small cars (29.2 percent), luxury cars (13.5 percent) and large cars (11.7 percent). Individual consumers bought the **most** cars in 1994 at 50.1 percent, but just barely more than businesses, at 48.7 percent. Government purchases represented just 1.2 percent of the total. With sales of 397,037, the Ford Taurus was the **most** popular passenger car of 1994. But the **most** popular vehicle of 1994 was actually the Ford F Series truck, with sales of 646,039.

SOURCE: American Automobile Manufacturing Association

Voted Most Popular by Sales

BASED on early estimates of total U.S. new-motor-vehicle sales in 1995, non-passenger-car sales are up overall. Americans purchased 5.5 million new cars and 5.3 million other new vehicles in 1995, and estimates are that non-passenger-car vehicles will actually outsell cars for the first time ever in 1996. In 1994, however, the following passenger cars sold the **most** in the U.S.

	Make and Model	Classification	Number of Sales
1.	Ford Taurus	Family Sedan	397,037
2.	Honda Accord	Import Luxury	367,615
3.	Ford Escort	Subcompact	336,967
4.	Toyota Camry	Family Sedan	321,979
5.	Saturn	Subcompact	286,003
6.	Honda Civic/CRX	Subcompact	267,023
7.	Pontiac Grand Am	Family Sedan	262,310
8.	Chevrolet Corsica/Beretta	Subcompact	222,129
9.	Toyota Corolla	Subcompact	210,926
10.	Chevrolet Cavalier	Family Sedan	187,263

In 1994, the following non-passenger-car vehicles sold the **most** in the U.S.

	Make and Model	Number of Sales
1.	Ford F Series	646,039
2.	Chevrolet C/K	580,445
3.	Ford Ranger	344,744
4.	Ford Explorer	278,065
5.	Dodge Caravan	268,013
6.	Chevrolet S10 Pickup	250,991
7.	Jeep Grand Cherokee	238,512
8.	Dodge Ram Pickup	232,029
9.	Plymouth Voyager	211,494
10.	Toyota Compact Pickup	204,212

SOURCE: American Automobile Manufacturer's Association

Spending the Most to Make the Most

WITH the help of catchy ads starring Lindsay Wagner, the **most** popular car of 1994 was a Ford. However, four of General Motors' lines made it into the top ten, compared to just two for Ford. Ford Motor Company also spent the **most** on advertising and media to promote Ford car and truck lines, a little under double that of the next highest spender, Toyota.

What companies spent the **most** to promote their cars in 1994? Read on.

	Car Line	Company	Number of Total Sales	Media Expenditures (millions)
1.	Ford	Ford	3,171,649	$1,550
2.	Chevrolet	General Motors	2,180,800	561
3.	Dodge	Chrysler	1,064,750	363
4.	Toyota	Toyota Motor Sales	1,000,663	865
5.	Nissan	Nissan North America	722,956	477
6.	Honda	American Honda Motor	676,093	481
7.	Pontiac	General Motors	621,184	222
8.	Buick	General Motors	546,836	220
9.	Mercury	Ford	467,237	164
10.	Oldsmobile	General Motors	448,945	187

SOURCE: America Automobile Manufacturers Association

The Most Popular Car Colors

SOMEONE buying a new car might select a bright color so the car will be easy to spot across a crowded parking lot. Another might choose neutral tones so the car will be less conspicuous on the street. Whatever the basis for the selection, the popularity of car colors changes from year to year, so the color of the car parked next to you at the grocery store may not be this year's top tint. On the other hand, you might be surprised at just how many of the cars you see on the road are painted one of the top two or three colors. In 1994, green and white headed Du Pont Automotive Products' list of the **most** popular colors for different sizes of new passenger autos as well as trucks and vans. But in the future, depending on your perspective, this choice will become either much easier or much more difficult. At the 1996 Los Angeles Auto Show, Saleen Performance displayed a one-of-a-kind supercharged Mustang called the Saleen Speedster, featuring a new finish known as Mystic, developed by BASF Corporation's

Automotive Finish Group. As the angle of view changes, the color of the car appears teal green, emerald green, blue, violet, or gold. Far superior in its color-shifting effects to the current tri-coat systems, Mystic offers a whole new trend in specialty automotive colors. But don't worry yet about having to choose *five* colors for your new car. Mystic won't be commercially available for some time.

The **most** popular motor vehicle colors for the 1995 model year were:

Luxury Cars

	Color	Percent
1.	White	14.9
2.	Light Brown	13.4
3.	Dark Green	13.0
4.	Black	9.7
5.	Medium Red	9.1
6.	White Metallic	7.8
7.	Silver	7.7
8.	Light Green	4.7
9.	Dark Red	4.5
10.	Dark Blue	3.9

Full- and Medium-Size Cars

	Color	Percent
1.	White	18.9
2.	Dark Green	17.3
3.	Medium Red	11.2
4.	Light Brown	9.7
5.	Black	5.9
6.	Silver	5.4
7.	Teal/Aqua	4.6
8.	Medium Blue	4.4
9.	Bright Red	4.4
10.	Light Blue	4.3

Compact and Sport Cars

	Color	Percent
1.	Dark Green	15.2
2.	White	14.4
3.	Medium Red	11.3

Color	Percent
4. Black	11.2
5. Bright Red	9.5
6. Purple	7.8
7. Teal/Aqua	6.6
8. Silver	6.3
9. Light Brown	4.4
10. Dark Blue	3.7

Light Trucks and Vans

Color	Percent
1. White	23.8
2. Dark Green	15.9
3. Black	9.1
4. Bright Red	8.5
5. Medium Red	7.5
6. Teal/Aqua	7.4
7. Medium/Dark Blue	5.2
8. Light Brown	5.1
9. Silver	4.3
10. Dark Red	2.8

SOURCE: American Automobile Manufacturers Association

The Most Expensive Production Car Available in the U.S.

LOOKING for a sporty little car, maybe something in red, perhaps even a convertible? Your local Ferrari dealer just might have a suggestion for you: the 1995 Ferrari F50. At around $487,000, the F50 is the **most** expensive production passenger car available in the U.S. The F50 can reach a top speed of 202 miles per hour, go from 0 to 60 miles per hour in 3.7 seconds, and travel a mile from a standing start in 30.3 seconds. With its 513-horsepower, 4.7-liter V-12 engine, the F50 gets just 10 miles per gallon in the city and 12 miles per gallon on the highway—not that you'd ever really drive this particular two-seater on a city street or freeway. It is street-legal, but the only place you can drive it to its potential is on a track. In reality, the majority of these cars wind up as showpieces in auto collections and are never driven by their owners. If you're looking for options, though, you may be a little disappointed. The F50 only comes in red with a black-and-red interior. It doesn't come with a sound system, and there's no air bag. It does, however, come with both a hard top and a soft top, so it can be driven as a convertible.

Purchasing an F50 isn't a simple matter of walking into a showroom and writing a check. Only fifty-five were made available in the U.S., and the competition to own one is fierce. Dealers first submit the names of potential buyers to Ferrari, then the company itself decides who will own the car. To qualify, prospective buyers must have what Ferrari calls "a high profile," be worth at least $200 million, and already have purchased several Ferraris. In fact, one owner selected from California had bought five new Ferrari models a few months earlier just to qualify for an F50.

SOURCE: American Automobile Manufacturers Association

The Most Expensive Production Car in the World

CALLING the McLaren F1 a "car" seems somehow a gross understatement. Selling for a cool $1 million, the F1 is the world's **most** expensive and **most** powerful production car. At 627 horsepower, the F1 can reach a top speed of 231 miles per hour and go from 0 to 60 miles per hour in just 3.2 seconds. In March 1989, based on a series of sketches, timetables, and budget projections submitted by Technical Director Gordon Murray, McLaren officially announced the F1 project. During the next several months, Murray met with a team of designers and engineers, outlining his ideas for the new car. He also called on Paul Rosche of BMW to develop a unique V-12, 6.1-liter, four-cam, 48-valve engine. From the driver's seat position at the center of the cockpit to the carbon-composite chassis, every detail was designed to increase the driver's involvement with the car and to eliminate unnecessary weight. This is why the car doesn't include such amenities as traction control, power steering, power brakes, or ABS brakes.

However, the car does come with the world's lightest and smallest ten-disc CD player, specially designed for the F1 by Kenwood. The very first F1 was completed in December 1989. With a production rate of just 3 per month, McLaren says that it will build a total of 300 F1s (though recently McLaren has announced it will stop building the F1 in 1997 as only 100 have sold). Individually built, each F1 takes about 4.5 months to manufacture and assemble. But if you'd like to buy an F1, you'll have to be patient. First, you'll need to put down a 20 percent deposit ($200,000) just to get on the waiting list. The next 30 percent ($300,000) is due eight months prior to delivery, and the balance is due when you go to get the car. Each new owner visits McLaren a few weeks before the scheduled delivery date to be fitted for the custom-built seat, and to be measured so the steering wheel and pedals can be properly adjusted. The car even comes with its own set of luggage, a tool set, a battery charger, and a car cover. A golf bag and suitcase designed to fit in one of the passenger seats are optional. The F1 development driver, Dr. Jonathan Palmer, will even give new owners tips on driving this unique auto. The car isn't being marketed in the U.S. right now because of the high cost of certification. Only a few F1s have been permitted into the country for exhibition or to become part of museum or private collections.

Who would buy such an expensive car? Although McLaren is very protective of the identity of its customers, one book about the supercar includes a picture of former Beatle George Harrison eyeing the dashboard of a new F1.

SOURCES: *Arena,* Apr. 1996;
Business Review Weekly, Mar. 4, 1996; *Road and Track,* Mar. 1996; McLaren

The Bug Is the Most Popular

ON the other hand, if you've ever owned a Volkswagen Beetle, you're certainly not alone. The VW Bug is easily the **most** popular car of all time. With over 22 million sold in more than 100 countries since the company's founding in 1937, the Bug is the best-selling passenger car ever. Designed by engineer Ferdinand Porsche, the car was Adolf Hitler's idea for a "people's car" *("Volks-wagen").*

However, manufacturing ceased during World War II because the factory was being pounded by Allied air bombings. It wasn't until 1949 that the first Beetle reached the United States. Sales were slow until 1959, when an ad agency came up with the "Beetle" name to describe the car's funny shape. The Bug caught on in the 1960s as cheap, fuel-efficient transportation. It was also inexpensive to repair, since there were so few changes in the basic design—parts could easily be swapped from year to year. In 1968, at the height of its popularity, sales reached 423,008. Beginning that same year with *The Love Bug,* Disney Pictures released four films starring a VW Bug named Herbie. CBS even aired five episodes of a series called *Herbie the Love Bug* in 1982. For years it was the best-selling car in the U.S., but with a flood of Japanese economy imports in the 1970s, sales died off. Only 10,681 were sold in 1979, the last year the Beetle was available in the U.S. But Volkswagen has given a new look to an old favorite by updating the Beetle for the nineties. With a sleek, new exterior and a whole package of technological innovations, Volkswagen expects to have what it has dubbed "Concept 1" in showrooms by 1997. The hope is that the new design will get the attention of both those who grew up with the Beetle and Generation Xers who will be buying their first new cars around that time. Volkswagen hasn't yet come up with a name for the new model, but it definitely won't be the "Bug." Still, the original Beetle hasn't lost its popularity yet. Disney Studios has just finished production on a new television movie featuring Herbie, set to air soon.

SOURCE: David A. Fetherson, *Volkswagen Customs and Classics,* Motorbooks International, 1995

The Most Reliable New Cars

As automobile consumers pay higher and higher prices for their new cars, expectations for increased quality are also rising. New-car buyers are less tolerant than in the past of even minor imperfections in appearance or performance. That little whirring noise that once went ignored is now reason enough to take the car in to be checked. For nine years, J. D. Power and Associates has been conducting its *New Car Initial Quality Study,* the nation's only independent survey of new-vehicle owners. If you've bought a new car recently, you probably received one of J. D. Power's survey forms in the mail a few months after your purchase. The 1995 study analyzed the problems experienced by over 50,000 consumers surveyed during their first three months of new-car ownership. A record 55 models achieved or exceeded the old standard of excellence—"100 problems per 100 cars"—including autos of all sizes, price ranges, and countries of origin. The 1995 overall average was 103 problems per 100 cars, a seven-point improvement over 1994, when the average was 110 problems per 100 cars. Overall, American Honda Motor Company, including both its Acura and Honda divisions, was the top-ranked corporation, with an average of just 70 problems per 100 cars. Infiniti was named "Best Overall Car Line," with an average of just 55 problems per 100 cars.

The ten **most** problem-free car models in 1995 according to surveys conducted by J. D. Power and Associates are listed below.

	Make and Model	Problems per 100 Cars
1.	Honda Prelude	48
	Infiniti J30	48
3.	Lexus SC 300/SC 400	49
4.	Acura Legend	50
5.	Lexus LS 400	51
6.	Geo Prizm	56

	Make and Model	Problems per 100 Cars
7.	Infiniti G20	62
	Volvo 940	62
9.	Honda Accord	63
10.	Cadillac DeVille	64

Get the Most for Your Money: Buy the Best!

Most of us have limited budgets and we have to put our dollars to the best possible use. A great place to start is with our next auto purchase. Using our heads is using our money wisely.

So if you're looking for the **most** value out of your next new car, look for the best-made cars for the price you're willing or able to pay.

Following are the leaders in each price category, according to the same J. D. Power and Associates surveys for 1995.

Price Range	Make and Model	Problems per 100 Cars
under $13,000	Mercury Tracer	95
$13,001–$17,000	Geo Prizm	56
$17,001–$22,000	Honda Accord	63
$22,001–$29,000	Honda Prelude	48
over $29,000	Infiniti J30	48

The Most Satisfied New-Car Customers

J. D. Power and Associates also surveys customers one year after the purchase of a new car. Focusing on the "people" aspects of car ownership, this survey asks not only how satisfied the customers are with their car (Vehicle Repair/Reliability), but how well they feel they were treated by their dealership (Customer Handling). In 1995, the car business overall achieved a Customer Satisfaction Index score of 138. For the third consecutive year, three car lines placed at the top of J. D. Power's CSI. Based on a survey of over 32,000 car and light-truck owners nationwide, Lexus had the **most** satisfied customers, with a CSI of 173, followed by Infiniti (172) and Saturn (150).

More than 9,500 light-truck owners participated in the 1995 survey, and owners of the five Toyota truck models were by far the **most** satisfied, awarding their trucks an overall CSI score of 172. If the tremendous improvement in scores on these surveys in the last ten years are any indication, auto manufacturers seem to be listening, building better cars, and treating their customers better.

Following is J. D. Power and Associates' 1995 Customer Satisfaction Index for both cars and light trucks.

	Car Line	CSI		Light-Truck Line	CSI
1.	Lexus	173	1.	Toyota	172
2.	Infiniti	172	2.	Honda	154
3.	Saturn	159	3.	Oldsmobile	153
4.	Acura	155	4.	Ford	150
	Volvo	155	5.	Geo	146
6.	Audi	152	6.	Mazda	144
7.	Cadillac	150		Plymouth	144
8.	Honda	149	8.	Nissan	143
	Mercedes-Benz	149	9.	Mitsubishi	142
10.	Toyota	148			

The Most Value Retained

LET'S say you just purchased a new car and you're about to start paying for it. You've probably sat down with your spouse or parent or friend or whoever and have rationalized those monthly payments. But have you given any thought to what that brand-new beauty out in the driveway is going to be worth over time? Whether you have or haven't, you might want to know which new cars out there today will retain **most** of their value after five years.

Subcompacts

	Car	Resale Value (percent of purchase price)
1.	Saturn SC Coupes	69
2.	Acura Integra RS Coupe	64
3.	Toyota Celica ST Liftback	62

Compacts

	Car	Resale Value (percent of purchase price)
1.	Saturn SL Sedan series	65
2.	Honda Accord DX Sedan	64
3.	VW Jetta GL Sedan	61

Midsize

	Car	Resale Value (percent of purchase price)
1.	Nissan Maxima series	61
2.	Toyota Camry XLE Sedan	58
3.	Volkswagen Passat GLX	55
	Mazda 626 DX Sedan	55

Large

	Car	Resale Value (percent of purchase price)
1.	Buick LeSabre Custom	53
2.	Chrysler Concorde	51
	Dodge Intrepid Sedan	51

Luxury

	Car	Resale Value (percent of purchase price)
1.	Lexus LS 400	67
	Lexus GS 300	67
3.	Mercedes-Benz E420	66

Sport

	Car	Resale Value (percent of purchase price)
1.	Porsche 911 Carrera Cabriolet	64
2.	Mitsubishi 3000GT	61
3.	Chevrolet Corvette	59
	Mercedes SL 320 Roadster	59

Small Wagon

	Car	Resale Value (percent of purchase price)
1.	Honda Accord LX	65
	Saturn SW	65
3.	Toyota Corolla DX	62

Midsize-to-Large Wagon

Car	Resale Value (percent of purchase price)
1. Toyota Camry LE	58
2. Subaru Legacy L	57
3. Volkswagen Passat GLX	55

SOURCE: *The Complete Car Cost Guide,* IntelliChoice, 1995

Losing the Most Resale Value

MAYBE you read the above and didn't see your brand-new car on it. Don't panic. It's probably still a very fine car. However, you might think twice about reading on.

The cars below are projected to lose the **most** value after five years, beginning on the date the car is purchased. Percentages are based on how much the original value of the car is retained after those first five years.

Subcompact

Car	Resale Value (percent of purchase price)
1. Hyundai S Coupe	47
2. Eagle Summit DX Coupe	48
3. Chrysler LeBaron GTC Convertible	48

Compact

Car	Resale Value (percent of purchase price)
1. Oldsmobile Achieva S Ser. II Coupe	43
2. Dodge Spirit Sedan	45
3. Buick Skylark Custom Sedan	46

Midsize

Car	Resale Value (percent of purchase price)
1. Ford Taurus SHO Sedan	43
2. Oldsmobile Cutlass Sierra SL	45
Mercury Sable LS Sedan	45

Large

Car	Resale Value (percent of purchase price)
1. Oldsmobile 88 LSS Sedan	46
2. Buick Roadmaster Lmt. Sedan	48

Luxury

Car	Resale Value (percent of purchase price)
1. Alfa Romeo 164	46
2. Lincoln Continental	47
Cadillac DeVille	47

Sport

Car	Resale Value (percent of purchase price)
1. Pontiac Firebird Formula Coupe	49
Porsche 928 GTS	49
3. Subaru SVX L	50
4. Nissan 300ZX 2+2 Coupe	52

Small Wagon

Car	Resale Value (percent of purchase price)
1. Ford Escort LX	52
Mercury Tracer	52
Subaru Impreza AWD	52

Midsize-to-Large Wagon

Car	Resale Value (percent of purchase price)
1. Ford Taurus LX	47
2. Volvo 940	48
3. Mercury Sable LS	49

SOURCE: *The Complete Car Cost Guide,* IntelliChoice, 1995

The Most-Reliable Used Cars

LOOKING for a car that looks new but isn't? Then look at the used-car market. But because you won't be getting a warranty, make sure to look extra hard. Fortunately, a few people out there have put together information to show you the way and keep you from questioning your sanity later on. One such book actually tells you what the **most** reliable used-car buys are. Following are the cars that made it.

Subcompact

Car	Years
Acura Integra	1986–95
Chevrolet Nova	1986–88
Geo Prizm	1990–95
Dodge/Plymouth Colt	1986–93
Mitsubishi Mirage	1986–93
Honda Civic	1986–95
Mazda 323	1986–89
Mercury Tracer	1988–89
Nissan Sentra	1988–95
Toyota Tercel	1986–95

Compact

Car	Years
BMW 3-Series	1986–95
Dodge Aries	1986–89
Plymouth Reliant	1986–89
Dodge Spirit	1990–93
Plymouth Acclaim	1990–93
Honda Accord	1986–95

Intermediate

Car	Years
Ford Taurus	1988–95
Mercury Sable	1988–95
Toyota Camry	1992–95
Volvo 240 Series	1986–93

Large

Car	Years
Buick LeSabre	1988–95
Oldsmobile 88 Royale	1988–95
Pontiac Bonneville	1988–95
Chevrolet Caprice	1986–95
Dodge Caravan	1987–95
Plymouth Voyager	1987–95
Ford Crown Victoria	1986–95
Mercury Grand Marquis	1986–95

Luxury

Car	Years
Lexus LS 400	1990–95
Lincoln Town Car	1986–95
Volvo 740/900	1987–95

Sporty

Car	Years
Honda Prelude	1986–95
Mazda RX-7	1988–91
Toyota MR2	1986–95

As the suggested years for the above models vary, so will the prices.

SOURCE: Jack Gills, *The Used Car Book,* 8th edition (1995)

A Used-Car Most

So, you think you paid a bit too much for your last used car? Your price, however, probably doesn't even come close to the **most** ever paid for a used auto. On April 12, 1990, the Meitec Corporation of Japan bought a 1931 Bugatti Type 41 Royale Sports Coupé by Kellner for $15 million, which included the dealer's commission.

Burning the Most, Conserving the Most

IF you're like the majority of drivers, you probably don't really know what kind of mileage your car gets. What you do know, though, is how much it costs to fill the tank each time you pull up to the gas pump. Of course, those who can afford to drive a Lamborghini DB132/Diablo, which guzzles the **most** gas per mile of any production car, probably aren't all that concerned with their car's mileage. Those concerned with fuel efficiency and the environment, however, will more likely be found checking out a car like the Geo Metro, which gets the **most** miles per gallon of fuel.

Each year the Environmental Protection Agency tests the fuel economy of new cars, which the Department of Energy then reports in a comparative guide. The EPA, however, suggests that their figures are to be used more for comparison than as an exact indicator of a car's mileage. That is, a car rated at 25 miles per gallon will nearly always get better mileage than one rated at 20 miles per gallon.

Below are the mileage figures you'll see printed on the window stickers of cars for the 1996 model year, both the fuel misers and the gas guzzlers, along with their estimated average annual fuel cost based on driving 15,000 miles per year.

The 1996 Fuel Economy Winners (aka "The Misers")

	Gas Misers (engine displacement/ cylinders/transmission)	Miles per Gallon: City/Highway	Annual Fuel Cost
1.	Geo Metro (1.0L/3/M5)	44/49	$391
2.	Honda Civic HB HX (1.6L/4/M5)	39/45	$439
3.	Geo Metro (1.3L/4/M5)	39/43	$439
	Suzuki Swift (1.3L/4/M5)	39/43	$439
5.	Honda Civic HX (1.6L/4/AV)	35/39	$486
6.	Ford Aspire (1.3L/4/M5)	34/42	$486
7.	Toyota Tercel (1.5L/4/M4)	34/40	$500
8.	Honda del Sol (1.6L/4/M5)	34/39	$500
9.	Honda Civic (1.6L/4/M5)	33/38	$515
10.	Mitsubishi Mirage (1.5L/4/M5)	32/39	$515
	Mazda Protege (1.5L/4/M5)	32/39	$515
	Eagle Summit (1.5L/4/M5)	32/39	$515

M4 = manual four-speed, M5 = manual five-speed, AV = Automatic

The 1996 Fuel Economy Losers (aka "The Guzzlers")

Gas Guzzlers (engine displacement/ cylinders/transmission)	Miles per Gallon: City/Highway	Annual Fuel Cost
1. Lamborghini DB132/ Diablo (5.7L/12/M5)	9/14	$1,841
2. Rolls-Royce Silver Spur Limo (6.8L/8/L4)	11/15	$1,557
Rolls-Royce Bentley Limo (6.8L/8/L4)	11/15	$1,557
Rolls-Royce Bentley Azure (6.8L/8/L4)	11/15	$1,557
5. Rolls-Royce Bentley Continental (6.8L/8/L4)	11/16	$1,557
6. Rolls-Royce Turbo R/ Turbo RL (6.8L/8/L4)	12/16	$1,446
Jaguar XJ12 (6.0L/12/L4)	12/16	$1,446
Rolls-Royce Bentley Brookland/LWB (6.8L/8/L4)	12/16	$1,446
9. Rolls-Royce Silver Spur/ Silver Dawn (6.8L/8/L4)	12/17	$1,446
10. Mitsubishi Mirage (6.0L/12/A5)	13/19	$1,446
Porsche 911 Turbo (3.6L/12/M6)	13/19	$1,351

M5 = manual five-speed, M6 = manual six-speed, A5 = automatic five-speed, L4 =Automatic

SOURCE: Environmental Protection Agency; Department of Energy

Mileage Mosts

THINK what the world would be like if all production autos could even come close to the mileage achieved by a team of students from Lycée St. Joseph LaJoliverie in Nantes, France. On July 17, 1992, this group achieved an incredible 7,591 miles per gallon, the **most** miles per gallon ever, while driving in the Shell Mileage Marathon held at Silverstone, Great Britain. Of course, their car was specially designed for that purpose. However, later that month, between July 26 and 29, Stuart Bladon and Robert Procter drove an unmodified Audi 100TDI filled with one tank of diesel fuel (17.62 gallons) all the way from John o'Groats in Scotland to Land's End, England, the entire length of Great Britain, and back into Scotland. The fuel finally ran out some 35 hours and 18 minutes later, after the car had driven 1,338.1 miles, the **most** ever driven on a single tank of gas for a production car. The car had achieved a very efficient 75.94 miles per gallon.

SOURCE: *The Guinness Book of Records 1996,* Bantam, 1996

Cars with the Most Overall Protection in a Crash

EACH year as part of its New Car Assessment Program, the National Highway Traffic Safety Administration (NHTSA) tests cars in simulated 35-mile-per-hour head-on collisions in order to measure the effects of the impact on a passenger's head, chest, and legs. The cars carry specially designed "crash-test dummies" to record the force transferred to each of the three areas of the body during the crash. The results then show just how much protection the car offers for each area. For example, a car might provide good protection from head injury but slightly less for the chest and legs. *The Car Book* then publishes its annual summary of the NHTSA's crash-test data and provides a single index number reflecting all of the forces measured by the tests. The lower the index number, the better the car's overall performance in the crash test compared to others of the same approximate weight and size. Results can vary, though, based on how the car is equipped and whether it has two or four doors. The Ford Thunderbird and the Mercury Cougar, each with an index rating of 1362, provide their driver and passenger with the **most** overall protection in the event of an accident. Of course, these are both large cars.

Listed below by weight class are the index numbers for the 1996 cars for which crash test information is available.

Subcompact

	Car Model	Index
1.	Geo Metro 4-dr.	3080
	Suzuki Swift 4-dr.	3080
3.	Mitsubishi Mirage 4-dr.	3224
	Eagle Summit	3224

Compact

	Car Model	Index
1.	Chrysler Sebring	1760
	Dodge Avenger	1760
3.	Honda Prelude	1959
4.	Ford Probe	2026
	Mazda MX-6	2026

Intermediate

	Car Model	Index
1.	Chevrolet Camaro	1705
	Pontiac Firebird	1705
3.	Mazda Millenia	2085
4.	Audi A6/S6	2143
5.	Chrysler Concorde	2323
	Dodge Intrepid	2323
	Eagle Vision	2323

Large

	Car Model	Index
1.	Ford Thunderbird	1632
	Mercury Cougar	1632
3.	Ford Crown Victoria	2116
	Mercury Grand Marquis	2116
5.	Chevrolet Lumina	2173

Minivan

	Minivan Model	Index
1.	Ford Windstar	1911
2.	Honda Odyssey	2889
3.	Chevy Lumina Minivan	3263
	Oldsmobile Silhouette	3263
	Pontiac Trans Sport	3263

SOURCE: *The Car Book,* 1996

Mosts in the Underworld of the Auto World

IF you live in California, own a red Mustang that's about three years old, and leave it parked in the driveway, watch out! It's a prime target for auto thieves. In September 1995, LoJack, a company that operates an electronic stolen-auto-recovery system, released a report showing the **most** commonly stolen Lojack-equipped vehicles and the **most** common circumstances under which they are taken from their owners. It is true that **most** stolen cars, about 80 percent, are taken by professionals for parts.

However, and contrary to the myth that new, luxury autos are the main targets of auto theft, the average stolen car is over three years old and worth about $17,000.

Another myth dispelled by LoJack's study is that stolen cars are driven long distances across state or international borders. It seems that car thieves would rather limit the time they're in the vehicle, so **most** stolen autos are driven just fifteen miles from the scene of the crime. Also, car thieves rarely dismantle stolen cars immediately, preferring instead to leave them on residential side streets for a day or so to "cool off." No single day of the week fares much better than any other when it comes to auto theft, with each day averaging between 12 and 16 percent of the week's total. **Most** cars (52 percent) are reported as having been stolen in broad daylight, between 8:00 A.M. and 4:00 P.M., with 30 percent being stolen between 4:00 P.M. and midnight and just 18 percent between midnight to 8:00 A.M.

In Washington, D.C., and the eleven states where LoJack operates, the **most** popular location from which cars are stolen is the owner's driveway, followed by places of employment, then shopping malls. The **most** popular color for stolen vehicles is red, representing 27 percent of the total, followed by black (23 percent), white (14 percent), gray (10 percent), and green (9 percent).

What's the **most** popular vehicle to steal? That depends on whether you live on the West Coast or the East Coast. Here are the top five LoJack-equipped vehicles reported stolen on both coasts.

West Coast	East Coast
1. Ford Mustang	1. Toyota Corolla
2. Honda Accord	2. Oldsmobile Cutlass
3. Honda Prelude	3. Ford Mustang
4. Jeep Wrangler	4. Chevrolet Camaro
5. Honda Civic	5. Toyota Celica/Supra

SOURCE: LoJack

The Most Rolls-Royces

BEFORE his deportation in 1985, the followers of the Bhagwan Shree Rajneesh (1931–90) had provided the Indian mystic with 84 Rolls-Royces. His collection contained the **most** Rolls-Royces ever owned by a single individual. So consider this. If Rajneesh were to have ridden in a different car every day, it would have taken nearly three months before he had to use the first car again!

SOURCE: *Economist,* Feb. 29, 1992

The Most Car Wrecks

BEING in just one car accident can be traumatic, even if you're lucky enough to walk away. But can you imagine destroying 2,003 cars in a lifetime and on purpose? That's how many Dick Sheppard of Gloucester, England, managed to demolish during his 40-year career as a stuntman— the **most** ever wrecked by a single individual.

SOURCE: *The Guinness Book of Records 1996,* Bantam, 1996

Where to Hail the Most Cabs

NEED a cab? You should be able to find one fairly easily in Mexico City. With 60,000 pesaros (regular taxis) and settas (airport taxis), Mexico City has the **most** taxis of any city in the world. In the United States, New York City has the **most** cabs, with 11,787 (as of January 1, 1994) registered yellow medallion cabs and 40,000 licensed drivers serving approximately 226 million passengers each year. The city also has about 30,000 for-hire vehicle (FHV) cabs working out of 600 bases within the city's five boroughs.

SOURCE: Mexico City Department of Tourism/New York City Transit Authority

Mosts
from the World of
Pets and Animals

SOME WE LOVE and hug, others we eat. Some we watch with fascination, others turn our stomachs. What are we talking about? Animals. Pretty varied subject, huh? You better believe it. So have a glance below and check out all the **mosts** the animal kingdom has to offer.

The Most Popular Pets by Household

WHETHER they run on the ground, slip silently through the water, or fly gracefully through the air, pets contribute so much to our lives. Their companionship and unconditional love provide stability and a tremendous feeling of being needed. Owning a pet teaches a child the responsibility of feeding and caring for another living creature. And just what are the **most** popular pets in the United States? According to a survey by the American Veterinary Association, dogs can be found as pets the **most** often in U.S. households. However, pet owners frequently have more than one pet, averaging 1.5 dogs and 2.0 cats per household. So, in terms of the actual number of pets in the U.S., cats are the **most** popular, outnumbering dogs 57,000,000 to 52,500,000.

In the following, though, we only look at households owning one particular type of pet, not at how many of such pets are owned by a household.

	Pet	Percent of U.S. Households
1.	Dogs	36.5
2.	Cats	30.9
3.	Birds	5.7
4.	Fish	2.8
	Horses	2.8
6.	Rabbits	1.5
7.	Hamsters	1.0

Pet	Percent of U.S. Households
8. Guinea pigs	0.5
9. Gerbils	0.3
10. Ferrets	0.2

SOURCE: American Veterinary Association

The Most Popular Dogs

WITH an estimated 52.5 million dogs in the U.S. alone, it should be easy to find a puppy that would make a good pet. But some people spend hours studying the characteristics of the breed of dog they'd like to have as a pet, carefully selecting a breeder and then waiting patiently until an AKC registered puppy is available. Others fall in love at first sight with the cutest little tail-wagger that looks up from a cage at the local Humane Society. Either way, according to the Pet Food Institute, an estimated 37.7 percent of U.S. households have dogs as pets. But which breed is the **most** popular? According to the AKC, the top ten registered breeds in 1995 were:

Breed	No. Registered by the AKC
1. Labrador retriever	132,051
2. Rotweiler	93,656
3. German shepherd	78,088
4. Golden retriever	64,107
5. Beagle	57,063
6. Poodle	54,784
7. Cocker spaniel	48,065
8. Dachshund	44,680
9. Pomeranian	37,894
10. Yorkshire terrier	36,881

SOURCE: American Kennel Club

The Most Overworked Sire

A champion greyhound from London named Low Pressure, nicknamed Timmy, is the **most** prolific sire of all time. Between December 1961 and his death on November 27, 1969, he fathered over 3,000 puppies. We believe he passed away as a happy pooch.

SOURCE: *The Guinness Book of Records 1996,* Bantam, 1996

Fido's Most Commonly Performed Tricks

THE Pet Food Institute and a U.S. pet food manufacturer conducted a survey including 25.3 million of the 52.5 million dogs in the U.S. to determine the **most** common tricks they are taught to perform. Here are a few of Fido's **most** favorite maneuvers.

	Trick	Dogs Performing
1.	Sit	5,313,105
2.	Shake paw	3,795,075
3.	Roll over	2,884,257
4.	"Speak"	2,681,853
5.	Lie down	1,872,237
5.	Stand on hind legs	1,872,237
7.	Beg	1,821,636
8.	Dance	1,543,331
9.	"Sing"	759,015
10.	Fetch newspaper	430,508

SOURCE: Pet Food Institute

The Most Intelligent Pups

PSYCHOLOGY professor and pet trainer Stanley Coren created a series of work and obedience tests to determine the intelligence of different breeds of dogs. Coren's 1994 book *The Intelligence of Dogs* describes the results of the tests he conducted on 133 different breeds. The border collie ranked as the **most** intelligent breed. Poodles came in second, while German shepherds and golden retrievers tied at third. The list continued with Doberman pinschers, Shetland sheepdogs, Labrador retrievers, papillons, rottweilers, and Australian cattle dogs. Amazingly, the bloodhound, often used to help track missing people, ranked a disappointing 128th, and the Afghan hound was at the very bottom of the list, its only consolation being that it's cute.

SOURCE: Stanley Coren, *The Intelligence of Dogs,* Bantam, 1994

The Most Popular Dog Names

A recent survey of U.S. dog licenses shows that terms of royalty account for half of the names on a list of the top ten doggy monikers. The **most** popular name is Lady, followed by King, Duke, Peppy, Prince, Pepper, Snoopy, Princess, Heidi, Sam, and Coco. The list also reveals some unusual names, including Beowulf, Rembrandt, and Twit. The name of television and film star Lassie came 82nd. Rover made it onto the list at 161st place.

The Breed with the Most Killer Instinct

IN a twenty-seven-year study conducted in New York City, the breed of dog that bites the **most** is the German shepherd, followed by the chow, the poodle, the Italian bulldog, and the fox terrier. But which breed is the deadliest? One pit bull is credited with killing the **most** human beings, seventeen, during its life of twenty-two years. This gruesome total was three times that for all of the study's next-deadliest breed, German shepherds.

SOURCE: Barbara Berliner, *The Book of Answers:* The New York Public Library. Simon and Schuster, 1990

The Most Decorated Dog

DURING World War II, a dog named Chips, a German shepherd–collie mix, was awarded the most military honors of any canine in military history. On the night of July 10, 1943, the soldiers who landed on a beach in Sicily were being held down by machine-gun fire. Chips, a member of the K9 Corps, risked his life by storming the machine-gun nest. Within moments, with Chips growling and barking, the handful of Italian soldiers manning the guns surrendered. Chips was wounded but soon recovered, and in a special ceremony held on November 19, 1943, he was awarded the Purple Heart, the Silver Star, and the Distinguished Service Medal for "bravery in action against the enemy."

SOURCE: Department of the Army, Office of Public Affairs

The Most Popular Cats

ANCIENT Egyptians worshiped cats as sacred to Bast, the cat-headed goddess of pleasure. Killing a cat meant instant death, and cat funerals were so common and kitty cemeteries so numerous that until recently such final resting grounds were profitably used as sources of fertilizer.

In the U.S. today, the Cat Fancier's Association lists 71,036 registered cats classified into 39 different breeds. The following list shows the 10 **most** popular registered breeds of cat in 1994.

	Breed	Cats Registered
1.	Persian	47,022
2.	Maine coon	3,852
3.	Siamese	2,881
4.	Abyssubuab	2,447
5.	Exotic shorthair	1,507
6.	Scottish fold	1,250
7.	American shorthair	1,143
8.	Oriental shorthair	1,123
9.	Birman	957
10.	Burmese	884

SOURCE: Cat Fancier's Association

The Most Popular Cat Names

WORDS describing the way cats look dominate the list of the **most** popular cat names in the U.S. Names like Patches, Tiger, Boots/Bootsie and Cali/Calico easily describe a cat's markings, while Misty, Ginger, Smokey, Pepper, Rusty/Rusti and perhaps even Punkin/Pumpkin can describe the color of a cat's soft, furry coat.

Here's a list of the top ten names for both male and female cats. Maybe your own little precious will make the list.

	Female		Male
1.	Samantha	1.	Tiger/Tigger
2.	Misty	2.	Smokey
3.	Patches	3.	Pepper
4.	Cali/Calico	4.	Max/Maxwell

	Female		Male
5.	Muffin	5.	Simon
6.	Angel/Angela	6.	Snoopy
7.	Ginger	7.	Morris
8.	Tiger/Tigger	8.	Mickey
9.	Princess	9.	Rusty/Rusti
10.	Punkin/Pumpkin	10.	Boots/Bootsie

SOURCE: Cat Fancier's Association, Manasquan, New Jersey

Mama Cats' Mosts

A tabby named Dusty, of Bonham, Texas, is the **most** prolific mother cat of all time. Born in 1935, she produced a record 420 kittens during her breeding life, giving birth at age seventeen to her last litter, a single kitten, on June 12, 1952. In 1970, a Burmese-Siamese-mix mother cat living in Westcote, England, gave birth to 19 kittens, the **most** ever born in a single litter, although 4 of them were stillborn.

SOURCE: *The Guinness Book of Records 1996,* Bantam, 1996

The Most Intelligent Animals

EVERYONE loves to brag about how smart their dog or cat is, but the truth is that dogs and cats don't even rank in the top ten of animals in intelligence! According to a study which defined intelligence as the speed and extent of learning performance over a wide range of tasks (also accounting for the ratio of brain size to body bulk), the following animals are the **most** intelligent outside of human beings (some, anyways).

1. Chimpanzee
2. Gorilla
3. Orangutan
4. Baboon
5. Gibbon
6. Monkey
7. Smaller-toothed whale
8. Dolphin
9. Elephant
10. Domestic hog

As you can see, primates are the smartest of the lot.

The Most per Litter

ANIMAL babies are certainly cute, and it can be fun to watch a litter of puppies or kittens grow. But what mammals have the **most** babies? Although instances of pigs having litters of 30 or more have been recorded, such occurrences certainly aren't common. With an average of 20 young per litter, the tiny, tailless tenrec from Madagascar produces the most babies at a time. The golden hamster, which has only a 15-day gestation period, is second, with an average of 10 or more babies per litter.

SOURCES: David MacDonald, *The Encyclopedia of Animals*, Facts on File, 1984; Helen Piers, *Taking Care of Your Hamster*, Borron's, 1992

The Most Romantic Spot in the Animal Kingdom

EACH year, a gathering of the **most** members of a single species of mammal takes place on the Pribilof Islands in the Bering Sea off Alaska. This is the breeding ground of the Alaskan fur seal, and an estimated 1.5 million of them arrive each year and produce approximately 600,000 seal pups.

SOURCE: *Grzimek's Animal Life Encyclopedia*, Dr. Bernhard Grzimek, editor, Van Nostrand Reinhold Co., 1975

Hamsters Have the Most Relatives

NOT just **most,** but actually all of the pet hamsters in the world today are descended from just one female golden hamster found with a litter of twelve babies in Syria in 1930. Scientists named the species in 1839 when a single animal was found, also in Syria, but they hadn't seen the breed for nearly 100 years when the mother and her babies were discovered. Since then, a number of color variations have been produced through selective breeding.

SOURCE: *Grzimek's Animal Life Encyclopedia*, Dr. Bernhard Grzimek, editor, Van Nostrand Reinhold Company, 1975

The Most Adaptable

OVER 2,000 years ago, around the time of Aristotle, scientists discovered that certain species of fish are able to change gender when there aren't enough members of the opposite sex available. But such changes were thought to be irreversible. Recently, however, scientists discovered that at least three species of fish are able to change both their genitalia and their brain in an average of four days and as often as their social environment requires it. Of the three species that are able to change gender the **most** often, one, studied by biologist Matthew Grober of the University of Idaho, is a variant of the gobi called *Trimma okinawae*. It was discovered by marine biologist Tokomi Sunobe of the Natural History Museum and Institute in Chiba, Japan. In this species of fish, the lone male is also the primary caregiver for the group's young. But when a larger male moves in on the group, the first male stops caring for the young and begins taking on the female role in courtship. In a few days, its sexual organs change and it begins producing eggs. If the new male is removed from the group, the process is reversed, and the female fish becomes male once again. According to researchers, the complete cycle takes about ten days. Grober has been studying the brains of the fish at different points during the cycle, and hopes that certain similarities between these fish and vertebrates will provide meaningful insights into human behavior.

SOURCE: Matthew Grober; University of Idaho

Eating the Most Meat

MOVE over *Tyrannosaurus rex!* The **most** massive meat-eating dinosaur of them all was recently discovered in Argentina. Called *Giganotosaurus carolini,* this new king of the prehistoric beasts weighed between 6 and 8 tons and stretched 42 feet long. Amateur fossil hunter Reuben Carolini discovered the first remains in 1993, and its skull, backbone, pelvis, and leg bones were subsequently located by a pair of Argentine paleontologists, who reported their findings in the journal *Nature.* Bones of one of the largest plant-eating dinosaurs, called *Argentinosaurus,* were also found at the same site. Estimates are that these giants lived nearly 30 million years before the evolution of *Tyrannosaurus rex.*

SOURCE: *Nature*

Mosts
from the World of the
Movies

MOST PEOPLE WATCH them, **most** people talk about them, and at one time or another in our lives, **most** of us have wanted to be in them. What are they? Does "lights, camera, action!" sound familiar? If so, you know you're in the Movies! Read on to see where you and your favorite movies and moviemakers fit in when compared to **most** others in the world of stars and magic—the movies.

Making the Most

IN March 1915, a huge headline in *Moving Picture World* magazine proclaimed Hollywood the "Motion Picture Mecca." Even now, people still think of Hollywood as the entertainment capital of the world. But what country actually produces the **most** full-length feature films a year? To answer that one, we'll need to set our sights a bit further east, actually quite a ways east—all the way to India, to be exact.

India's filmmakers have produced the **most** feature-length films yearly since 1971. In 1990, that total reached 948, the **most** movies ever produced by any country in a single year. In the U.S., the **most** productive year ever was 1921, when "the industry" (as it is known to Hollywood insiders) produced 854 feature films, 94 movies short of India's record.

Not surprisingly, India also holds the record for the **most** full-length motion pictures produced overall, with a grand total of 27,361 between 1913 and 1994. And this feat was accomplished using 51 different languages. The U.S., though, does spend the **most** on film production, accounting for a whopping 74 percent of the worldwide total. The **most** prolific film-producing countries in 1994 were:

	Country	Films Produced
1.	India (southern India only)	499
2.	United States	420

	Country	Films Produced
3.	Japan	251
4.	Hong Kong	192
5.	China	148
6.	France	115
7.	Italy	95
8.	Russian Federation	90
9.	United Kingdom	70
10.	South Korea	65

SOURCE: *Variety*

The Most Powerful Movie Moguls

LOOKING for your big break in Hollywood? It may help to know one of these guys. *Entertainment Weekly* named them their top ten power brokers in Hollywood in 1996.

1. Rupert Murdoch, Chairman, NewsCorp. (20th Century–Fox)
2. Michael Eisner, Chairman, Walt Disney Company
3. Gerald Levin, Chairman, Time Warner (Warner Bros.)
4. Ted Turner, Vice Chairman, Time Warner (Warner Bros.)
5. Sumner Redstone, Chairman, Viacom (Paramount)
6. Edgar Branfman Jr., President, The Seagram Company (Universal)
7. Nobuyuki Idei, President, Sony Corp. (Columbia)
8. Bob Daly, Co-CEO, Warner Bros.
   Terry Semel, Co-CEO, Warner Bros.
10. Bob Wright, Don Ohlmeyer & Warren Littlefield, NBC

SOURCE: "Power 101," *Entertainment Weekly,* Oct. 25, 1996

The Whiz-Kid with Jaws to Match

BEGINNING with *Jaws* in 1975 and continuing with the success of *Schindler's List* in 1993, Steven Spielberg has earned the title of world's **most** successful filmmaker. Worldwide, his films have grossed over $2.17 billion. In fact, four of the top ten international all-time favorites are Spielberg films, with *Jaws* (1975) only now, after twenty years, slipping into eleventh position. *Schindler's List,* his 1993 dramatic black-and-white depiction of the Holocaust, earned the Best Picture Oscar that year and earned Spielberg his first Oscar for Best Director.

SOURCE: *Variety*

The Most International B.O.

No, that's not B.O. as in body odor. By no means. We're talking *box office* here, baby, and it's the big talk in Tinseltown. Curious what the big winners are? Read on.

Jurassic Park, Steven Spielberg's 1993 megahit about dinosaurs being re-created from prehistoric DNA, is the **most** successful film in motion picture history in terms of international box-office gross revenues.

Adventures of all kinds dominate the list, including several that address questions of epic proportions: Is there life after death? Is there intelligent life on other planets? Can our world survive the future? Can we reconstruct life from its **most** basic elements? Would you die for someone you love? These themes have been the mainstay of literature over the centuries, but it's good to see that they flourish in an industry where even getting a picture made is a miracle.

The top ten international box-office hits of all time are:

Film Title (Year Released)	Box Office Gross Through 8/24/95 (millions)
1. *Jurassic Park* (1993)	$913.1
2. *The Lion King* (1994)	773.3
3. *E.T. The Extra-Terrestrial* (1982)	701.1
4. *Forrest Gump* (1994)	673.7
5. *Ghost* (1989)	517.6
6. *Star Wars* (1977)	513.0
7. *The Bodyguard* (1992)	507.6
8. *Indiana Jones and the Last Crusade* (1989)	494.8
9. *Aladdin* (1992)	490.0
Terminator 2: Judgment Day (1991)	490.0

SOURCE: *Variety*

The Most B.O. When Accounting for Inflation

BOX-OFFICE-REVENUE statistics for **most** early films are at best incomplete, and confusing matters even more is the fact that methods for calculating these numbers have changed over the years. Also, inflated ticket prices have meant that newer films earn much more than older films. However, adjusted for inflation, the much-loved film adaptation of Margaret Mitchell's *Gone with the Wind,* starring Vivien Leigh and Clark Gable, remains the all-time box-office champ. According to a July 1995 study by Exhibitor Relations, the films that have earned the **most** adjusted gross revenues are those below:

Film Title (Year Released)	Box Office Adjusted Gross Revenue
1. *Gone with the Wind* (1939)	$827,745,000
2. *Star Wars* (1977)	602,125,561
3. *The Ten Commandments* (1958)	546,270,000
4. *The Sound of Music* (1965)	535,349,040
5. *Jaws* (1975)	534,088,670
6. *E.T. The Extra-Terrestrial* (1982)	529,265,056
7. *Dr. Zhivago* (1965)	517,644,850
8. *Jungle Book* (1967)	463,059,892
9. *Snow White and the Seven Dwarfs* (1937)	454,530,000
10. *101 Dalmatians* (1961)	414,101,557

SOURCE: Exhibitor Relations, July 1995

The Most Profitable Movie Series

THE **most** profitable film series of all time is the *Star Wars* trilogy. Collectively, it includes *Star Wars* (1977), *The Empire Strikes Back* (1980), and *Return of the Jedi* (1983), and it has earned over $800 million in North America alone and over $4 billion worldwide, inclusive of all rights (*before* its 1997 rerelease!). Next are the nineteen James Bond films, beginning in 1962 with *Dr. No* starring Sean Connery, and continuing in 1995 with *Golden Eye* starring Pierce Brosnan.

SOURCE: Variety

The Most Grosses Among Foreign-Language Movies

FOR over twenty years, the list of top-grossing foreign-language films in the U.S. was led by the Swedish soft-porn import, *I Am Curious (Yellow),* and the Italian classic, *La Dolce Vita.* But when the delightful Mexican film *Like Water for Chocolate* was released in the U.S. in 1993, it became so hugely popular that its box-office revenues exceeded $20 million in early 1994, making it the **most** popular foreign-language film of all time.

According to *Variety,* the following foreign-language films have generated the **most** grosses of all time:

Film Title (Year Released)	Country	Director
1. *Like Water for Chocolate* (1993)	Mexico	Arau
2. *I Am Curious (Yellow)* (1969)	Sweden	Sjoman
3. *La Dolce Vita* (1960)	Italy	Fellini
4. *La Cage aux Folles* (1979)	France/Italy	Molinaro
5. *Z* (1969)	France	Costa-Gavras
6. *A Man and a Woman* (1966)	France	Lelouch
7. *Cinema Paradiso* (1990)	Italy/France	Tornatore
8. *Emmanuelle* (1975)	France	Jaeckin
9. *Das Boot* (1982)	Germany	Peterson
10. *Story of O* (1975)	France	Jaeckin

SOURCE: *Variety*

The Most Screenings

"LET'S do the time warp again!" Get out your high heels and tux—or your favorite monster costume—and don't forget the rice! For twenty years now, fans of the cult movie classic *The Rocky Horror Picture Show* have gathered at Friday and Saturday midnight screenings dressed in costume. And when the film rolls, the costumed audience begins imitating and playing along with the movie characters, right there in the theater aisles! The movie bombed when it was first released in 1975 but has since grossed over $150 million and has continued running for the **most** weeks of any film, making it the longest-running movie in motion picture history. In fact, some fans have actually seen the film between four and five hundred times. Several Internet web sites are devoted exclusively to the film, and at least two offer complete scripts (both with and without audience participation lines).

The film stars Barry Bostwick and Susan Sarandon as the nerdy Brad Majors and Janet Weis. After their car breaks down on a rainy night they seek shelter in the castle of Dr. Frank N. Furter, played by Tim Curry. And it just so happens that this is the night of the annual gathering of visitors from Dr. Frank's home planet, Transsexual. The movie, filled with music, dancing, and a truly weird cast of characters, is probably still playing on weekend nights at a theater near you—just look for the **most** outrageously dressed ticket buyers and listen for the **most** boisterous audience.

SOURCE: *Variety*

The Most Boardroom Tears

PICTURE this. Several studio executives gather around the boardroom table on a Monday morning to discuss weekend box-office returns. They've just released one of the following, and whether it was meant to be a tear-jerker or not, the **most** tears shed aren't over who triumphed, died, broke up, or got back together again in the movie.

United Artists' ill-fated *Heaven's Gate* (1980) is considered the **most** financially disastrous motion picture of all time. Its losses, estimated at $34.2 million, ultimately caused the demise of United Artists, which was eventually sold to MGM for a mere $340 million. However, comparing North American box-office earnings to production costs, the film that lost the **most** money in motion picture history, an incredible $48.1 million, is the 1988 Warner Brothers release *The Adventures of Baron Münchhausen*. The following list of the biggest movie flops of all time is proof positive that big-name stars don't always mean big returns at the box-office.

The ten **most** disastrous movies of all time, in terms of being flops, are:

Film Title (Year Released)	Estimated Losses (millions)
1. *The Adventures of Baron Münchhausen* (1988)	$48.1
2. *Ishtar* (1987)	47.3
3. *Hudson Hawk* (1991)	47.0
4. *Inchon* (1981)	44.1
5. *The Cotton Club* (1984)	38.1
6. *Santa Claus—The Movie* (1985)	37.0
7. *Heaven's Gate* (1980)	34.2

8.	*Billy Bathgate* (1991)	33.0
9.	*Pirates* (1986)	30.3
10.	*Rambo III* (1988)	30.0

SOURCE: *Variety*

Budget Busters

WITH final production costs estimated at $175 million, Kevin Costner's *Waterworld* is the **most** expensive motion picture ever made. Filming was often delayed aboard the massive floating sets off the coast of Hawaii due to unpredictable weather. That and the fact that no expense was spared in caring for the safety of the cast, crew, and the environment added up to make this one the behemoth of budget busters. Ultimately, Costner himself ended up financing part of the production. Incidentally, Universal Studios executives are stating that it turned a profit.

Adjusted for inflation, however, the 1963 Elizabeth Taylor–Richard Burton extravaganza *Cleopatra* is the **most** expensive film of all time. The film's actual cost of $44 million would now be well over $200 million. Taylor's costumes alone amounted to a hefty $194,800, the most ever spent on outfitting a performer in a single film.

Interestingly, four of the films on the list of all time budget busters starred action hero Arnold Schwarzenegger.

The top ten **most** expensive films of all time (not adjusted for inflation) are:

	Film Title (Year Released)	Estimated Cost (millions)
1.	*Waterworld* (1995)	$175.0
2.	*True Lies* (1994)	110.0
3.	*Inchon* (1981)	102.0
4.	*War and Peace* (1967)	100.0
5.	*Terminator 2: Judgment Day* (1991)	95.0
6.	*Total Recall* (1990)	85.0
7.	*The Last Action Hero* (1993)	82.5
8.	*Batman Returns* (1992)	80.0
9.	*Alien³* (1992)	75.0
10.	*Who Framed Roger Rabbit* (1988)	70.0
	Die Hard 2 (1990)	70.0
	Hook (1991)	70.0
	Wyatt Earp (1994)	70.0

As a note, keep in mind that a few of the films released in 1996 incurred production costs that should cause them to make the above list.

SOURCE: *Variety*

The Most Money for Those Rights

IN 1975, Columbia Pictures paid Charles Strouse $9.5 million for his highly successful Broadway musical *Annie.* That $9.5 million made *Annie* the **most** expensive film rights ever sold. Columbia went into production with high expectations for the movie, but, alas, it was a box-office bust. The fee for the rights alone represented 27 percent of the film's $35 million budget and was, according to one critic, just about all Columbia should have spent on the entire film.

SOURCES: *The Guinness Book of Records 1996,* Bantam, 1996, and *Variety*

Screenplay Mosts

SCREENWRITER Shane Black, who wrote the 1987 action blockbuster *Lethal Weapon,* earned a record-setting $1.75 million in April 1990 for *The Last Boy Scout.* Joe Eszterhas topped that amount just a few months later when Carolco paid him $3 million for the screenplay for the sexy thriller *Basic Instinct.* In July 1994, however, New Line Cinema agreed to pay Black $4 million for a script entitled *The Long Kiss Goodnight,* setting a new record for the **most** ever paid for a screenplay. Since then, Joe Eszterhas has been at work on a project for which he could equal Black's record.

SOURCE: *Variety*

The Novels Selling for the Most

JOHN Grisham's first novel, *A Time to Kill,* was rejected by twenty-five publishers before it was finally purchased by Bill Thompson, an editor at Wynwood Press who had earlier discovered a little-known writer named Stephen King. Only 5,000 copies of the book were printed, and Grisham himself bought 1,000 of them. What he couldn't sell at book signings in nearby small towns he gave away as Christmas gifts to family and friends.

Today, those first editions Grisham had such a hard time getting rid of are worth $3,900 apiece.

In August 1994, New Regency Productions paid Grisham $6 million for *A Time to Kill,* the **most** ever paid for the film rights to a novel. Although *A Time to Kill* was John Grisham's first novel, it wasn't the first novel he had sold to Hollywood.

Author Nicholas Evans had been making a living as a producer and screenwriter for ten years, but even he was surprised when a bidding war erupted for the rights to his first novel, *The Horse Whisperer,* which he hadn't even finished yet. Joining the fray were such luminaries as Robert Redford, Peter Guber at TriStar, and Jon Peters at Warner Brothers. The battle began with a bid from Paramount for $200,000 and quickly reached $3 million.

"These were people, you know, for ten years their eighteenth assistant would not have returned my calls," Evans said. "And I had to decide whether I would allow them to give me $3 million." When the dust settled, Evans decided to let Robert Redford and his production company, Wildwood Enterprises, buy the rights for $3 million, the **most** ever paid to a novice novelist for the rights to a first book.

SOURCE: *Variety*

The Actors Getting the Most

UNIVERSAL Studios recently announced a three-picture deal with Sylvester Stallone for $60 million. Both Jim Carrey and Tom Cruise also signed deals in 1995 that will earn them $20 million each for their upcoming films, making them among the **most** highly paid actors in Hollywood. And as if that wasn't enough, many actors also receive a percentage of their film's profits.

What makes these actors able to command such huge salaries? The answer is that their films are big international hits. Three of Stallone's recent films, *Cliffhanger, Demolition Man,* and *The Specialist* all earned roughly twice their North American revenues overseas. Jim Carrey's film, *The Mask,* earned $120 million in North America and $200 million overseas. With that kind of international drawing power, it's no wonder that studios are willing to meet these actors' salary demands. But how much is the **most** an actor has ever earned for performing in a single film? Well, including his share of the profits, Jack Nicholson reportedly earned over $50 million for playing the diabolical Joker in *Batman.* Sylvester Stallone's total earnings for both writing and acting in *Rocky V* were estimated to be the same, putting these two stars in a category beyond even those with the **most.**

SOURCE: *Variety*

The Actresses Getting the Most

SALARIES for leading actresses are still considerably lower than those for leading actors. But in March 1995, Demi Moore signed to star in Castle Rock's *Strip Tease* for $12.5 million, the **most** ever paid to an actress for a performance in a film. And filmmakers seem to think she's worth it. Her recent films, *Ghost, Indecent Proposal, A Few Good Men,* and *Disclosure,* have all been huge international blockbusters (though the same cannot be said about *The Scarlet Letter*). This recent deal is expected to raise the salaries for other leading actresses—including Sharon Stone, Julia Roberts, Meg Ryan, and Academy Award winner Jodie Foster—a bit closer to those of their male counterparts. In fact, Sandra Bullock, whose films include *Speed, The Net,* and *While You Were Sleeping,* recently signed for $12 million to star in New Line Cinema's *In Love and War* as the Red Cross nurse who inspired Ernest Hemingway to write *A Farewell to Arms.*

SOURCE: *Variety*

Young and Rich and Loving Life

MACAULAY Culkin was just ten years old in 1990 when he starred as Kevin McCallister in the wildly successful Christmas hit *Home Alone.* The following year, Columbia Pictures signed him for $1 million to appear in *My Girl.* In 1992, Twentieth Century–Fox paid the twelve-year-old Culkin $5 million plus a percentage of the profits to re-create the role of Kevin in *Home Alone II: Lost in New York,* the **most** ever paid to a child performer.

SOURCE: *Variety*

Many Mosts at the Oscars

THE Academy of Motion Picture Arts and Sciences (AMPAS) presented its first Academy Awards on May 16, 1929. "The Statuette," as it was then known, depicts a man holding a sword standing on a reel of film. In 1931, AMPAS librarian Margaret Herrick remarked, "He looks like my Uncle Oscar," and the name stuck.

The Academy's **most** honored film of all time is the 1959 Charlton Heston epic *Ben Hur.* The film received eleven Oscars, including Best Picture, Best Director, Best Actor, Best Supporting Actor, Cinematography, Art Direction, Sound, Musical Score, Film Editing, Special Effects, and Costume Design.

Including *Ben Hur,* the **most** awarded films of all time (with a minimum of nine "Bests") are:

	Film (year released)	Oscars
1.	*Ben Hur* (1959)	11
2.	*West Side Story* (1961)	10
3.	*Gigi* (1958)	9
	The Last Emperor (1987)	9

SOURCE: The Academy of Motion Pictures Arts and Sciences

The Most Nominations

THE motion picture to receive the **most** Oscar nominations is the 1950 release *All About Eve.* It won in six of the fourteen categories in which it was nominated.

SOURCE: The Academy of Motion Pictures Arts and Sciences

The Most Almosts

WHAT do *The Turning Point* (1977) and Steven Spielberg's *The Color Purple* (1985) have in common? Well, the good news is that they both received eleven Academy Award nominations. The bad news is that neither movie won a single Oscar.

SOURCE: The Academy of Motion Pictures Arts and Sciences

The Most Sweeps

THE top five Oscars are generally regarded as Best Picture, Best Director, Best Screenplay, Best Actress, and Best Actor awards. Yes, this is a little unfair to the cinematographers, composers, editors, costume designers, set dressers, and so on, but that's the way they see it in Hollywood and we don't want to start any fights here.

In 1934, *It Happened One Night* became the first film to sweep all top five Oscars. It was forty-one years before a second film, *One Flew over the Cuckoo's Nest,* could match that feat, and another sixteen before a third, *The Silence of the Lambs,* was so honored. These three films are the **most** such honored in Oscar history. Read on to see who was a part of this particular **most.**

Best Picture	Best Actor	Best Actress	Best Director	Best Screenplay
It Happened One Night (1934)	Clark Gable	Claudette Colber	Frank Capra	Robert Riskin
One Flew over the Cuckoo's Nest (1975)	Jack Nicholson	Louise Fletcher	Milos Forman	Lawrence Hauben & Bo Goldman
The Silence of the Lambs (1991)	Anthony Hopkins	Jodie Foster	Jonathan Demme	Ted Tally

SOURCE: The Academy of Motion Pictures Arts and Sciences

Mosts in the Wonderful World of Mosts

IN 1953, Walt Disney, the man, received Oscars in the categories of Documentary Feature, Documentary Short Subject, Cartoon Short Subject, and Two-Reel Short Subject. These four Academy Awards are the **most** ever won by one person in a single year. Overall, Disney personally received twenty-six Academy Awards, as well as a set of miniature Oscars for *Snow White and the Seven Dwarfs,* making him the Academy's **most** honored individual.

SOURCE: The Academy of Motion Pictures Arts and Sciences

Kate's Oscars

KATHARINE Hepburn is the Academy's **most**-honored motion picture performer of all time. Hepburn has won the **most** Best Actress Oscars, a total of four times, for her performances in *Morning Glory* (1933), *Guess Who's Coming to Dinner* (1967), *The Lion in Winter* (1967), and *On Golden Pond* (1981). She has also received the **most** Academy Award nominations ever, a grand total of thirteen. And Hepburn's award-winning career spans the **most** time of any performer, an incredible forty-eight years between her first and latest Oscar wins.

SOURCE: The Academy of Motion Pictures Arts and Sciences

The Actors in Oscar's League of Mosts

SIX actors share the honor of having received the **most** Oscars for their performances in film. Spencer Tracy, Fredric March, Gary Cooper, Marlon Brando, Dustin Hoffman, and Tom Hanks have each won two Academy Awards. Tracy and Hanks are the only two actors in motion picture history to win the Best Actor award for two consecutive years. Tracy was honored for his performances in *Captains Courageous* (1937) and *Boys Town* (1938), and Hanks received his awards for *Philadelphia* (1993) and *Forrest Gump* (1994). Neither Richard Burton nor Peter O'Toole have ever won an Oscar, but they share the distinction of having received the **most** non-winning Oscar nominations, with seven each.

SOURCE: The Academy of Motion Pictures Arts and Sciences

The Most Nominations Before the Big Win

GERALDINE Page received her first Oscar nomination in 1953 as Best Supporting Actress for her performance in the Paul Newman film, *Hud*. By the time Page won the Oscar as Best Actress some thirty-two years later, in 1985, for her moving portrayal of a woman returning to the home of her youth in *The Trip to Bountiful,* Page had received a total of 8 Oscar nominations (5 as Best Supporting Actress and 3 as Best Actress), the **most** ever received by a performer before winning an Oscar.

SOURCE: The Academy of Motion Pictures Arts and Sciences

Directing His Way to the Most

LEGENDARY motion picture director John Ford has received the **most** Best Director Oscars ever. His four Academy Awards were for *The Informer* (1935), *The Grapes of Wrath* (1940), *How Green Was My Valley* (1941), and *The Quiet Man* (1952).

SOURCE: The Academy of Motion Pictures Arts and Sciences

The Most Words

IN 1942, Greer Garson gave the **most** lengthy Academy Award acceptance speech of all time, lasting a full five and a half minutes, as she received the Best Actress Oscar for her performance in *Mrs. Miniver.*

SOURCE: The Academy of Motion Pictures Arts and Sciences

The Most Air Time

THE 1984 Awards ceremony holds the distinction of being the **most** lengthy—a tedious 3 hours and 40 minutes, with winners taking an average of 99 seconds to thank 7.8 people on average. No wonder the Academy began limiting Oscar acceptance speeches to 45 seconds in 1990! Since then, a red light flashes after 25 seconds, then loud music rises if the recipient is still thanking family or colleagues or taking a stab at world peace when his or her time is up.

SOURCE: The Academy of Motion Pictures Arts and Sciences

The Most Enduring Performers

Manorama

INDIAN comic actress Manorama began her film career in 1958. Having completed her 1,000th film in 1985, and working on as many as 30 films at one time, she has played the **most** leading roles of any performer in motion picture history.

SOURCE: *Guinness Book of Movie Facts and Feats,* 5th ed., Abbeville Press, 1993

The Duke

BEGINNING with *The Drop Kick* in 1927 and ending with *The Shootist* in 1976, Hollywood star John Wayne (1907–1979) had the leading role in 142 of his 153 movies, the **most** of any American performer. And in each of them, according to Wayne himself, he always played John Wayne, regardless of the character.

SOURCE: The Academy of Motion Picture Arts and Sciences

Tom London

AN actor by the name of Tom London (1883–1963) holds the record for performing in the **most** American motion pictures. Beginning with the *Great Train Robbery* in 1903 and ending with *The Lone Texan* in 1959, London appeared in over two thousand films.

SOURCE: The Academy of Motion Picture Arts and Sciences

The First Lady of the Movie Theater

WITH a career spanning 78 years, Helen Hayes (1900–1993) is the **most** enduring American actress of all time. Hayes made her film debut in 1910 in the film *Jean and the Calico Doll* and performed last in the 1988 religious docudrama *Divine Mercy, No Escape.*

SOURCE: The Academy of Motion Picture Arts and Sciences

Lillian Gish

HOWEVER, since much of Hayes's later work was produced for the small screen—television—Lillian Gish (1893–1993) actually holds the record as the **most** enduring actress on the big screen. Gish first starred in *An Unseen Enemy* in 1912 at age nineteen, and co-starred with Bette Davis seventy-five years later in her last film, *The Whales of August,* in 1987.

SOURCE: The Academy of Motion Picture Arts and Sciences

The Most Tests for the Best Scarlett

THE **most** extensive screen test in motion picture history was conducted in 1939 for the role of Scarlett O'Hara in *Gone with the Wind.* Producer David O. Selznick tested over sixty actresses before he finally narrowed his choices to four, including popular film stars Paulette Goddard, Joan Bennett, and Jean Arthur, and a relatively unknown actress named Vivien Leigh. Shooting was already under way on the film before Selznick tested and ultimately cast Vivien Leigh in the role that remains one of the **most** memorable of all time. Held in 1939, the screen tests cost $105,000, the entire budget for **most** of the feature films of the time.

SOURCE: Metro-Goldwyn-Mayer

Kiss Me, You Fool

SCREEN legend Lionel Barrymore is credited with giving the **most** kisses ever in a single film. His 127 embraces were shared with actresses Mary Astor and Estelle Taylor in the 1926 film *Don Juan.*

Cast of Thousands

ON January 31, 1981, in Delhi, India, Sir Richard Attenborough assembled a crowd of over 300,000 extras (94,560 paid extras and over 200,000 volunteers) to film the funeral scene for his epic motion picture *Gandhi.* This scene, which lasts 125 seconds, contains the **most** extras ever to appear in a motion picture. But will such "casts of thousands" be necessary much longer? In the Vietnam War protest scene in *Forrest Gump,* just 1,000 live extras actually appear in the foreground of the reflecting pool on the Washington Mall. The wizards at Industrial Light and Magic (a special-effects company started and run by filmmaker George Lucas) digitally reproduced the group of extras, changing certain elements such as the colors of their signs and placards, and then superimposed them on both sides of the pool and back toward the Washington Monument. In the movie, it appears as though over 100,000 antiwar protesters have gathered there that day. Not a bad idea considering the savings on the craft services (food) bill.

SOURCE: *The Guinness Book of Records 1996,* Bantam, 1996;
Industrial Light and Magic, San Mateo, CA

And Noah Thought His Ark Was Full?

THE **most** animals ever assembled for a motion picture were the 8,552 sheep, buffalo, donkeys, horses, monkeys, bulls, elephants, skunks, and

ostriches which appear in the 1956 film *Around the World in Eighty Days.*
But can you imagine what it must have been like on the set of Irwin
Allen's *The Swarm,* with 22 million bees, the **most** living creatures ever
to appear in a film, all playing the starring role?

The Most Character Effects

THE 1995 film *Casper* has the **most** minutes of 3-D character animation
ever to appear in a live-action motion picture. Eighty technicians at Industrial Light and Magic worked for 18 months preparing the 42 minutes
of animation for the film. This was a phenomenal effort, considering that
the earlier record holder, *Jurassic Park* (1993), contained just 6.5 minutes of animated dinosaurs, and the computer-generated effects for the
liquid-metal terminator in *Terminator 2: Judgment Day* (1991) took up
just 4 minutes on the screen.

SOURCES: Industrial Light and Magic, San Mateo, CA;
Lightstorm, Inc., Los Angeles, CA

Movie Music Mosts

OVER thirty-seven years, Max Steiner created music for more than 188
motion pictures, making him the **most** prolific film composer in motion
picture history. His work included the music for such Hollywood classics as *Gone with the Wind* (1939) and *King Kong* (1933). Steiner also
won Oscars for three of the films he scored: *The Informer* (1935), *Now,
Voyager* (1942), and *Since You Went Away* (1944).

SOURCES: James L. Limbacker, *Film Music: From Violins to Video,* Scarecrow Press, 1974;
The Academy of Motion Pictures Arts and Sciences

Composer John Williams has written the music for more than half of
the top ten highest-grossing films in motion picture history, easily earn-
ing him the title of **most** successful film composer of all time. Perhaps
best known for having written the themes for the *Star Wars, Indiana
Jones,* and the *Superman* film series, Williams has also won five Academy Awards for Best Original Film Score: *Fiddler on the Roof* (1971),
Jaws (1975), *Star Wars* (1977), *E.T. The Extra-Terrestrial* (1982), and
Schindler's List (1993). Among Williams's eighteen other Oscar nominations are those for *JFK* (1991), *Home Alone* (1990), *Born on the Fourth
of July* (1989), *The Witches of Eastwick* (1987), *The River* (1984), *The*

Towering Inferno (1974), *The Poseidon Adventure* (1972), and *The Reivers* (1969).

SOURCE: The Academy of Motion Pictures Arts and Sciences

The Most Soundtracks Sold

MOVIE soundtracks often become big recording hits as well. According to album sales figures, the following are the **most** popular movie soundtracks of all time.

	Film Soundtrack	Copies Sold
1.	*The Bodyguard*	16,000,000+
2.	*Purple Rain*	13,000,000
3.	*Dirty Dancing*	11,000,000
	Saturday Night Fever	11,000,000
5.	*The Lion King*	10,000,000
6.	*Footloose*	8,000,000
	Grease	8,000,000
7.	*Top Gun*	7,000,000

It's interesting to note that the story lines for five of these eight films are centered around music, focusing on either singing or dancing.

SOURCE: *Billboard* June 15, 1996 and January 11, 1997

The Most Singles Sold

BING Crosby's recording of Irving Berlin's "White Christmas" in 1942 is not only the **most** popular song ever sung in a movie, but is also the **most** popular single of all time. It has been sung in three different motion pictures and to date has sold over 171 million copies in North America alone.

SOURCE: *The Guinness Book of Records 1996,* Bantam, 1996

348 Versions to Date

WITH 348 motion pictures based on his works, William Shakespeare is the **most** filmed author of all time. Although the majority of these movie versions are relatively true to the original plays, there are also 41 contemporary adaptations, such as *West Side Story* (1961) and a 1970 British soft-porn film called *The Secret Sex Life of Romeo and Juliet.*

Hamlet is the **most** frequently adapted of Shakespeare's plays, with 74 movie versions. Among the more unusual of these is a 1977 Turkish film titled *Female Hamlet* and a rather bizarre 1968 Italian film in which Hamlet is portrayed as gunfighter in the American West. Next is *Romeo and Juliet,* which has been made into 51 motion pictures, and *Macbeth,* which has been adapted for the screen 33 times.

SOURCES: James Limbacker, *Haven't I Seen You Somewhere Before?,* Pierian Press, 1991; *Leonard Maltin's 1997 Movie & Video Guide,* Signet, 1996

The Most-Adapted American Author

BEST known for his terrifying short stories and poems, Edgar Allan Poe is the **most** filmed American author. His diabolical tales have been made into 111 feature films, including *The Murders at the Rue Morgue, The Pit and the Pendulum,* and *The Fall of the House of Usher.*

SOURCE: James Limbacker, *Haven't I Seen You Somewhere Before?,* Pierian Press, 1991

The Most-Beloved Characters

IT's no mystery that the **most** frequently portrayed character in motion picture history is Sir Arthur Conan Doyle's Sherlock Holmes. This character has appeared in 211 films and been played by 75 different actors between 1900 and 1993, including Basil Rathbone (who starred in 14 of the films), Peter Cushing, and Nicol Williamson. The films haven't always been adapted directly from Conan Doyle's stories, however, and liberties have certainly been taken in the portrayal of the character. Holmes has been depicted as everything from a heartsick school boy in Steven Spielberg's *Young Sherlock Holmes* (1985) to a recovering drug addict played by Nicol Williamson in *The Seven Percent Solution* (1976). Still, audiences continue to love that moment toward the end of the film when Holmes solves the mystery and explains to Watson the simplicity of the reasoning that led to his conclusion.

As the following list of other **most** frequently portrayed characters shows, many of them started out much like Holmes, presented first within the pages of a book.

	Character	Times Portrayed on Film
1.	Sherlock Holmes	211
2.	Count Dracula	160
3.	Frankenstein's Monster	115
4.	Tarzan	98
5.	Zorro	70
6.	Hopalong Cassidy	66
7.	The Durango Kid	64
8.	Robin Hood	58
9.	Charlie Chan	49

SOURCE: James Limbacker, *Haven't I Seen You Somewhere Before?*, Pierian Press, 1991

The Most-Filmed Stories

THE **most-**filmed story of all time is *Cinderella*. This rags-to-riches story has been the subject of 95 motion pictures to date, including Walt Disney's classic animated film and such comedy adaptations as Jerry Lewis's 1960 *Cinderfella*.

Following are the stories which have been remade the **most.**

	Story	Times Remade
1.	*Hamlet*	74
2.	*Carmen*	58
3.	*Dr. Jeckyl and Mr. Hyde*	52
4.	*Faust*	51
5.	*Romeo and Juliet*	51
6.	*Robinson Crusoe*	44
	The Three Musketeers	44
8.	*Don Quixote*	36

SOURCES: James Limbacker, *Haven't I Seen You Somewhere Before?*, Pierian Press, 1991; *Leonard Maltin's 1997 Movie & Video Guide*, Signet, 1996

The Most Often Used Names

YOU go to the movies and what names are you hearing the **most?** Read on.

Based on a study of feature films released between 1983 and 1993, and according to Simon Rose's *One FM Essential Film Guide,* the ten **most** common names of film characters are the following.

	Name	Movie Characters
1.	Jack	126
2.	John	104
3.	Frank	87
4.	Harry	72
5.	David	63
6.	George	62
7.	Michael	59
	Tom	59
9.	Mary	54
10.	Paul	53

Interestingly, only one woman's name appears on the list. Either screenwriters are more creative when choosing the names of their female characters or there are too few women's roles to count.

SOURCE: Simon Rose, *One FM Essential Film Guide,* 1994

Actors' On-Screen Jobs

You ever notice in the movies that everyone seems to be a police officer or a singer or dancer or a lawyer or an actress? Why is that? In the movies, you rarely see stars playing characters that are working at the kinds of jobs we (you know, us) typically go to each day. That's because most of us don't go to jobs in which life and death or the fate of society or fame and fortune routinely hang in the balance. Our jobs do not allow us to seem larger than life. Movies with larger-than-life characters are the movies that tend to be the **most** popular and make the **most** money, so they're the kind of characters that moviemakers depict the **most.**

In a study of 2,305 motion pictures between 1920 and 1990, *The Guinness Book of Movie Facts and Feats* reported that the **most** common professions of leading characters in film were the following.

Jobs Held by Men	Percent	Jobs Held by Women	Percent
Policeman/sheriff/agent	12.7	Singer/dancer	21.5
Physician/psychiatrist	5.7	Actress	10.0

Jobs Held by Men	Percent	Jobs Held by Women	Percent
Armed forces officer	5.0	Office worker	8.0
Lawyer	5.0	Nurse	4.6
Noncommissioned armed services personnel	3.9	Journalist	3.9
Journalist	3.6	Prostitute/madam	3.9
Businessman	3.6	Hotel/restaurant/bar worker	3.3
Sportsman	3.4	Student	3.3
Musician/songwriter	3.1	Secret agent	3.1
Farmer/rancher	3.1	Teacher	3.1

SOURCE: *The Guinness Book of Movie Facts and Feats*

The Most Ever

OVER 110,000 people gathered in Central Park on the afternoon of June 10, 1995, for the premiere of Walt Disney's *Pocahontas,* the **most** ever to view a film at the same time. Now that's some crowd! One hundred thousand ticket holders were admitted inside the great lawn area, while the others watched from the perimeter. Several children even came to the screening dressed as characters from the movie.

In preparation for the showing, it took 54 men a full week to stack railroad cars 10 high and 3 deep to accommodate the four special screens, each measuring 80 feet by 120 feet. With typical Disney flair, this special event featured roving performers, food vendors, and live stage performances prior to the screening.

SOURCE: *New York Times,* June 11, 1995

The Most Screens, Seats, and Theaters to Go To

DESPITE the popularity of video rentals, going to the movies remains a favorite American leisure-time activity. An estimated 59 percent of adults attend at least one movie each year. And increasingly, going to the movies means going to a local multiplex offering as many as 10, 15, or even more films at once. Currently, Deatron's Kineopolis in Brussels, Belgium, with 24 auditoriums, is tied with AMC's The Grand in Dallas, Texas, which also has 24 screens, for the **most** screens of any multiplex worldwide. The Grand is a prototype for the newer style of multiplex offering "stadium seating," where moviegoers enter the auditorium at the bottom of the steps and climb up to select their seat. These theaters also feature retractable armrests so you can snuggle with the person sitting next to you more easily.

So-called entertainment centers, with even more screens, are in the works. In 1996 AMC plans to open two multiplexes with 30 screens, one in Kansas City, Missouri, and one in Plano, Texas, just outside Dallas. Such are owned and operated by a fairly small number of theater chains. United Artists Theaters leads the list of top U.S. movie houses with the **most** screens, but the chain with the **most** theaters is Carmlike Cinemas, while Cinemark, with an average 7.46 screens per theater, Cinemark has the **most** per-theater screens of any chain.

Read on to see who owns the **most** theaters and screens in the U.S.

	Chain	Screens	Theaters	Average Number of Screens per Theater
1.	United Artists Theaters	2,295	423	5.43
2.	Carmlike Cinemas	2,037	467	4.36
3.	AMC Entertainment	1,632	233	7.00
4.	Cineplex Odeon	1,631	357	4.57
5.	Cinemark, USA	1,224	164	7.46
6.	General Cinema Theaters	1,202	202	5.95
7.	Sony Theatre Management	946	170	5.56
8.	National Amusements	870	98	8.88
9.	Regal Cinemas	861	116	7.42
10.	Act III Theatres	575	116	4.96

SOURCES: National Organization of Theater Owners

The Most Spacious Marquee Needed

TRY fitting the name of this movie on a theater marquee! The film title with the **most** words ever is the 1993 American film *Night of the Day of the Dawn of the Son of the Bride of the Return of the Revenge of the Terror of the Attack of the Evil, Mutant, Hellbound, Zombified, Flesh-eating, Sub-Humanoid Living Dead—Part 4.*

The Most-Comfortable Seats Needed

LET'S hope any theater that shows this film has comfortable seats! The **most** lengthy motion picture of all time is the 85-hour U.S. film *The Cure for Insomnia,* shown at the Art Institute of Chicago from January 31 to February 3, 1987. The movie consists mainly of L. D. Groban reading his 4,080-page poem by the same title, but is mixed with rock music and what the filmmaker described as some X-rated footage.

The **most** lengthy commercial U.S. production to be released in America is the 1963 film *Cleopatra,* lasting 4 hours and 3 minutes. Next is *The Greatest Story Ever Told* (1965) at 3 hours and 45 minutes, followed by *Gone with the Wind* (1939), and *Exodus* (1960), both exactly 3 hours and 40 minutes long. However, the original length of the British film *Lawrence of Arabia* (1962) was just 1 minute longer, at 3 hours and 41 minutes.

Where Do You Put the Most Fan Mail Ever?

IN 1928, Walt Disney himself provided the high-pitched voice of Mickey Mouse in his debut film, *Steamboat Willie.* Within a year, Mickey Mouse fan clubs across the U.S. had more than a million members. Disney estimates that in 1933, Mickey received 800,000 fan letters, over 66,000 each month, the **most** ever received by a "motion picture star" in a single year.

However, it was seven-year-old Shirley Temple who received the **most** fan mail of any human in motion picture history. By 1933, the curly-haired moppet was receiving 60,000 letters a month.

But it was cowboy singing legend Roy Rogers who received the **most** fan letters in any single month. In July 1945, Rogers received 74,852 pieces of fan mail, while his horse Trigger received 200.

The Most Ardent Movie Fan

BY the end of March 1993, newspaper photographer Gwilym Hughes of Dolgellau, Wales, claimed to have seen 21,157 movies, the **most** seen by a single individual not associated with the motion picture industry. Hughes saw his first film, *King Solomon's Mines* (1950), in 1953 at the hospital where he was being treated for a bone disease. He now watches 500 movies or so each year, **mostly** on videocassette.

SOURCE: *The Guinness Book of Records 1996,* Bantam, 1996

The Most Videos Sold

FAMILY films dominate the list of all-time best-selling videos in the U.S. In fact, the top four best-selling videocassettes of all time and seven of the top ten are animated features produced by Disney. *The Lion King* leads the pack, with sales of over 27.5 million, the **most** copies sold of any videocassette ever—enough to have dethroned *Snow White and the Seven Dwarfs* in just six days after its release in February 1995.

Read on to see what other videos are selling the **most** in North America.

Film (Year Originally Released)

1. *The Lion King* (1994)
2. *Aladdin* (1992)
3. *Beauty and the Beast* (1991)
4. *Snow White and the Seven Dwarfs* (1937)
5. *Forrest Gump* (1994)
6. *101 Dalmatians* (1961)
7. *Jurassic Park* (1993)
8. *The Little Mermaid* (1989)
9. *Pinocchio* (1940)
10. *E.T. The Extra-Terrestrial* (1982)

SOURCE: Alexander & Associates/Video Flash, New York, N.Y.

Mosts
from the World of
Television

WE'RE TALKING THE tube here. That thing we stare into for hours on end. Dancing elephants slipping on banana peels couldn't hold our attention so long. Maybe it's all the good programming, or just all those fascinating commercials, but whatever it is, we like our television.

The Most TVs

WORLDWIDE, China claims the **most** homes with televisions, at 227.5 million, followed by the U.S., at 94.2 million. By population, though, the U.S. has the **most** television sets, 790 per 1,000 people, compared to China's 31 sets per 1,000. Following are the top ten countries with a penchant for the tube.

	Country	Homes with Televisions
1.	China	227,500,000
2.	U.S.	94,200,000
3.	Russia	48,269,000
4.	Japan	41,328,000
5.	Brazil	38,880,000
6.	Germany	36,295,000
7.	India	35,000,000
8.	U.K.	22,446,000
9.	France	21,667,000
10.	Italy	20,812,000

SOURCE: UNESCO *Statistical Yearbook,* 41st edition, 1996

Who's in Front of the TV the Most?

IN 1996, Americans watched an average of 7 hours and 17 minutes of television each day, just ten minutes more than the daily average in 1985. But within that average, who actually watches television the **most**? A 1993 study by Nielsen Media Research shows the average weekly viewing hours for different categories of viewers based on age and sex.

	Category	Avg. TV Viewing per Week
1.	Women 55 and older	44 hrs 11 min
2.	Men 55 and older	38 hrs 28 min
3.	Women 25–54	30 hrs 35 min
4.	Men 25–54	28 hrs 04 min
5.	Women 18–24	25 hrs 42 min
6.	Children 2–5	24 hrs 32 min
7.	Men 18–24	22 hrs 31 min
8.	Teenage Boys	21 hrs 10 min
9.	Teenage Girls	20 hrs 50 min
10.	Children 6–11	19 hrs 59 min

SOURCE: Nielsen Media Research, 1993

The Most-Watched TV Episodes

THE final episode of *M*A*S*H,* a two-and-a-half-hour special entitled "Goodbye, Farewell, and Amen," was broadcast by CBS on February 28, 1983. An audience estimated at 125 million tuned in as the men and women of the 4077th prepared to leave Korea as the "police action" came to an end, making this the **most**-watched television episode of all-time. Hawkeye Pierce (Alan Alda) suffered a dramatic nervous breakdown, from which he would recover, but Major Charles Winchester (David Ogden Stiers) was traumatized by the senseless killing of a group of P.O.W. musicians whose playing had touched him. Cross-dressing Corporal Maxwell Klinger (Jamie Farr) met, fell in love with, and married a beautiful Korean woman named Soon-Lee. The other characters, including Major Margaret Houlihan (Loretta Swit), Father Mulcahy (William Christopher), Captain B. J. Hunnicut (Mike Farrell), and Colonel Sherman Potter (Harry Morgan), each departed Korea to re-enter civilian life.

Other **most**-watched TV episodes are the "Who Shot J.R.?" episode of *Dallas;* the one-hour special episode of *Friends* aired after the 1996 Superbowl; the final episode of *The Fugitive,* in which Dr. Richard Kimble finds the one-armed man who murdered his wife; the final episode of CBS's *Cheers,* in which Diane returns but decides not to marry Sam; and the night the Beatles made their American television debut on the *Ed Sullivan Show.*

In the following list, the "Overall Ranking" is where the programs fall in Nielsen's list of the fifty **most**-watched television shows of all time, which includes series, mini-series, theatrical movies, sporting events, and made-for-television movies.

	Series	Overall	Network	Date	Percent of Households Viewing	Number of Viewers
1.	*M*A*S*H* (finale)	1	CBS	02/28/83	60.2	50,150,000
2.	*Dallas*	2	CBS	11/21/80	53.3	41,470,000
3.	*Friends*	17	NBC	01/28/96	46.0	n/a
4.	*The Fugitive* (finale)	19	ABC	08/29/67	45.9	25,700,000
5.	*Cheers* (finale)	23	NBC	05/20/93	45.5	42,360,000
6.	*Ed Sullivan Show*	25	CBS	02/09/64	45.3	23,240,000
7.	*Beverly Hillbillies*	34	CBS	01/08/64	44.0	22,570,000
8.	*Ed Sullivan Show*	35	CBS	02/16/64	43.8	31,190,000
9.	*Beverly Hillbillies*	42	CBS	01/15/64	42.8	21,960,000
10.	*Beverly Hillbillies*	45	CBS	02/26/64	42.4	21,750,000

n/a = not available

SOURCE: Nielsen Media Research

The Most-Watched Movies on TV

THE two-part broadcast of Margaret Mitchell's *Gone With the Wind* was the **most** watched theatrical film broadcast in television history. The 1972 adaptation of Erich Segal's tearjerker *Love Story* starring Ali Mac-Graw and Ryan O'Neal, and the 1973 adaptation of Arthur Hailey's *Airport,* featuring Burt Lancaster and Dean Martin, tie as the second-highest-rated theatrical releases on television. However, taking into account the five network broadcasts of Frank Baum's *The Wizard of Oz* (1939), which earns consistently high ratings, this classic Judy Garland film would be the **most** popular theatrical release overall ever shown on television.

The chilling made-for-television movie *The Day After,* starring Jason Robards and JoBeth Williams, depicted the painful drama of a family trying to survive in a town slowly dying of radiation poisoning after a nuclear bomb strike. This was the **most**-watched television movie of all time. It is followed by ABC's broadcast of all four evenings of the television adaptation of Colleen McCullough's romantic epic *The Thorn Birds,* which starred Richard Chamberlain and Rachel Ward. Although seven of the eight broadcasts of the televised adaptation of Alex Haley's *Roots* rank among the top fifty, ABC described the miniseries as a "drama" rather than a "made-for-television movie," so it isn't included in the following list.

According to Nielsen, the following are the **most** watched movies on prime-time network television ever.

Film (Year Released)	Date Aired	Percent of Households Viewing	Number of Viewers
1. *Gone with the Wind,* part 1 (1939)	11/07/76	47.7	33,960,000
2. *Gone with the Wind,* part 2 (1939)	11/08/76	47.4	33,750,000
3. *The Day After** (1983)	11/20/83	46.0	38,550,000
4. *The Thorn Birds,* part 3* (1983)	03/29/83	43.2	35,990,000
5. *The Thorn Birds,* part 4* (1983)	03/30/83	43.1	35,900,000
6. *The Thorn Birds,* part 2* (1983)	03/28/83	42.5	35,400,000
7. *Airport* (1970)	11/11/73	42.3	28,000,000
Love Story (1970)	11/01/72	42.3	27,410,000
9. *The Thorn Birds,* part 1* (1983)	03/27/83	39.5	32,900,000
10. *The Godfather, Part II* (1974)	11/18/74	39.4	27,422,400

*Indicates a made-for-television movie

SOURCE: Nielsen Media Research

The Most-Watched Sporting Events

No wonder advertisers pay big bucks to run television ads during playoffs and championship games. Heavily promoted sporting events tend to attract huge television audiences. Of Nielsen's top ten programs, four of them are Superbowls. Although it ranked just sixteenth in Nielsen's overall listings based on the percentage of the viewing audience, Superbowl XXX, held in Tempe, Arizona, on Sunday, January 28, 1996, was the **most**-watched television event of all time in the U.S. An estimated 138,488,000 viewers watched at least part of the game, with an average audience of 94.1 million viewers tuning in to watch the Dallas Cowboys beat the Pittsburgh Steelers 27 to 17.

Following are Nielsen's **most**-watched sporting events on television in the U.S. (by percentage of households viewing).

	Event	Contestants	Date Aired	Percent of Households Viewing	Number of Viewers
1.	Superbowl XVI	49ers 26, Bengals 21	01/24/82	49.1	40,020,000
2.	Superbowl XVII	Redskins 27 Dolphins 17	01/30/83	48.6	40,480,000
3.	XVII Winter Olympics	Women's Figure Skating	02/23/94	48.5	45,690,000
4.	Superbowl XX	Bears 46, Patriots 10	01/26/86	48.3	41,490,000
5.	Superbowl XII	Cowboys 27, Broncos 10	01/15/78	47.2	34,410,000
6.	Superbowl XIII	Steelers 35, Cowboys 31	01/21/79	47.1	35,090,000
7.	Superbowl XVIII	Raiders 38, Redskins 9	01/22/84	46.4	38,800,000
	Superbowl XIX	49ers 38, Dolphins 16	01/20/85	46.4	39,390,000
9.	Superbowl XIV	Steelers 31, Rams 19	01/20/80	46.3	35,350,000
10.	Superbowl XXX	Cowboys 27, Steelers 17	01/28/96	46.1	n/a

n/a = not available

SOURCE: Nielsen Media Research

Joey and Amy Make for the Most

TRUE-LIFE stories (the sleazier the better) are the mainstay of made-for-television movies, but in early 1992 all three networks scrambled to produce movies about one particular story. On May 19, 1992, New York teenager Amy Fisher tried to kill the wife of her boyfriend, Joey Buttafuoco. A shot was fired at Mrs. Buttafuoco, though she survived the bullet wound to her skull. The media dubbed Fisher "The Long Island Lolita," and before long the three major networks were scrambling to produce made-for-television movies about her. NBC aired *Amy Fisher: My Story* on December 28, 1992, while ABC's *The Amy Fisher Story* and CBS's *Casualties of Love* both aired on January 3, 1993. These three movies are the **most** ever broadcast by the networks on the same subject during one week, and this is the only time in television history that two different TV movies on the same subject aired on competing networks at the same time. Of the three movies, ABC's earned the highest ratings (19.5), followed closely by NBC's (19.1), with CBS's coming in a distant third (14.3).

SOURCE: Nielsen Media Research

PBS and Those Fascinating Animals

WITH questions about funding for public broadcasting at the forefront of congressional debate, along with accusations that PBS tends to favor politically liberal programming, it's interesting to note that eight of the top ten **most** popular PBS programs of all time are National Geographic specials, which focus mainly on wild animals.

The **most** popular PBS programs ever, as of May 1994, are:

	Program (Year Released)	Viewers
1.	*NGS: The Sharks* (1982)	24,100,000
2.	*NGS: Land of the Tiger* (1985)	22,400,000
3.	*NGS: The Grizzlies* (1987)	22,300,000
4.	*Great Moments with National Geographic*	21,000,000
5.	*Best of Wild America: The Babies*	19,300,000
6.	*NGS: The Incredible Machine* (1975)	19,000,000
7.	*The Music Man*	18,700,000
8.	*NGS: Polar Bear Alert* (1982)	18,400,000
9.	*NGS: Lions of the African Night* (1987)	18,100,000
10.	*NGS: Rain Forest* (1983)	18,000,000

"NGS" stands for National Geographic Special.

SOURCE: Nielsen Media Research

The Most Game Shows Equals the Most Shows

GAME-SHOW producer Mark Goodson (1915–92) is the **most** prolific producer in television history. His highly popular game shows included *Beat the Clock* (1950–58), *What's My Line* (1950–67), *I've Got a Secret*

(1952–76), *To Tell the Truth* (1956–67), and *The Price Is Right,* which aired on prime-time from 1957 to 1986 and is still seen during the day on CBS. Goodson produced over 39,000 broadcasts totaling more than 21,240 hours. A Goodson-produced show has been aired at least once each week since February 1950.

SOURCE: Nielsen Media Research

Prime Time's Most Prolific Producer

SINCE writing his first script for Dick Powell's *Zane Grey Theater* in 1956, Aaron Spelling has provided a record 3,000 hours of television entertainment, making him prime time's **most** prolific producer. For a person viewing eight hours a day, five days a week, it would take over a year and a half to screen all of Spelling's series, miniseries, television movies, and theatrical films.

A brief list of just some of Spelling's **most** popular series shows his tremendous impact not only on television history but on popular American culture as well. His police-detective series have included *The Mod Squad* (1968–72), *Starsky and Hutch* (1975–79), *Charlie's Angels* (1976–81), *S.W.A.T.* (1975–76), *Vegas* (1978–84), *Hart to Hart* (1978–84), and *T. J. Hooker* (1982–85). Among his romantic-adventure series are *The Love Boat* (1977–87), *Fantasy Island* (1978–84) and *Hotel* (1983–88). His legendary prime-time soap operas include the Emmy Award–winning series *Family* (1976–80), *Dynasty* (1981–89), *The Colbys* (1985–87), *Beverly Hills 90210* (1990–), and *Melrose Place* (1992–). Spelling's television movies have often dealt with important issues. *Day One* (1989) recounted the building of the first atomic bomb and the decision to drop it on Hiroshima. *Best Little Girl in the World* (1981) was a revealing look at the eating disorder anorexia nervosa. His highly acclaimed television film *And the Band Played On* (1993) dramatized the early days of AIDS research, drawing one of the largest audiences in television history for a single special program and receiving the 1993–94 Emmy for Best Television Movie.

SOURCE: Nielsen Media Research

Meet the Most-Seasoned Program

FOR over forty-seven years, the panelists on NBC's *Meet the Press* have conducted interviews with world leaders and U.S. politicians, eliciting spontaneous and sometimes surprising reactions to tough questions. The program first aired on November 6, 1947, and has been broadcast each week since September 12, 1948. As of September 10, 1995, a total of 2,431 shows had been aired over forty-seven years, the **most** seasons of any program in television history.

SOURCE: Nielsen Media Research

Blame This Most on Jack, Johnny, and Jay

BEFORE television came along, Americans typically listened to the radio, and it was by habit that we went to sleep before midnight. Then along came television and immediately our habits changed. In fact, the popularity of *The Tonight Show* just might be one reason for our sudden reluctance to nod off by midnight.

Broadcast now for over thirty-eight years on NBC, *The Tonight Show* has been on the air the **most** seasons of any nightly show in television history. The program first aired with host Jack Parr from 1957 to 1962. Then, Johnny Carson kept audiences awake for the next thirty years, right to 1992. Today Jay Leno continues entertaining late-night audiences with a blend of gentle but insightful humor and lively celebrity interviews.

SOURCE: Nielsen Media Research

Walt Giving the Most

EACH week for over thirty-four years ABC's broadcast of *Walt Disney's Wonderful World of Color* presented children and parents with the best in animated characters, including Jiminy Cricket, Donald Duck, and Goofy, and stories about such historical American figures as Davy Crockett (played by Fess Parker) and the "Swamp Fox" (Francis Marion, played by Leslie Nielsen). The show was the first venture by any major motion picture studio into television production, and Disney changed the face of entertainment by proving that such a venture could be successful. Previously, studios refused to provide programming for television and would even deny the television industry access to their best films or current releases. For many years, until his sudden death in 1966, Walt Disney himself introduced the telecasts, and soon the show turned the master showman into a national celebrity. When it left the prime-time lineup in

1988, *Walt Disney's Wonderful World of Color* had aired for the **most** seasons of any prime-time network series.

SOURCE: Nielsen Media Research

The Most Broadcasts, Bozo!

"HOWDY, this is your old pal Bozo. Just keep laughing!" The television program with the **most** broadcasts of all time is the children's show *Bozo the Clown*. Airing daily on 150 stations in the U.S. and abroad, the show has broadcast over 150,000 episodes since it was first created some fifty years ago. As a character, Bozo was actually developed for a series of children's story albums by Capitol Records. The character was first played by Pinto Colvig, who also did the voice of Goofy for Walt Disney. But when Capitol needed someone to play the character at live appearances, they held auditions and selected Larry Harmon to be the clown. Soon, Harmon began appearing as Bozo on Los Angeles television station KTLA. Recognizing the commercial possibilities of the character, Harmon purchased the rights to Bozo from Capitol. Before long, he began franchising Bozos for other cities. In fact, the first franchised Bozo was NBC *Today Show* weatherman Willard Scott, who played the character in Washington, D.C. Since then Harmon has trained 203 others to play Bozo, cloning himself in every American television market. Today, the character airs nationally on Chicago Superstation WGN-TV as well as a few local stations. Parents still wait years for tickets, signing their children up to meet Bozo even before they are born. At age seventy, Harmon remains actively involved with marketing the character. He was even behind the "No Bozos" fad a few years ago, in which the international "No" symbol (a circle with a diagonal line) was placed over the image of the famous clown. In 1996, for the first time in ten years, Harmon donned the bright red wig and size 83AAA shoes once more for the January 1 Tournament of Roses Parade, riding atop a float entitled "Clowning Around."

SOURCES: Nielsen Media Research;
Harmon Marketing

The Most-Watched Babes

Now aired in over 110 countries, *Baywatch* is the **most**-watched weekly program in television history. *Baywatch* is the first American series ever to air in mainland China, and estimates are that it now reaches a weekly audience of over 2.3 billion. Starring David Hasselhoff as Lieutenant Mitch Buchannon, the series captures the relationships and adventures of a team of Los Angeles County lifeguards who patrol the mile-long stretch of beach at Malibu, California. *Baywatch,* with its unique blend of gorgeous characters, pop music, dramatic rescues, and romance, has become the number one U.S. imported television program in at least seven countries.

SOURCES: Nielsen Media Research

Jim Henson's *The Muppet Show,* with its whimsical combination of puppets and human guests, comes in second to *Baywatch*'s **most** viewers. The show now reaches an estimated weekly audience of 235 million in 106 countries. Well-loved characters like Kermit and Miss Piggy, popular guests like Elton John, Tony Bennett, and George Burns, as well as running features like "Pigs in Space," have made the show a favorite with adults as well as children.

Downs's 10,000-Plus Is a Most

DURING a distinguished television career spanning forty-eight years, Hugh Downs, co-host of ABC's newsmagazine *20/20,* has appeared for the **most** hours on network commercial television. As of May 19, 1994, Downs had been on camera 10,347 hours. Although he had already been a radio broadcaster for several years, Downs began his work in television in July 1957 by helping launch NBC's *Tonight Show* with Jack Parr, where he stayed for five years, followed by nine years as host of NBC's *Today* (1962–71). Since 1978, Downs has been the host, and now co-host with Barbara Walters, of *20/20.* Downs has often been honored for his coverage of environmental issues, medical breakthroughs, challenges related to aging, and developments in the treatment of mental illness. But there is also a daring side to this veteran communicator. Exciting adventure stories have become his trademark on *20/20.* He once risked his life by diving in a cage off the Australian coast to film the great white shark. Downs is also the author of several books, including an autobiography called *On Camera: My 10,000 Hours on Television,* and an account of sailing a sixty-five-foot ketch across the Pacific entitled *A Shoal of Stars.*

SOURCE: Nielsen Media Research

60 *Minutes* of Mosts

WITH its distinctive ticking stopwatch, ground-breaking investigative style, and provocative stories, the weekly CBS news magazine *60 Minutes* is considered the **most** popular television program of all time. First broadcast on September 24, 1968, *60 Minutes* holds a record eighteen straight seasons in Nielsen's top ten, and it was actually the highest-rated prime-time program for the years 1979, 1982, 1991, and 1992. During twenty-seven years on the air, *60 Minutes* has received fifty Emmys in such categories as news analysis, investigative reporting, interviewing, and news or documentary programming. The show's strong appeal can be credited in part to the tremendous human drama of many of its stories, to the remarkable diversity of stories each week, and to the show's correspondents, who manage to keep their audiences both entertained and informed year after year.

SOURCE: Nielsen Media Research

All in the Family Mosts

NORMAN Lear's *All in the Family* was the top-rated show for five straight seasons from 1971 through 1976, capturing the largest audience for the **most** consecutive years of any prime-time series. *All in the Family* is also the television series spin-off champ, with the **most** spin-offs ever generated by one show. The program, broadcast on CBS from 1971 to 1983, changed television comedy forever by bringing into the homes of middle America the stark reality of racial, religious, and ethnic bigotry. Archie Bunker, played to outrageous perfection by Carroll O'Connor, was blatantly prejudiced. His outspoken opinions were not so much made fun of as contrasted by those of the other characters, including Archie's wife, Edith (Jean Stapleton), their daughter, Gloria (Sally Struthers), and son-in-law Michael Stivic (Rob Reiner), as well as the other regulars on the series. The Bunkers lived next door to a black family named the Jeffersons, whose patriarch, George Jefferson (Sherman Hemsley) was as bigoted and outspoken as Archie. Eventually George's dry-cleaning business became successful, and he and his wife, Louise (Isabel Sanford), and their son, Lionel (played by both Mike Evans and Damon Evans), moved to Manhattan and onto their own show, *The Jeffersons* (1975–85). Edith's cousin, the ultra-liberal Maude Findlay (Beatrice Arthur), was soon given her own series, *Maude* (1972–78). When Gloria and Michael's move to California saw the end of their marriage, Gloria headed to upstate New York and began a new life as a veterinarian's assistant in the series *Glo-*

ria (1982–83). Maude's housekeeper, Florida Evans (Esther Rolle), and her family were featured in *Good Times*. Then the Jefferson's maid, Florence Johnston (Marla Gibbs), became the executive housekeeper of a large Manhattan hotel, and a short-lived series entitled *Checking In* was based on her relationships with the hotel's staff and manager. Directly and indirectly, *All in the Family* was the basis for five new series, the **most** spin-offs in television history.

SOURCES: Nielsen Media Research

Saturday Night Live Mosts

"LIVE from New York, it's . . ." Since its debut in 1975 with guest host George Carlin, NBC's *Saturday Night Live* has provided its audience with outrageous moments, great characters, and a totally unique perspective on culture and politics. And that "wild and crazy guy" Steve Martin has been *SNL*'s **most** frequent guest host, delivering the show's opening monologue a grand total of thirteen times.

The cast member with the **most** years on *Saturday Night Live* is Kevin Nealon, whose nine-year stint began with the 1986–87 season and ended in 1994–95.

Singer-songwriter Paul Simon has been *SNL*'s **most** frequent musical guest. Beginning with his appearance on the show's second broadcast, October 18, 1975 (during which he sang with former partner Art Garfunkel), Simon has been the musical guest 9 times and guest host 4. Other frequent *SNL* guest hosts have been Buck Henry (10 times); Chevy Chase (7 times), John Goodman, Tom Hanks, and Elliott Gould (6 times each); and Candice Bergen, Alec Baldwin, and Danny DeVito (5 times each).

SOURCE: *Saturday Night Live,* NBC

The Clapper with the Most

As the hostess of *Wheel of Fortune,* Vanna White flashes her bright smile throughout each show as contestants call out a letter or solve one of the game show's word puzzles. According to *The Guinness Book of Records,* Vanna also claps some 720 times per show, or 28,080 times each year, which earns her the title of television's **most** frequent clapper.

SOURCE: *The Guinness Book of Records*

The Most Charitable Pledges

FOR over thirty years, the *Jerry Lewis Labor Day Telethon* has been raising funds for the Muscular Dystrophy Association. Lewis hosts the $21^{1}/_{2}$-hour broadcast each year with the help of local stations, which try to coordinate their own participation with the national event. Between corporate and individual contributions, the 1989 *Jerry Lewis Labor Day Telethon* holds the distinction of being the **most** successful telethon ever, receiving $78,438,573 in pledges.

SOURCE: The Muscular Dystrophy Association

The Rights That Cost the Most

ON August 7, 1995, NBC announced that it would pay a total of $1.27 billion for the exclusive U.S. broadcast rights of the 2000 Summer Olympic Games in Sydney, Australia, and the 2002 Winter Games in Salt Lake City, Utah. Then, on December 13, 1995 the network announced a second agreement with the International Olympic Committee in which it would pay an additional $2.3 billion to broadcast the Summer Games in 2004 and 2008 and the Winter Games in 2006, the first time ever that a network has bought the rights to the Games without knowing the host city in advance (the IOC doesn't select the site until seven years before the games). NBC agreed to offer viewers free coverage of significant events, telecasting the games over its broadcast network and its two cable networks, CNBC and America's Talking. This total $3.57 billion investment represents the **most** ever paid by a network for television rights to an event or events. It also means guaranteed support for the U.S. Olympic Committee through 2008, which receives 10 percent of the U.S. television fees.

Here's what NBC will pay for the broadcast rights for each of the Olympics between 2000 and 2008.

	Olympic Games	Year	Host City	Amount (millions)
1.	Summer Olympics	2000	Sydney, Australia	$705
2.	Winter Olympics	2002	Salt Lake City, Utah	545
3.	Summer Olympics	2004	(site to be selected)	793
4.	Winter Olympics	2006	(site to be selected)	613
5.	Summer Olympics	2008	(site to be selected)	894

SOURCES: U.S. Olympic Committee and International Olympic Committee

Paying the Most to Push Their Products

IF $3.57 billion seems like a lot of money for broadcast rights, just imagine what advertisers will have to pay to promote their products during the Olympics. ABC reportedly charged a whopping $2.2 million per minute of advertising during the broadcast of Superbowl XXIX on January 29, 1995, watched by over 120 million American consumers. This was the **most** expensive advertising rate of all time.

SOURCE: Cap Cities/American Broadcasting Corporation

Scarlett Gets the Most

IN November 1991, CBS and a group of U.S. and European investors hoped to take advantage of the popularity of *Gone with the Wind* by producing a television movie of Alexandra Ripley's sequel, *Scarlett.* The rights cost the investors $8 million, making these the **most** expensive television story rights ever. The telefilm, broadcast in November 1994, starred Joanne Walley-Kilmer as Scarlett O'Hara Butler and Timothy Dalton as Rhett Butler, and followed Scarlett to Ireland as she began to rebuild her life.

SOURCE: *The Guinness Book of Records 1996,* Bantam, 1996

The Most Miniseries $

THE 1997 NBC miniseries *The Odyssey* is the **most** expensive television production of all time. The thirty-hour miniseries *War and Remembrance* was the second **most** expensive television production of all time. The final cost for *The Odyssey* exceeds the $110 million spent by ABC when, after three years of filming, ABC aired the fourteen-part World War II epic in November 1988 and March 1989. *War and Remembrance* was a sequel to the more-successful *The Winds of War,* both based on novels by Herman Wouk. The cast included dozens of well-known stars, with Robert Mitchum reprising his role as Admiral Victor "Pug" Henry, now named ambassador to Germany, and Polly Bergen starring as his wife. Sir John Gielgud, Peter Graves, Jane Seymour, David Dukes, and Victoria Tenant also had featured roles. The production won the Emmy for best miniseries that year but lost an estimated $20 million, marking what appears to be an end to such extravagant miniseries.

SOURCE: National Broadcasting Co., Capital Cities Inc./American Broadcasting Co.

Immys, Emmys, and the Most Wins

THE National Academy of Television Arts and Sciences (NATAS) awarded its first Emmy on January 25, 1949. Academy president Harry Lubcke named the award after the image orthicon tube, known as an "immy," which allowed cameras to transmit images without the intense light previously required. During 1976 and 1977, the Hollywood chapter split from the national organization, and the Emmys were divided into two categories. The Academy of Television Arts and Sciences (ATAS) in Los Angeles became responsible for awarding the prime-time Emmys, and the National Academy in New York took on awarding the daytime Emmys.

Producer-director Dwight Hemion is the **most**-honored individual in Emmy history. Among his 17 awards are those for musical specials, including *Frank Sinatra: A Man and His Music* and *Barbra Streisand . . . and Other Musical Instruments.* Hemion is also Emmy's **most**-nominated individual, with 42 nominations.

SOURCES: The National Academy of Television Arts and Sciences;
The Academy of Television Arts and Sciences

The Most-Watched and Most-Honored Miniseries

THE eight-part, twelve-hour adaptation of Alex Haley's *Roots,* which dramatized the story of Haley's African ancestry, won nine Emmys in 1977, making it the **most**-honored television miniseries of all time. It was also the **most**-watched dramatic special in television history, with nearly half of the U.S. population assembled in front of their TV sets to watch. The concluding episode was watched by 51.1 percent of the viewing audience, an estimated 100 million people, and is the third-highest-rated show of all time. Not even ABC was prepared for its unprecedented success. In fact, one reason the network scheduled the miniseries over eight consecutive nights was that if it flopped it would be over quickly.

The story of *Roots* began with the birth of Kunta Kinte (LeVar Burton and John Amos) in Gambia, West Africa, through his capture by white slave traders and transport to America aboard a slave vessel. The episodes continued with the lives of successive generations of his family, ending with Kunte Kinte's great-grandson, Tom (George Stanford Brown), finding freedom after the Civil War. Overall, the themes and characters in the miniseries had a profound effect on the way viewers felt about their own ancestry as well as that period of American history.

SOURCES: Nielsen Media Research;
The Academy of Television Arts and Sciences

The Series with the Most Emmy Nominations and Wins

WITH 29 prime-time Emmys, the **most**-honored series in television history is *The Mary Tyler Moore Show,* which aired on CBS from 1970 to 1977. Both critics and viewers loved Mary Richards, the quintessential independent woman of the 1970s. Mary worked as an assistant producer at Minneapolis television station WJM-TV, along with her boss, the irascible but lovable Lou Grant (Ed Asner); bumbling news anchor Ted Baxter (Ted Knight); and head newswriter, Murray Slaughter (Gavin MacLeod). Mary lived in an older apartment building where she became friends with neighbors Rhoda Morgenstern (Valerie Harper) and Phyllis Lindstrom (Cloris Leachman). Over the years, there were changes in Mary's career and relationships, but what never changed was the openness and vulnerability that made her such a favorite with audiences.

NBC's comedy hit *Cheers* (1982–93) is second to Mary's **most**, with 27 Emmys. *Cheers,* which starred Ted Danson, Shelley Long, Rhea Perlman, Kelsey Grammer, Woody Harrelson, George Wendt, Kirstie Alley, Nicholas Colasanto, and John Ratzenberger as the regulars at a Boston bar called Cheers, is also the **most**-nominated series of all time, having received 117 Emmy nominations.

In 1994, Stephen Bochco's *NYPD Blue* (ABC, 1993–   ) received an unprecedented 26 Emmy nominations, the **most** of any series in a single year. In 1981, *Hill Street Blues* (NBC 1981–87), another of Bochco's riveting police dramas, received 8 Emmys, setting a record for the **most** Emmy wins in a single year. That record stood for fourteen years, until 1995 when Michael Crichton's gritty hospital drama *ER* (NBC, 1994–   ) also won 8 Emmys.

SOURCES: The National Academy of Television Arts and Sciences;
The Academy of Television Arts and Sciences

The Most Emmys Won by a Performer

DURING her career as a musical-variety hostess on several shows, Dinah Shore received the **most** Emmys ever awarded to an individual for performing on television. Her trademark kiss blown to the audience at the end of each show, her friendly style, and her warm voice earned her eight Emmys.

SOURCE: The National Academy of Television Arts and Sciences

Mosts for Mary, Murphy, Lou, and Hawkeye

WITH seven Emmys each, Mary Tyler Moore and one-time co-star Ed Asner share the record for having won the **most** Emmys for acting. They both won for their performances in *The Mary Tyler Moore Show,* and Asner later won for playing the same role in the series *Lou Grant* (CBS, 1977–82). Moore also received Emmys as Series Actress of the year in 1974 and as Outstanding Supporting Actress for her role in the television movie *Stolen Babies* in 1993. Asner's Emmys include those for his performances in the miniseries *Rich Man, Poor Man* (CBS, 1976) and *Roots* (ABC, 1977).

Mary Tyler Moore is also tied with Candice Bergen for winning the **most** Emmys as Best Actress in a series. Moore won twice for *The Dick Van Dyke Show* (CBS, 1961–66) and three times for *The Mary Tyler Moore Show.* Bergen's five wins have all been for CBS's *Murphy Brown* (1988–   ).

Best known for his eleven years as Captain Benjamin Franklin "Hawkeye" Pierce on CBS's *M*A*S*H,* Alan Alda has received a total of five Emmys for his full range of acting, writing, and directing, the **most** won by any performer in these diverse categories.

SOURCES: The National Academy of Television Arts and Sciences;
The Academy of Television Arts and Sciences

The Most Daytime Emmys

IN 1971, the Television Academy began honoring the best in daytime dramas with their own awards. The Daytime Emmy awards ceremony moved to prime time in 1991 and placed an amazing second in the ratings for the week it was broadcast. The **most**-honored soap opera in daytime Emmy history is the revolutionary drama *The Young and the Restless,* which has earned a total of 49 daytime Emmys. Since 1974, the show has also received five Emmys as Outstanding Daytime Drama Series, the **most** awarded to any soap opera. *The Guiding Light* has the second-highest number of Emmys, with 38, followed by *All My Children,* with 37, *Santa Barbara,* with 23, and *One Life to Live,* with 22.

SOURCE: The National Academy of Television Arts and Sciences

The Most Daytime Emmys to a Soap Actress

FOR over 24 years, Erika Slezak has played both the illustrious Victoria Lord (Buchanan) and her evil split personality Nicki Smith on ABC's *One Life to Live*. During those 24 years she has become the **most**-honored actress in daytime television, winning four Emmys for Outstanding Actress in a Daytime Drama. Kim Zimmer (Reva Lewis in *The Guiding Light*) is next, with three Outstanding Daytime Actress Emmys. Helen Gallagher (Maeve Ryan in *Ryan's Hope*) and Judith Light (Karen Wolek in *One Life to Live*) have won two Emmys each.

SOURCE: The National Academy of Television Arts and Sciences

The Daytime Actress with the Most Almosts

SHE is certainly a favorite among soap opera fans, but actress Susan Lucci just can't seem to win an Emmy for her performance as the archetypal femme fatale Erica Kane in ABC's *All My Children*. Her incredible 17 daytime Emmy nominations in twenty-three years of performing the role are the **most** ever for which an actress has been nominated but not won.

And if Susan's case isn't frustrating enough, she has company. Angela Lansbury, who plays mystery novelist Jessica Fletcher on *Murder She Wrote,* ties that record in prime time. She has also not received any of the 15 awards for which she has been nominated, which include 11 for her work in *Murder She Wrote,* one for *Sweeney Todd,* one for *Little Gloria, Happy at Last,* and two for hosting the Tony Awards ceremony.

SOURCES: The National Academy of Television Arts and Sciences;
The Academy of Television Arts and Sciences

The Most Daytime Emmys to a Soap Actor

THE **most**-honored actor in daytime drama also plays two completely contrasting roles. David Canary joined the cast of ABC's *All My Children* in 1983 and has received four Emmys as Outstanding Actor in a Daytime Drama playing twin brothers Adam and Stuart Chandler. While Adam is wealthy and ruthless, his brother Stuart is kind-hearted and naive. Adam's marriage to Erica Kane was fiery and tumultuous, but Stuart's marriage to Cindy, who was dying of AIDS, was one of the more touching periods in soap opera history.

Macdonald Carey (Dr. Thomas Horton in *Days of Our Lives*), Larry Bryggman (John Dixon in *As the World Turns*), Douglas Watson (Mackenzie Cory in *Another World*), and Peter Bergman (Jack Abbott in *The Young and the Restless*) have each won two Outstanding Actor Emmys.

SOURCES: The National Academy of Television Arts and Sciences

The Best Writing Gets Most Emmys

DURING its fourteen years on the air, ABC's *Ryan's Hope* won six Emmys for Outstanding Writing in a daytime drama, the **most** of any soap opera. Its involving story lines and compelling performances also earned the show two Emmys as Outstanding Daytime Drama.

SOURCES: The National Academy of Television Arts and Sciences

Oprah and Phil Share the Most

OPRAH has won seven Emmys as Outstanding Daytime Talk Show, the **most** of any daytime talk show. However, Phil Donahue outdoes Oprah Winfrey with the **most** Emmys as Outstanding Daytime Talk Show Host. He's won nine compared to Oprah's five.

SOURCE: The National Academy of Television Arts and Sciences

The Thrill of the Most Victories

FOR thirty-five years, *ABC's Wide World of Sports* has brought viewers the "thrill of victory and the agony of defeat" in its live coverage of a variety of sports the world over. During its broadcast history, the program has been awarded seventeen Emmys as Outstanding Sports Series, the **most** in daytime Emmy history.

SOURCES: The National Academy of Television Arts and Sciences;
The Academy of Television Arts and Sciences

Emmys for Sportscasters

THE first Emmys for Sportscaster were awarded in 1968. Since then, John Madden has received the **most** Emmys for Sportscasting, all for Outstanding Sports Analyst. Jim McKay is second, with 9 Emmys for Sportscasting, 8 as Outstanding Host/Commentator and 1 as Outstanding Host/-Play-by-Play. Bob Costas is third with 6 Emmys, 4 for Outstanding Play-by-Play and 2 as Outstanding Studio Host. Dick Enberg is fourth with 4 Emmys for Outstanding Host/Play-by-Play. However, Jim McKay has also won 2 Emmys for Sports Writing and 1 for News Commentary for an overall total of 12 Emmys. He was also awarded a special Life Achievement Emmy Award in 1989.

SOURCES: The National Academy of Television Arts and Sciences;
The Academy of Television Arts and Sciences

The Most Daytime Emmys for a Children's Show

FIRST broadcast in 1970, Public Television's *Sesame Street* has won seventeen Emmys as Outstanding Children's Series, the **most** of any children's show.

SOURCES: The National Academy of Television Arts and Sciences;
The Academy of Television Arts and Sciences

Putting the Most Suds into Soaps

IN 1930, former schoolteacher Irna Phillips persuaded radio station WGN in Chicago to air a fifteen-minute drama she had created called *Painted Dreams.* When WGN refused an offer to carry the show nationally, Phillips quit and went to work for NBC. WGN wouldn't part with the rights to *Painted Dreams,* so Phillips re-created the basic story line and characters in a new drama called *Today's Children,* which was one of the genre's great early successes. By the late 1930s more than 40 million people each day were listening to more than thirty serials, sponsored **mostly** by soap companies. Phillips went on to create *The Guiding Light* for radio in 1937 and then oversaw its transition to television in 1952. With over 12,290 broadcasts (as of November 1995) and over forty-three years on CBS, *The Guiding Light* is television's **most** enduring soap opera.

Phillips has created a number of daytime dramas since then, including three others (aside from *The Guiding Light*) that are still on the air today: *As the World Turns* (1956–   ), *Another World* (1964–   ) and *Days of Our Lives* (1965–   ).

SOURCES: Nielsen Media Research; Individual Producers

The Soap Viewed the Most Around the World

ARE romance and intrigue the real international languages? If the world-wide popularity of American soap operas (and the hot, sexy *telenovelas* from South America) is any clue, the answer is a resounding yes! Set in glamorous Beverly Hills, *The Bold and the Beautiful* is the world's **most** popular American soap opera. The show was developed by the husband-and-wife team of William Bell and Lee Phillip Bell (who also created *The Young and the Restless*).

First aired in March 1987, the story chronicles the lives and loves of two fashion dynasties, the distinguished Forrester Creations and the up-start Spectra Fashions. Among the series regulars are John McCook, Susan Flannery, Darlene Conley, Ron Moss, Katherine Kelly Lang, Michael Sabatino, and Hunter Tylo. Seen by an estimated daily world-wide audience of 200 million, *The Bold and the Beautiful* currently airs in over 79 countries on 6 continents and is dubbed into a number of for-eign languages. It is often broadcast under a different title and is edited in some countries because of themes that are a bit too mature for certain national tastes.

SOURCE: Nielsen Media Research

The Soap Watched the Most in America

SINCE its debut in 1973, *The Young and the Restless* has changed the face of daytime drama. While traditional soap operas delved into the scan-dalous affairs of the older characters, creators William Bell and Lee Phillip Bell placed greater emphasis on more frank and open sexuality among the younger characters. The Bell's also insisted on using movie-quality production values and artistic photography, setting a whole new standard for the look of daytime drama. The show is also known for mak-ing the **most** of the musical talents of popular performers like Michael Damian, who starred on Broadway in Andrew Lloyd Webber's *Joseph and the Amazing Technicolor Dreamcoat.* Story lines for these characters often include episodes with elaborately staged rock concert sequences.

Originally aired as a half-hour drama, *The Young and the Restless* ex-panded to an hour in 1980. As the number-one-rated daytime drama since 1988 and having achieved an incredible 313 weeks at the top of Nielsen's ratings as of March 3, 1995, *Y&R* is easily the **most** popular soap opera in America. The show's fan club hosts their annual luncheon in July and offers the fans an opportunity to meet their favorite cast members.

SOURCES: Nielsen Media Research; *The Young and the Restless*

Soap's Most Enduring Performer

ON April 2, 1956, Helen Wagner, playing the role of Nancy Hughes, spoke the first line ("Good morning, dear.") of the premier telecast of CBS's *As the World Turns*. To honor her and the show's ten thousandth episode, aired May 12, 1995, Wagner was given the same lines to speak once again. With the exception of a few brief absences, Wagner has played the character over forty years (as of December 1996), making her daytime drama's **most** enduring performer.

SOURCE: CBS "Eye Point"; CBS, Inc.

Thirteen Toms Makes for the Most

WHEN a performer leaves a soap opera, the show's producers will often recast the part rather than write out an important character. Also, there are times when a child actor will be replaced by an older child or teenager as a story line develops. Over the years, the role of Tom Hughes on CBS's *As the World Turns* has been played by thirteen different actors, the **most** of any soap opera character. The actors who have played Tom Hughes are James Madden, Jerry Schaffer, Frankie Michaels, Richard Thomas, Paul O'Keefe, Peter Link, Peter Galman, C. David Colson, Tom Tammi, Justin Deas, Jason Kincaid, Gregg Marx, and Scott Holmes.

SOURCE: CBS, Inc.

The Most Moves by a Soap Opera Star

PERFORMERS occasionally leave one soap opera to join another. At least 33 actors have been veterans of 4 or more soap operas. Sometimes, however, they continue playing the same role on the new show, causing the character to simply move from one fictional town to the next. Nicholas Coster has played 8 roles on 9 different shows, the **most** of any performer in soap opera history. He has appeared in *Young Dr. Malone, The Secret Storm, Our Private World, As the World Turns, Somerset, Another World, One Life to Live, All My Children, Santa Barbara,* and recently back to *As the World Turns* (but this time as a different character).

SOURCE: Soap Opera Digest

The Most Trips to the Chapel

ERICA Kane (Susan Lucci) of ABC's *All My Children* is daytime television's **most**-married character. Her eight weddings have been to medical intern Jeff Martin, Phil Brent, ex–football star Tom Cudahy, wealthy businessman Adam Chandler, Travis Montgomery, Travis Montgomery a second time, and businessman Dimitri Marick, whom she married in 1993 and 1995.

SOURCE: *All My Children*

Luke and Laura and the Most Viewers Ever

ON ABC's *General Hospital,* Laura Baldwin (Genie Francis) was still a teenager and had just recently married Scotty Baldwin (Kin Shriner) when she was raped by Luke Spencer (Anthony Geary). For months, Luke chased Laura trying to make up for what he'd done, and eventually Laura fell in love with him. Their love affair, set within a story line filled with danger and intrigue, became such a cultural phenomenon that Geary and Francis made the cover of *Newsweek* magazine. Luke and Laura's wedding on November 16–17, 1981, which featured a highly publicized cameo appearance by Elizabeth Taylor as the evil Helena Cassadine, was the **most**-watched event in daytime television history, seen by an estimated 17 million viewers.

SOURCE: Nielsen Media Research

The Most Talked About on Talk Shows

"GET Bigger Breasts or Else!" *(Rolanda)* "He Slept with the Babysitter!" *(Sally Jessy Raphaël)*. These are just two of the outrageous topics covered in recent TV talk shows, and it seems the more outrageous the better. Talk show guests have included everyone from skinheads to high-priced hookers, from women who marry convicted murderers to women who murdered their husbands, from unhappy transsexuals to people who have masqueraded for years in relationships as members of the opposite sex. Several hosts were embarrassed in early 1995 when one couple disclosed to the press that they had appeared together as guests on several shows, making up completely different backgrounds and stories to suit each appearance. But it was a single event in March 1995 that seems to have awakened people to just how low talk shows had sunk. Invited to appear on *Jenny Jones,* John Schmitz, twenty-four, was told only that he would meet a "secret admirer." During the taping of the episode, another young man, Scott Amadore, 32, revealed that it was he who had a crush on Schmitz. Humiliated and embarrassed by having been confronted with this on a nationally televised program, Schmitz carried a shotgun to Amadore's apartment three days later and murdered him. That particular *Jenny Jones* episode never aired, but instead of providing a reason to stop such poor judgment in topics, a torrent of even more sensational ambush-style episodes soon flooded the airways. It got so bad that former secretary of education William Bennett, along with Senators Sam Nunn and Joseph Lieberman, took out their own ads in October calling for the end the "cultural rot" of television talk shows. In the long run, it seems these programs have chosen to survive by ratings rather than conscience. Lately, however, several of the newer talk shows have been cut, and others have promised to cut back on the sleaze. We can only wonder if the extremes taken by some of these shows aren't what caused the retirement of one of the earlier pioneers of the genre, Phil Donahue.

With around twenty-three talk shows airing daily, many advertisers have grown more selective about which ones they will sponsor. But what do these hosts and their guests really spend their time talking about? Although topics overlap, a study by the Henry J. Kaiser Foundation found that parent-child relations are the **most** popular topic of discussion on television talk shows. This includes shows on unwed dads who won't take responsibility for their children, kids who are embarrassed by the way their parents dress, children who abuse their parents, parents who don't like their child's girlfriend or boyfriend—the whole range of parent-child issues.

Following is a percentage breakdown of the **most**-talked-about "issues" on talk shows.

	Topic	Percent of Programs
1.	Parent-Child Relations	48
2.	Dating	36
3.	Marital Relations	35
4.	Sexual Activity	34
5.	Reconciliations	25
6.	Physical Health	24

	Topic	Percent of Programs
7.	Abuse	23
	Alienation	23
	Physical Appearance	23
10.	Criminal Acts	22

SOURCE: Henry J. Kaiser Foundation

Fessing Up the Most on Talk Shows

"I'M pregnant with your husband's baby." "I just can't stop cheating on my wife." Personal revelations are the grist of television talk shows. The Henry J. Kaiser Foundation studied the top 11 talk shows and found an average of 16 personal disclosures during each hour-long program. Of those, the **most** common were revelations about sexual activity and personal attributes (health problems, addictions), averaging 4 disclosures per hour, followed by 3 revelations of abuse, 2 each of criminal activity and embarrassing situations, and 1 disclosure of sexual orientation.

SOURCE: Henry J. Kaiser Foundation

Television Theme Songs

IT'S hard to think about a certain television series without remembering its theme song. Just a few notes of the intro or the first few words to any one of them brings nearly instant recognition, such as the theme from *The Beverly Hillbillies* ("Come and listen to a story 'bout a man named Jed . . ."), *The Brady Bunch* ("Here's the story, of a lovely lady . . ."), *Gilligan's Island* ("Sit right back and you'll hear a tale, a tale of a fateful trip . . ."), *The Courtship of Eddie's Father* ("People let me tell you 'bout my best friend . . ."), and the wonderful whistling on *The Andy Griffith Show.* Successful theme songs can earn their composers huge royalties. Sherwood Schwartz, who wrote both *The Brady Bunch* and *Gilligan's Island* themes, says he earns about $60,000 each year from those two theme songs alone, some of it from unusual sources. Schwartz once received a royalty check for under $1 when a marching band played the *Gilligan's Island* theme at halftime during a football game.

Sometimes television theme songs become big radio hits. The top ten television theme songs are listed below by chart position and by the year they were released. According to *Billboard Magazine,* the theme from *Miami Vice* is the **most** successful television theme of all time, based on the number of weeks it stayed at the top of the charts.

	Song	Show	Performer	Year - Chart	
1.	"S.W.A.T."	*S.W.A.T.*	Rhythm Heritage	1975	1
2.	"Welcome Back"	*Welcome Back, Kotter*	John Sebastian	1976	1
3.	"Miami Vice"	*Miami Vice*	Jan Hammer	1985	1
4.	"I'll Be There for You"	*Friends*	The Rembrandts	1995	1
5.	"Believe It or Not"	*Greatest American Hero*	Joey Scarbury	1981	2
6.	"Dragnet"	*Dragnet*	Ray Anthony Orchestra	1953	3
7.	"Secret Agent Man"	*Secret Agent Man*	Johnny Rivers	1966	3
8.	"Hawaii Five-O"	*Hawaii Five-O*	The Ventures	1969	4
9.	"Happy Days"	*Happy Days*	Pratt and McClain	1976	5
10.	"Makin' It"	*Makin' It*	David Naughton	1979	5

SOURCE: *Billboard*

Making the Most of a Title

THE title of a television show can often mean the difference between a big hit and a flop, particularly in a time when series' live and die in their first few airings and grabbing that debut audience is crucial. Though it's also true that including the name of the show's star in the title might just be enough of a drawing card to attract viewers.

Lucille Ball's name has appeared in the titles of the **most** television series. Her 7 series were *Here's Lucy, I Love Lucy, Life with Lucy, Love That Lucy, The Lucy-Desi Comedy Hour, Lucy in Connecticut,* and *The Lucy Show.* Next is Dick Clark, whose full name appears in the title of 5 different shows, followed by Tim Conway and Mary Tyler Moore, with 4 each. Coming in with 3 apiece are Bob Newhart, Bill Cosby, and the Smothers Brothers.

SOURCE: *International Television and Video Almanac 1996,* 41st Edition. Quigley Publishing Co., 1996

Mostly, the First Word's Easy

ASIDE from articles (for example, *a* and *the*) and network initials (ABC, CBS, NBC), the word "You" in all of its forms is the first word in the titles of 26 prime-time show—a **most**. "You" itself begins 9 series titles, including *You Asked for It, You Are There,* and *You Bet Your Life.* "Your" begins 13 titles, including the 1950's Sid Caesar–Imogene Cocoa hit *Your Show of Shows.* "You're" is the first word in three short-lived series, including a Jackie Gleason quiz show, *You're in the Picture,* which lasted just one broadcast and for which Gleason spent the entire half hour the following week apologizing. "Yours" appears just once in Bert Parks's quiz show, *Yours for a Song.*

The word "Mr." is second, appearing in the titles of 24 television series, including *Mr. Ed, Mr. Novak, Mr. Magoo, Mr. Lucky, Mr. Roberts,* and *Mr. Belvedere.* The word "New" is third, beginning the titles of 24 series, several of which were revamps of earlier shows, as in *The New Gidget, The New Mike Hammer, The New Dick Van Dyke Show, The New Monkees* and *The New Leave It to Beaver.* Fourth on this list of **mosts** are the words "It" and "It's," starting 21 series titles, including *It's a Living, It's About Time* and *It's Garry Shandling's Show.* The word "Big" begins the titles of 20 shows, such as *The Big Valley, Big Town,* and *Big Shamus, Little Shamus.* Lastly, the word "Man" begins the titles of 19 shows, including *A Man Called Hawk, A Man Called Shenandoah, The Man from U.N.C.L.E., Man from Atlantis,* and *Man of the People.*

SOURCE: *International Television and Video Almanac 1996,* 41st Edition, Quigley Publishing Co., 1996; Alex McNeill, *Total Television,* Third Edition, Penguin, 1991

What the Most Leading TV Characters Do

THE **most** prevalent occupations on prime-time television are law enforcement officer, then doctor, followed by lawyer. From *Dragnet* to *Kojak* to *N.Y.P.D. Blue,* from *Dr. Kildare* to *Marcus Welby, M.D.,* to *E.R.,* from *Perry Mason* to *The Defenders* to *Law and Order,* stories involving these three professions have been the mainstay of numerous shows over the years. This isn't exactly a reflection of society, however, since the U.S. Bureau of Labor Statistics lists the **most** common profession in the U.S. today as a salesperson.

SOURCE: Nielsen Media Research

The Most VCRs

ACCORDING to *Screen Digest,* since 1992, more than a third of all homes in the world with TVs also have VCRs. Based on a 1993 study, the countries with the **most** VCRs are:

	Country	Number of VCRs	Percent of TV-Owning Households with VCRs
1.	U.S.	66,560,000	70.2
2.	Japan	30,095,000	74.0
3.	Germany	21,770,000	61.5
4.	Brazil	20,669,000	45.4
5.	U.K.	16,354,000	72.6
6.	France	13,417,000	64.5
7.	Italy	8,851,000	40.6
8.	Canada	6,955,000	64.1
9.	Spain	5,866,000	51.7
10.	Former USSR	5,648,000	5.6
	World Total	275,055,000	36.9

SOURCE: *Screen Digest,* 1993

The Cable Networks with the Most Subscribers

CABLE television has brought to our homes the horrors of the war in Bosnia, coverage of popular sporting events, documentaries, children's programming, classic movies, and the debate that takes place in the U.S. Senate and House of Representatives. In many communities, cable television also provides coverage of city council meetings and other events. However, many cable providers have also been forced, by public access laws, to carry so-called adult programs as well. A report by Nielsen Media Research indicates that nearly 60.5 million households subscribe to basic cable services, representing 63.4 percent of households with television. In 1994 revenues for the U.S. cable industry reached over $28.8 billion, including $13.1 billion in basic cable subscriptions, $5.1 billion in subscriptions for premium services like HBO, and $4 billion in advertising. Not surprisingly, the cable networks provided by the majority of cable systems as a part of their basic cable package are seen in more homes than premium channels.

According to the National Cable Television Association, the following are the cable networks with the **most** subscribers, as of April 1995.

	Cable Network	Subscribers	Systems
1.	ESPN	64,900,000	26,700
2.	Cable News Network (CNN)	64,700,000	11,593
3.	TBS Superstation	64,400,000	11,688
4.	TNN (The Nashville Network)	63,600,000	13,639
5.	USA Network	63,000,000	12,500
	The Discovery Channel	63,000,000	10,036
	TNT (Turner Network Television)	63,000,000	9,840
8.	C-SPAN	61,700,000	5,162
9.	The Family Channel	61,400,000	10,555
10.	Arts & Entertainment Network	60,000,000	9,500

SOURCE: National Cable Television Association

The Pay Cable Networks with the Most Subscribers

PAY cable channels allow viewers access to recent Hollywood film releases, original movies, sporting events, and a wide variety of other kinds of programming not otherwise available. Unlike networks that broadcast on cable as part of a flat, all-inclusive fee (see above), the following are services that must be paid for separately.

Here are the **most** popular pay cable channels in the U.S., as of December 31, 1994.

	Cable Network	Subscribers
1.	Home Box Office	18,000,000
2.	The Disney Channel	17,830,000
3.	Showtime	7,600,000
4.	Cinemax	6,700,000
5.	Encore	5,100,000
6.	The Movie Channel	2,700,000
7.	Starz	1,000,000
8.	Flix	900,000
9.	TV-Japan	25,000
10.	ANA Television Network	10,000

SOURCE: National Cable Television Association

The Most Appearances in Commercials

As far as the public is concerned, Dick Wilson will always be Mr. Whipple, the storekeeper who tried to keep his customers from fondling his toilet paper by admonishing them with, "Please, don't squeeze the Charmin." The first of these commercials was filmed at a market in (where else) Flushing, New York. It was Wilson's own idea to soften the rather mean-sounding admonition by having the ladies catch Mr. Whipple squeezing the Charmin himself. The commercials aired between 1964 and 1989, and featured Whipple, along with various helpers including a dog and a parrot, doing his best to keep his customers from being enticed by the product's softness.

In France, they call her Françoise. In Germany, Austria, and Switzerland, she is called Tilly. Americans know her as Madge the Manicurist. Played by Jan Miner from 1965 to 1991, this wisecracking professional would reassure her customers who were about to soak their fingers in a small bowl of Palmolive dishwashing liquid with, ". . . Softens hands while you do dishes."

Madge and Mr. Whipple appeared the **most** in American television commercials, each having runs that lasted over twenty-five years. However, the pudgy little Pillsbury "Poppin' Fresh" Dough Boy has starred in commercials for over thirty years now, far longer than either of these two human beings.

SOURCE: Procter and Gamble, Colgate-Palmolive, The Pillsbury Co.

The Most Profitable Infomercials

"MAKE the call, now!" Some people consider them television's version of junk mail. But whether you pick up that telephone to call or the remote to switch channels, there's no denying that infomercials are becoming an increasing part of both broadcast and cable television. Large, well-respected corporations like Apple Computer, Toyota, Sony, Volvo, and Mattel have recently begun seriously considering the potential in presenting their products in thirty-minute segments rather than the traditional thirty-second commercial. Just how profitable are these half-hour-long commercials? As an example, between the infomercial and the two-minute direct-response ad featuring Dionne Warwick, the "Psychic Friends Network" brings in a cool $14 million a month and took in over $120 million between March 1994 and September 1995.

The following list from *Dworman's Infomercial Marketing Report* shows the **most** profitable infomercials of all time based on the revenues for their highest-grossing year.

1. Jane Fonda: Fitness Trends for the Nineties (treadmill)
2. Psychic Friends Network (1-900 psychic line)
3. Bruce Jenner: Powerwalk Plus (treadmill)
4. Connie Selleca and John Tesh: Growing in Love and Hidden Keys (videotapes)
5. Jake Steinfeld: Body by Jake (hip and thigh exercise machine)
6. Barbara De Angelis: Making Love Work (videotapes)
7. Health Rider (fitness machine)
8. Popeil Pasta Maker (kitchen appliance)
9. Anthony Robbins: Personal Power #4 (self-improvement)
10. Victoria Principal's Principal Secret (skin-care products)
    Your Psychic Experience (1-900 psychic line)
    Fantom Vacuum (household appliance)
    Mega Memory (self-improvement)
    Super Slicer (kitchen aid)

SOURCE: Dworman's *Infomercial Marketing Report,* Los Angeles

The Most-Celebrated Infomercials

CERTAINLY, infomercials have made household names of people like the "salesman of the century," Ron Popeil ("GLH" spray-on Hair, Ronco Food Dehydrator), Mike Levey ("Ask Mike," "Amazing Discoveries"), Victoria Jackson (her own line of make-up kits), and Susan Powter ("Stop the Madness"). They have also become second careers for celebrities like Cher, Victoria Principal, Dionne Warwick, and Dick Van Patten. These presenters and their infomercials have been honored since 1992 by the National Infomercial Marketing Association in their annual awards ceremony, held **most** recently in September 1995 during the NIMA International trade expo in Las Vegas. To show how much infomercials have grown in stature, it was no less than former NBC programming chief Brandon Tartikoff, now the chairman of New World Entertainment, who gave the keynote address.

As the following list of awards for the last four years shows, Jake Steinfeld has won the **most** NIMA awards thus far. He has received three awards as Best Male Presenter, and his "Body by Jake Ab & Back Plus" infomercial was named 1995's infomercial of the year.

Year	Infomercial of the Year	Best Female Presenter	Best Male Presenter
1992	"Personal Power," Tony Robbins	Victoria Jackson	Mike Levey
1993	"Stop the Insanity," Susan Powter	Susan Powter	Jake Steinfeld
1994	"Making Love Work," Barbara De Angelis	Kathy Smith	Jake Steinfeld
1995	"Body by Jake Ab & Back Plus," Jake Steinfield	Victoria Principal	Jake Steinfeld

SOURCE: National Infomercial Marketing Association

Mosts
from the World of
Music

WHO'S YOUR **MOST** favorite band or performer? What artist or group has sold the **most** records? How many **mosts** does The King (aka Elvis Presley) still retain? Maybe you already know, but if you don't, you're about to be educated.

The Most Successful Concerts

ACCORDING to Pollstar, the **most** successful individual concerts of all time based on box-office grosses are:

	Performer	Location (Year)
1.	Barbra Streisand	New York City (1994)
2.	Barbra Streisand	Las Vegas (1993)
3.	The Rolling Stones	New York City (1989)
4.	Bette Midler	New York City (1993)
5.	The Rolling Stones	East Rutherford, NJ (1994)
6.	The Rolling Stones	Los Angeles (1993)
7.	Paul Simon–Simon & Garfunkel	New York City (1993)
8.	Barbra Streisand	Auburn Hills, MI (1994)
9.	Billy Joel–Elton John	Philadelphia (1994)
10.	Bruce Springsteen and the E Street Band	East Rutherford, NJ (1985)

SOURCE: Pollstar; Fresno, CA

Making the Most on Tour

THE **most** successful North American concert tours of all time, based on box-office grosses through 1995, are:

	Performer	Year
1.	The Rolling Stones	1994
2.	Pink Floyd	1994
3.	Rolling Stones	1989
4.	Eagles	1994
5.	New Kids on the Block	1990
6.	U2	1992
7.	Eagles	1995
8.	Barbra Streisand	1994
9.	Grateful Dead	1994
10.	Elton John/Billy Joel	1994

SOURCES: Pollstar, Fresno, CA;
The World Almanac and Book of Facts 1997, World Almanac Books, 1996

Taking Home the Most Grammys

SIR Georg Solti, conductor of the Chicago Symphony Orchestra, holds the record for having received the **most** Grammys of any individual. His 31 wins have all been for albums of classical music and individual orchestral performances.

Outside the classical field, Quincy Jones has won the **most** Grammys of any individual, with 26 awards.

The Chicago Symphony Orchestra's 46 Grammys are the **most** awarded to any group or orchestra.

SOURCE: National Academy of Recording Arts and Sciences

Thriller's a Most

THE "King of Pop," Michael Jackson, holds the record for winning the **most** Grammys in a single year. In 1983, his eight awards included Album of the Year, *Thriller;* Record of the Year, "Beat It"; Best Rhythm and Blues Song, "Billie Jean"; and Best Recording for Children, "E.T. The Extra-Terrestrial."

SOURCE: National Academy of Recording Arts and Sciences

The Most Record of the Year Awards

SINGER-SONGWRITER Paul Simon has received Grammy's highest honor, Record of the Year, three times thus far, the **most** of any recording artist. With partner Art Garfunkel, he won in 1968 for "Mrs. Robinson" and again in 1970 for "Bridge Over Troubled Water." Then in 1987, he won for his solo album *Graceland*.

SOURCE: National Academy of Recording Arts and Sciences

The King Remains the Most Successful, But There's Still the Queen

ELVIS Presley is the **most** successful solo recording artist of all time. With 170 hit singles and over 80 best-selling albums since 1954, his achievements are unparalleled in recording history. In 1992, based on new audit figures, the Recording Industry Association of America presented Presley's estate with 110 gold and platinum records, making him the **most**-certified solo recording artist ever.

Barbra Streisand has received the **most** such awards of any female solo recording artist. To date, she has earned 7 gold singles, 30 gold albums, and 12 platinum albums, for a total of 57.

SOURCE: Recording Industry Association of America

Beatles and Stones Striking the Most Platinum

THE Beatles—Paul McCartney, John Lennon, George Harrison, and Ringo Starr—are the **most** successful recording group of all time. According to EMI estimates, the "Fab Four" had sold over 1 billion discs and tapes by May 1985, the **most** of any group. They have also received the **most** multiplatinum albums, 11 total. However, the Rolling Stones have received the **most** Recording Industry Association of America awards of any group, a total of 56 including 34 gold, 16 platinum, and 6 multiplatinum records.

SOURCES: Recording Industry Association of America; EMI

Making the Singles Charts the Most

BETWEEN 1956 and 1983, Elvis Presley had 149 singles on *Billboard's Hot 100,* the **most** ever to make the charts. The Beatles reached the top of *Billboard*'s single's charts 20 times, the **most** number one Rock singles ever. Conway Twitty has the **most** number one Country hits, with 40, and Aretha Franklin has the **most** number one Rhythm and Blues hits, with 20.

SOURCE: *Billboard*

The Most Number One Albums

THE Beatles have had the **most** number one albums of all time, with 15 of their records topping *Billboard*'s charts. Elvis Presley had 9 number one albums, the **most** of any male solo artist. Barbra Streisand has the **most** number one albums of any female solo artist, with 7 of her records making it to the top of the charts.

SOURCE: *Billboard*

The Most Albums on *Billboard*'s Charts

ELVIS Presley has had the **most** albums of any artist on *Billboard*'s charts. His astounding 92-album total is unlikely to be matched during this century. The second-highest total, held by Frank Sinatra, is 66 albums. Barbra Streisand's 43 albums is the **most** to reach the charts of any female artist.

SOURCE: *Billboard*

Michael and His Most Popular Album Ever

MICHAEL Jackson's 1982 smash hit album *Thriller* is easily the **most** popular album of all time. Both internationally and in the U.S., *Thriller* has sold the **most** copies of any album ever, with worldwide sales exceeding 47 million and U.S. sales reaching over 24 million. *Thriller* also spent the **most** time at the top of *Billboard*'s U.S. charts: a total of 37 weeks.

SOURCE: *Billboard*

The Most Listened To

WHOM do we listen to **most?** Our parents? Our bosses? Our spouses? Our children? No, Whitney Houston and Michael Jackson.

Read on to see which songs and albums have been the **most** listened to since *Billboard* began its charting system in 1958. The following **mosts** are good through June 1994.

	Song Title	Artist	Year
1.	"I Will Always Love You"	Whitney Houston	1993
2.	"End of the Road"	Boyz II Men	1992
3.	"The Sign"	Ace of Base	1993
4.	"You Light Up My Life"	Debby Boone	1977
5.	"Physical"	Olivia Newton-John	1981
6.	"The Twist"	Chubby Checker	1960
7.	"Mack the Knife"	Bobby Darin	1959
8.	"Endless Love"	Diana Ross & Lionel Richie	1981
9.	"Hey Jude"	The Beatles	1968
10.	"Bette Davis Eyes"	Kim Carnes	1981
11.	"That's the Way Love Goes"	Janet Jackson	1993
12.	"The Theme from A Summer Place"	Percy Faith	1960
13.	"Jump"	Kris Kross	1992
14.	"Can't Help Falling in Love with You"	UB40	1993
15.	"Dreamlover"	Mariah Carey	1993
16.	"Every Breath You Take"	The Police	1983
17.	"Night Fever"	Bee Gees	1978
18.	"Eye of the Tiger"	Survivor	1982
19.	"Tossin' and Turnin' "	Bobby Lewis	1961
20.	"I Want to Hold Your Hand"	The Beatles	1964

SOURCE: *Billboard*

How about the **most** popular albums of all time based on sales through June 1994? Before reading on, can you guess any that may have made this **most** of the **mosts** list? Think back, because some may surprise you with their lasting power.

	Album	Artist	Year
1.	*Thriller*	Michael Jackson	1984
2.	*My Fair Lady*	Original Cast	1964

3.	*Calypso*	Harry Belafonte	1975
4.	*Rumours*	Fleetwood Mac	1977
5.	*West Side Story*	Sound track	1961
6.	*South Pacific*	Sound track	1958
7.	*Please Hammer Don't Hurt 'Em*	M. C. Hammer	1990
8.	*Purple Rain*	Prince and the Revolution	1984
9.	*Dirty Dancing*	Sound track	1987
10.	*Saturday Night Fever*	Bee Gees—sound track	1977
11.	*Born in the U.S.A.*	Bruce Springsteen	1985
12.	*The Bodyguard*	Whitney Houston—Sound track	1992
13.	*Blue Hawaii*	Elvis Presley—Sound track	1961
14.	*Ropin' the Wind*	Garth Brooks	1991
15.	*The Sound of Music*	Sound track	1965
16.	*Some Gave All*	Billy Ray Cyrus	1994
17.	*Synchronicity*	The Police	1981
18.	*The Sound of Music*	Original Cast	1959
19.	*Mary Poppins*	Sound track	1964
20.	*The Button-Down Mind of Bob Newhart*	Bob Newhart	1960

SOURCE: *Billboard*

Dark Side Also in the Black the Most

PINK Floyd's rock epic *Dark Side of the Moon* has appeared on the charts for the **most** total (non-consecutive) weeks of any album, a total of 741 weeks since its release over twenty years ago.

SOURCE: *Billboard*

Whitney's First Is a Most

WITH international sales of over 14 million, including U.S. sales of over 9 million, Whitney Houston's first album, *Whitney Houston,* released in 1985, is the **most** popular debut album ever and the **most** popular album by a solo female artist. But, pulling into a dead-heat with it is Alanis Morisette's *Jagged Little Pill* (1995).

SOURCE: Recording Industry Association of America

Garth Selling Country's Most

GARTH Brooks exploded onto the country music scene in 1990, selling over 35 million albums in under four years. His album, *No Fences* (1995), was the first country record to sell more than 10 million copies, and has now sold over 13 million copies, the **most** of any country music album ever. Of the top ten country music albums of all time, five of them are by Garth Brooks. And, as of May 1996, Garth has sold over 60 million albums, second only to the Beatles 71 million certified sales of albums.

SOURCE: Recording Industry Association of America

True Blue Makes for an Overseas Most for the Material Girl

MADONNA'S album *True Blue* sold over 17 million copies and reached number one in 28 countries, the **most** of any album.

SOURCE: Recording Industry Association of America

The Most Soundtrack Albums Sold

WITH its sizzling combination of romantic and pop songs, the sound track from the 1992 hit film *The Bodyguard,* which starred Kevin Costner and Whitney Houston, in her acting debut, is the **most** popular movie sound track album of all time, with sales of over 15 million to date. Prince and the Revolution's 1984 sound track for *Purple Rain* is second with over 13 million sales as of May 1996. Before *Purple Rain* and *The Bodyguard,* The Bee Gees kept the sounds of seventies disco music alive with over 11 million sales of the sound track from the 1977 hit movie *Saturday Night Fever.* But this is a tie for third place with *Dirty Dancing,* also at 11 million sales.

SOURCE: Recording Industry Association of America

The Singles Selling the Most

THE Christmas season wouldn't be quite the same without the warm, nostalgic strains of Irving Berlin's "White Christmas." Recorded by Bing

Crosby on May 29, 1942, this is the **most** popular single of all time. The song has even been sung in three different motion pictures, and North American sales alone have exceeded 171 million copies!

Internationally, the classic rock-and-roll anthem "Rock Around the Clock" by Bill Haley and the Comets, which topped the charts in 1955, comes in second, with sales of 17 million. The British invasion of 1964 saw the Beatles' "I Want to Hold Your Hand" hit the charts with such strength that it remains the second-best-selling single of all time in the U.S., as well as the third-best seller internationally.

SOURCE: *The Guinness Book of Records 1996,* Bantam, 1996; *Billboard*

Whitney Houston's rendition of "I Will Always Love You" from *The Bodyguard* sound track is the **most** popular single by a female artist. Written by Dolly Parton, the song has sold over 10 million copies internationally and spent 14 weeks at number one on the U.S. charts.

SOURCE: Recording Industry Association of America

More Mosts for Dolly (and One for Kenny)

DOLLY Parton and Kenny Rogers teamed up for the country hit "Islands in the Stream," and it paid off. It is the **most** popular country single of all time, with sales of over 2 million copies. Next is the Oak Ridge Boys' "Elvira," followed by Billy Ray Cyrus's "Achy Breaky Heart."

SOURCE: Recording Industry Association of America

The Most Number Ones in a Row

BEGINNING in 1964 with "Where Did Our Love Go" and ending in 1969 with "Someday We'll Be Together," the Supremes had twelve straight number one hit singles, the **most** of any American singing group.

SOURCE: *Billboard*

The Most Popular Foreign-Language Singles Ever

OVER the years, several songs in languages other than English have done well on the U.S. charts. If we didn't speak the language, we listened carefully and learned the songs phonetically so we could sing along with the car radio. Domenico Modugno's 1958 Italian-language hit "Volare" is the **most** popular foreign-language single of all time in the U.S., with sales of over 2 million. "Dominique," recorded in French by the Singing Nun (Soeur Sourire, born Jeanine Deckers, 1932–85), comes next, then "Sukiyaki," sung in Japanese by Kyu Sakamoto. If sales of both the Richie Valens and Los Lobos versions of "La Bamba" were combined, that song would easily be the **most** popular foreign-language song to reach the charts in the United States.

SOURCE: *Billboard*

Our Most Popular Jukebox Singles

IN 1989, to celebrate the one hundredth anniversary of the jukebox, the Amusement and Music Operators Association conducted a poll of its membership to compile a list of the top forty jukebox singles of all time. Current hits come and go in jukeboxes, but this list, which spans several decades, includes the songs played the **most** often year after year—you know, the golden oldies that people still pay to tap their toes to in bars and diners all across North America.

There were some changes when the list was updated in 1992. Elvis Presley's double-sided "Hound Dog/Don't Be Cruel" dropped out of its number one position on the 1989 list to third in 1992, and Patsy Cline's "Crazy" moved up from number two to the number one spot. Although eleven "new" songs were added to the top forty, including The Righteous Brothers' "Unchained Melody" (number 12) and Jimmy Buffet's "Margaritaville" (number 14), none of them quite made it into the top ten. With the popularity of concert tours by groups like the Rolling Stones ("Honky Tonk Woman," number 15) and the Eagles ("Hotel California," number 27), there are likely to be a few more changes when the list is updated next.

However, here are the ten **most** popular jukebox singles as of 1992. And don't be embarrassed if you find yourself humming along with the list.

	Song	Artist	Year
1.	"Crazy"	Patsy Cline	1962
2.	"Old Time Rock and Roll"	Bob Seger	1979
3.	"Hound Dog/Don't Be Cruel"	Elvis Presley	1956
4.	"I Heard It Through the Grapevine"	Marvin Gaye	1968
5.	"Mack the Knife"	Bobby Darin	1959
6.	"Rock Around the Clock"	Bill Haley and the Comets	1955
7.	"Light My Fire"	The Doors	1967
8.	"The Dock of the Bay"	Otis Redding	1968
9.	"My Girl"	The Temptations	1965
10.	"New York, New York"	Frank Sinatra	1980

SOURCE: Amusement and Music Operators Association; 1989

The Beatles Take Up the Most Space

THE Beatles hold the record for the **most** songs to crowd the top of the *Billboard* charts in one week. For the week beginning April 4, 1964, the Beatles held positions one through five with the following songs:

1. "Can't Buy Me Love"

2. "Twist and Shout"

3. "She Loves Me"

4. "I Want to Hold Your Hand"

5. "Please Please Me"

SOURCE: *Billboard*

The Most-Sung Song

IN 1893, Mildred J. Hill, a concert pianist and church organist, wrote the music for a sweet little song called "Good Morning to All," and Patty Smith Hill, principal of the Louisville Kindergarten Training School in Kentucky, added the lyrics. The song was published in a book called *Song Stories for the Kindergarten.* Thirty-one years later, Robert H. Coleman included the song in a book called *Harvest Hymns,* but this time a second stanza was added which began with the now-familiar words "Happy

Birthday to you." The copyright for the **most**-sung song in the English language was registered in 1935 and remains in effect until the year 2010. Contrary to popular opinion, this song is not in the public domain, which means that every time you hear someone sing "Happy Birthday to You" in a movie or on television, the producers have paid royalties, which now go to the Hill Foundation in Chicago, Illinois.

SOURCE: Hill Foundation

The National Anthems with the Most in Common

IF you've ever watched the scene in *Casablanca* where the Germans begin singing "Die Wacht am Rhein" and the French drown them out with a stirring rendition of "La Marseillaise," you know how passionately people can feel about their national anthem. When Whitney Houston performed "The Star-Spangled Banner" at Superbowl XXV on January 27, 1991, she captured America's heart by epitomizing the country's surge of patriotism kindled by the Gulf War crisis. Demand for the song was so strong that Arista records released it as both a single and a video.

Congress officially chose "The Star-Spangled Banner" as America's national anthem in 1931. Prior to that, however, the honor was shared by "My Country 'Tis of Thee." Actually, the melody to "My Country 'Tis of Thee" is the same as that of Great Britain's national anthem, "God Save the Queen." Based on a keyboard piece written by British composer Dr. John Bull in 1619, that melody has been used in national anthems by the **most** countries of any song. Although they have different anthems now, the U.S., Germany (as well as a number of German states), Denmark, Sweden, Russia, and Switzerland have all used this as their national song at one time or another. Besides the U.K., the only other independent country still using this tune is Liechtenstein.

SOURCES: *Collier's Encyclopedia,* Macmillan Educational Company, 1992; Martin Shaw, *National Anthems of the World*, Blanford Press, London, 1960

The Most Performances for a Most Ill-Fitting Uniform

"GOD Save the Queen" also holds the distinction of being played the **most** times of any national anthem in a single non-stop performance. On the morning of February 9, 1909, a German military band performing at the Rathenau railroad station in Bandenburg, Germany, began playing the British national anthem to welcome Britain's King Edward VII. Meanwhile King Edward was inside the train struggling to get into a German field marshal's uniform. By the time the monarch finally stepped out onto the platform, the band had played the song as many as seventeen times.

Mosts
from the World of
Food and Drink

IF YOU LIKE to eat and drink like **most** of us do, then we think this chapter might just be for you. Don't study our **mosts** too hard though, you might just work up a thirst or a hunger and run off to man's best friend. And no, we're not referring to the dog. We're talking about the refrigerator. Of course, you might have to push the dog out of the way once you get the door open.

"I Scream, You Scream, We All Scream for Ice Cream": The Most Popular Chain and Flavor

WITH outlets in over fifty countries, including Russia and Vietnam, Baskin-Robbins is the **most** popular chain of frozen dessert stores in the world. The flavor experts at Baskin-Robbins even create ice creams to suit the particular tastes of their international consumers. For example, "Green Tea" ice cream is popular in Asia, and "Red Bean" ice cream is a favorite in India. Still the all-time international **most** popular Baskin-Robbins ice cream flavor is "Pralines n Cream" followed closely by "Jamoca Almond Fudge."

SOURCE: Baskin-Robbins

Our Most Popular Brands

FROM January through October 15, 1994, U.S. sales of the top ten brands of ice cream alone totaled more than $1.6 billion. Sales of private and store-label ice creams accounted for over half a billion dollars. According to *Dairy Foods Magazine,* the following are the ten **most** popular brands of ice cream, ranked by sales, in the United States (for the above-mentioned period).

Brand	Sales (millions)
1. Private label	$610.2
2. Good Humor–Breyers	269.1
3. Blue Bell	144.7
4. Dreyer's/Edy's	142.6
5. Häagen-Dazs	131.1
6. Ben & Jerry's	114.2
7. Sealtest	60.0
8. Borden	49.6
9. Kemps	45.9
10. Turkey Hill	40.2

SOURCE: *Dairy Foods Magazine,* 1994

The Most Popular Yogurt

SALES of frozen yogurt are still considerably lower than those for ice cream. However, here are the ten **most** popular brands of frozen yogurt in the U.S. based on sales from January to October 15, 1994.

Brand	Sales (millions)
1. Dreyer's/Edy's	$80.7
2. Private label	72.2
3. Kemps	68.2
4. Häagen-Dazs	40.9
5. Ben & Jerry's	39.3
6. Breyers	28.1
7. Columbo	25.2
8. Wells' Blue Bunny	21.8
9. Crowley	21.3
10. Turkey Hill	20.4

SOURCE: Individual Manufacturers

The Most Common M&M Colors

IN January 1995, consumers were given the unique opportunity to choose a new color for the "candy-coated" shell of M&Ms. By an overwhelming majority of 54 percent, **most** voters selected the new blue color over pink, purple, and the original tan. But what's the **most** frequently appearing color used in M&Ms? That depends both on the variety (plain, almond, or peanut) and the time of year. At Christmas, M&Ms come in red and green; on Valentine's Day, red, pink, and white; and at Easter, pastel shades of blue, yellow, green, pink, and purple.

For the **most** part, however, here's the scoop on what you'll find inside your next bag of M&Ms. One note: M&Ms bags are filled by weight, not by volume, so your package may not contain these precise proportions. Don't worry, though, maybe your individual bite-size bits are just bigger. So forget that diet and go ahead and enjoy!

Plain M&Ms			Peanut M&Ms			Almond M&Ms		
1.	Browns	30%	1.	Browns	20%	1.	Browns	20%
2.	Reds	20%		Yellows	20%		Reds	20%
	Yellows	20%		Reds	20%		Yellows	20%
4.	Greens	10%		Blues	20%		Blues	20%
	Oranges	10%	5.	Greens	10%		Greens	20%
	Blues	10%		Oranges	10%			

SOURCE: Mars Candy

What Junior Asks for the Most

WHAT food do kids like the **most?** In a recent Gallup Poll, 82 percent of kids aged three to eleven said they liked pizza more than any other food for lunch and dinner. *Parade Magazine* estimates that 94 percent of the U.S. population eats pizza. According to *Pizza Today,* an industry publication, pizza is a $30-billion-a-year industry. Pizza Hut has the **most** outlets of any pizza chain, with over 9,454 stores in more than 68 countries. In the U.S. alone, there are over 58,000 pizzerias, representing 17 percent of the restaurant industry.

SOURCES: Gallup Organization and *Parade Magazine* and *Pizza Today*

The Most Popular Pizza Toppings

NEARLY every kind of topping has been tried on pizza, including peanut butter and jelly, bacon and eggs, and mashed potatoes. In some parts of the country, gourmet toppings are gaining popularity and include such treats as oysters, chicken, crayfish, dandelions, sprouts, eggplant, Cajun shrimp, artichoke hearts, and tuna. Worldwide choices of toppings tend to reflect regional preferences. Numero Uno Pizzeria reports that eel and squid are favorites in Japan, curry is popular in Pakistan, red herring is preferred in Russia, and coconut is the topping of choice in Costa Rica. But what are America's **most** popular toppings? In order of popularity, they are pepperoni, mushrooms, extra cheese, sausage, green pepper, and onion.

SOURCE: *Pizza Today*

Reaching for Campbell's the Most

Mmm-mmm, good! America's **most** popular comfort food is Campbell's chicken noodle soup. In fact, of the top six best-selling dry grocery items, three of them are Campbell's soups. The next five items are Campbell's cream of mushroom soup, Kraft macaroni and cheese, Sun-Maid raisins, Star-Kist tuna, and Campbell's tomato soup.

Each year, Campbell sells over 350 million cans of chicken noodle soup, containing almost 1 million miles of noodles, enough to circle the equator almost forty times. During January, the height of the traditional cold-and-flue season, Americans buy an average of 100 cans of Campbell's soup every second of every day. But can chicken soup cure a cold? Despite the lack of conclusive scientific evidence, a recent Mayo Clinic Health Letter says, "Chicken soup is nutritious, tasty, inexpensive and has no known side effects." Well, not exactly proof positive, but nevertheless a respectable plug.

SOURCE: Campbell Soup Company

McDonald's Has the Most

"Two all-beef patties, special sauce, lettuce, cheese, pickles, onions on a sesame-seed bun." That's right, it's the Big Mac, "flagship sandwich" of McDonald's, the food service giant with the **most** restaurants in the world. Pittsburgh franchisee Jim Delligatti invented the Big Mac, and the sandwich was first introduced on the McDonald's menu in Uniontown, Pennsylvania, in 1968. Since then, worldwide sales of the Big Mac have topped 14 billion. If that many Big Macs were strung together side-to-side, the string would reach to the moon and back 2 times or circle the equator 35.5 times. In 1955 Ray Kroc (1902–1984) bought out brothers Dick and "Mac" McDonald, pioneers of the fast-food drive-in. Today, McDonald's Corporation of Oak Brook, Illinois, licenses or owns over 15,000 restaurants in 85 countries, including 9,928 in the U.S. More than 96 percent of Americans aged 16 to 65 have visited a McDonald's restaurant at least once, and 8 percent of American adults visit an average of once a day. McDonald's opens an average of one new restaurant every eight hours and somewhere between 600 and 800 outside the U.S. each year. The McDonald's with the **most** floor space, covering more than 80,000 square feet, is located in Beijing, People's Republic of China; the northernmost is in Fairbanks, Alaska; and the southernmost is in Gibson, New Zealand. McDonald's can even be found on trains in Germany and Switzerland.

What do they serve at McDonald's in other countries? In France you can order wine with your meal. In Thailand, the menu includes a Samurai Pork Burger marinated with teriyaki sauce. And in Norway, you can enjoy McLaks, grilled salmon served with dill sauce on a whole-grain bun.

Here's a list of the ten countries outside the U.S. with the **most** McDonald's.

	Country	Date the Country's First McDonald's Opened	Stores
1.	Japan	07/20/71	1,133
2.	Canada	06/01/67	717
3.	Germany	11/22/71	570
4.	U.K.	10/01/74	526
5.	Australia	12/30/71	454
6.	France	06/30/72	350
7.	Brazil	02/13/79	149
8.	Mexico	10/29/85	102
9.	Hong Kong	01/08/75	82
10.	Taiwan	01/28/84	81

SOURCE: McDonald's

The Most-Snacked-On Snacks

IF your tastes run to salty snacks like potato chips and pretzels rather than sweet and sticky munchies, you might be interested to know that this segment of the snack-food industry took in $15 billion in 1994 in the U.S. alone. U.S. consumers purchased 5.69 billion pounds of snack foods in 1994.

Each year, the Snack Food Association publishes its *State of the Industry Report,* which ranks snacks by their sales volume in supermarkets, bars, sports stadiums, and newsstands, and sold through street vendors, vending machines, and home delivery. Following are the snacks we're eating and sneaking the **most** (for 1994).

	Snack	Amount Spent (millions)
1.	Potato Chips	$4,699.0
2.	Tortilla Chips	3,033.0
3.	Snack Crackers	2,484.0
4.	Popcorn (popped & unpopped)	1,353.0
5.	Peanuts	1,346.0
6.	Pretzels	1,271.0
7.	Cheese Curls/Cheese Puffs	795.5
8.	Corn Chips	668.3
9.	Cracker Sandwiches	646.0
10.	Meat Snacks (jerky, etc.)	631.6

SOURCE: *State of the Industry Report,* Snack Food Association

The Most Expensive Food

No wonder they call it "vegetable gold"! Saffron powder, made from the dried stigmas of *Crocus sativus,* is used to flavor and color cakes, breads, and dressings and is a central ingredient in risottos and bouillabaisse. It is also the world's **most** expensive food. A single pound of the yellow-orange condiment sells for over $2,600.

SOURCE: Herbal Resources, Inc., Hutchinson, Kansas

The Most Beer Drinkers

WE'VE told you all about candy **mosts,** and you've made the resolution to drop sweets from your list of vices. But all of us need at least one vice, so you're out shopping for another. Does beer drinking come to mind? If so, consider moving to one of the following states to work on your beer belly. You'll find plenty of company, as these states rank highest in terms of the **most** beer consumed annually per capita.

	State	Beers per Capita Consumed Annually
1.	Nevada	431
2.	New Hampshire	355
3.	Wisconsin	322
4.	Arizona	309
5.	Florida	301

SOURCE: *USA Today*

Mosts
from the World of
Health

WHAT'S AILING YOU the **most?** What's the best exercise to help you get the **most** out of your years? Where's the best hospital to go to when you exercise a bit too hard? We'll tell you if you read on.

The Most Beneficial Exercise

Weight Control

THINKING of becoming Miss America? First, check your gender. Even in today's permissive society, if you're not female, forget it. Second, you'll want to start or continue exercising. Saddlebags and love handles are a no-no. We'll help you get a start by listing different exercises that will help you control your weight the **most.** They are (listed alphabetically):

> Bicycling
> Cross-country skiing
> Jogging and running
> Rowing and canoeing

Aerobic Training

MAYBE you're interested in aerobic training as well. Why not? The heart's a muscle too, and taking good care of it should be as important to us as having abs of steel, rock-hard glutes, or wondrous, diamond-shaped calves! Consider the following:

> Bicycling
> Cross-country skiing
> Jogging and running

Rowing and canoeing
Swimming

Stress Reduction

How about stress reduction? We're all aware now that stress is a killer, so how can we kill it first? Following are exercises that will help you reduce stress the **most.**

Bicycling
Cross-country skiing
Jogging and running
Rowing and canoeing
Sailing
Walking

SOURCE: Dr. David R. Stutz, *40+ Guide to Fitness,* Consumer Reports Books, 1994

Paying the Most to Become More Beautiful

ALL right, so you've given up on exercising and you've decided that you're going to do it the quick way. You'll just have those extra pounds vacuumed off via liposuction. But what's it going to cost? For that matter, what do any of the **most** popular "beauty enhancers" cost? And which cost the **most?**

Read on. Because if exercise isn't taking you to the heights you wanted to go, there's always the heights that can be achieved through breast augmentation or a nice buttocks lift. Now think of *those* heights!

Following are the average costs of various popular plastic-surgery procedures, from **most** to least expensive.

	Surgery	Average Cost (dollars)
1.	Breast reduction in women	4,525
2.	Facelift	4,156
3.	Tummy tuck	3,618
4.	Thigh lift	3,090
5.	Buttock lift	3,084
6.	Hair transplant (for male pattern baldness)	3,081
7.	Breast lift	3,063

8.	Nose reshaping (primary, open rhinoplasty)	2,997
9.	Breast augmentation	2,754
10.	Eyelid surgery (both uppers and lowers)	2,625
11.	Breast reduction in men	2,325
12.	Forehead lift	2,164
13.	Chin augmentation (osteotomy)	2,077
14.	Chemical peel (full face)	1,634
15.	Liposuction (any single site)	1,622

The above prices are national averages for 1994. Breast reconstruction was not included in the list because the cost varies widely and can easily exceed any of the above as the **most** expensive surgery of this sort undertaken.

SOURCE: American Society of Plastic and Reconstructive Surgeons, Inc., 1994

The Most Common Reasons for Emergency-Room Visits

WHAT'S making **most** of us jump into our cars at all hours of the day and night to get to the emergency room? The following are the **most** often cited reasons for making those harrowing trips.

1. Stomach cramps
2. Chest pains
3. Fever
4. Headaches
5. Injury (upper extremity)
6. Cough
7. Back symptoms
8. General pains in the body
9. Shortness of breath
10. Earache
11. Vomiting
12. Facial-area cuts
13. Head, neck, and face injury
14. Hand and finger symptoms
15. Labored breathing

SOURCE: National Center for Health Statistics, U.S. Department for Health and Human Services

The Most-Effective Nutritive Constipation Remedies

MORE and more people are turning to natural remedies for their ailments these days. We're finding we don't always have to take this or that drug, especially if the ailment is not immediately life-threatening. Take constipation, for instance. The next time you're suffering from it, you might want to try one of the following nutrients to help move things along some. They're said to be the **most** effective in clearing up intestinal matters.

Vitamin A	Pantothenic acid	Magnesium
Vitamin B complex	Vitamin C	Potassium
Vitamin B_1 (thiamine)	Vitamin D	Zinc
Vitamin B_6	Vitamin E	Fats
Choline	Unsaturated fatty acids	Water
Inositol	Fiber	Acidophilus
Niacin	Calcium	

Of, course, consult a physician or dietitian before relying too heavily on any of the above or any combination thereof.

SOURCE: Lavon J. Dunne, *Nutrition Almanac,* third edition

Nutrition to Control Bad Behavior

SO you've got a little troublemaker on your hands? Or maybe a big troublemaker? Why have them committed when you can try to curb their behavior in the **most** natural of ways. Following are nutrients that will help him or her control his or her bad behavior the **most** (prescription drugs not included).

Vitamin B complex
Vitamin B_1 (thiamine)
Vitamin B_6
Niacin
Vitamin C
Zinc

Note that the nutrients used to control criminal and delinquent tendencies in a person are also among the same nutrients used to alleviate constipation.

SOURCE: Lavon J. Dunne, *Nutrition Almanac,* third edition

The Best Hospitals in Most Categories

IN 1996, *U.S. News and World Report* ranked large hospitals on nearly all criteria. The hospitals that scored the highest **most** of the time are noted below.

Keep in mind that other hospitals around the country known for their excellent specialist programs may not have been included below, as the services offered are not as inclusive as those listed. Also, only major, academic hospitals have been considered.

	Hospital	Location
1.	Johns Hopkins Hospital	Baltimore
2.	Mayo Clinic	Rochester, MN
3.	Massachusetts General Hospital	Boston
4.	UCLA Medical Center	Los Angeles
5.	Duke University Medical Center	Durham, N.C.
6.	Cleveland Clinic	Cleveland
7.	University of California San Francisco Medical Center	San Francisco
8.	Brigham and Women's Hospital	Boston
9.	University of Texas M.D./Anderson Cancer Center	Houston
10.	Barnes Jewish Hospital	St. Louis
11.	Memorial Sloan-Kettering Cancer Center	New York City
12.	University of Washington Medical Center	Seattle
13.	University of Iowa Hospitals and Clinics	Iowa City
14.	New York University Medical Center	New York City
15.	Stanford University Hospital	Stanford, CA

SOURCE: "America's Best Hospitals" *U.S. News and World Report,* Aug. 12, 1996

The Most Common Causes of Poisoning

ACCORDING to a report in the September 1995 issue of the *Journal of Emergency Medicine,* the **most** common causes of poisoning are the following.

1. Household cleaning products
2. Analgesics
3. Cosmetics and personal-care products
4. Plants
5. Congestion and cold-relief products
6. Bites and venom

7. Topicals (creams and ointments)
8. Pesticides
9. Foreign bodies
10. Food products and food poisoning

Please note that **most** of the above are items that **most** people have in or around their households. Take care to note that with all their apparent good, these products are equally dangerous and should be stored in safe, childproof areas.

SOURCE: *Journal of Emergency Medicine,* September 1995

Drunk Driving's Horrid Mosts

BY far, the U. S. has the **most** deaths caused by drunk driving each year. Maybe this is because Americans travel by car far more often than people in other countries. But consider too that the U.S. is fourth in the world in consumption of alcohol. The result is that 17,274 Americans died in 1995 from alcohol-related deaths. That's a 4% increase over 1974 figures—perhaps due to higher speed limits.

SOURCE: National Highway Traffic Administration

The Most Common Causes of Death

WHAT is it in the U.S. that is killing people the **most?** The following diseases and ailments are. But keep in mind that all deaths have to be attributable to something, so when an elderly person passes on, that death will also be classified as one of the following.

	Cause of Death	Percent of Total Deaths
1.	Heart Disease	32.1
2.	Cancer	23.5
3.	Stroke	6.8
4.	Lung Diseases	4.5
5.	Accidents	3.9
6.	Pneumonia and Influenza	3.6
7.	Diabetes	2.4

8.	HIV	1.8
9.	Suicide	1.4
10.	Liver Disease	1.1

Figures are for 1994.

SOURCE: National Center for Health Statistics, U.S. Department of Health and Human Services

The Most Hiccups

THE **most** lengthy attack of hiccups ever began in 1922, when Charles Osborn (1894–1991) of Anthon, Iowa, was slaughtering a hog. Osborn hiccupped thereafter every 1½ seconds for 69 years and 5 months, finally stopping at age 85, in February 1990. Despite his affliction, Osborn managed to marry twice and father eight children.

SOURCE: *The Guinness Book of Records 1996,* Bantam, 1996

The Most "Bless Yous"

IT would have been impossible for those near Donna Griffiths (born in 1969) of Pershore, Great Britain, to say, "Bless you" every time she sneezed during her amazing 978-day-long sneezing fit. The unfortunate young woman began sneezing on January 13, 1981, and wasn't able to stop until September 16, 1983. In the first year alone, Donna was estimated to have sneezed one million times. That's an average of 1.9 sneezes every minute, or about 2,740 each day. Donna's consolation for all that sneezing is that she made *The Book of Mosts.*

SOURCE: *The Guinness Book of Records 1996,* Bantam, 1996

Mosts
from the World of
Human Interest

SEARCHING FOR THAT little tidbit of information? Something to keep in the back of your mind for the right cocktail party? Then you're going to find this chapter just right. Of course, there will be more facts, figures, current trends, and gobs of everyday things, but **most** importantly, there will be more **mosts.**

Read On!

WHAT magazines have you been reading **most** lately? If you're like **most** readers in America, you've been reading one or more of the following the **most.**

	Magazine	Circulation
1.	*Parade*	37,604,285
2.	*Modern Maturity*	21,716,727
3.	*USA Weekend*	18,502,858
4.	*Reader's Digest*	15,126,664
5.	*TV Guide*	14,037,062
6.	*National Geographic*	9,203,079
7.	*Better Homes*	7,613,661
8.	*Good Housekeeping*	5,223,935
9.	*Ladies Home Journal*	5,048,081
10.	*Family Circle*	5,005,301
11.	*Woman's Day*	4,724,500
12.	*McCall's*	4,611,848
13.	*Time*	4,063,146
14.	*Prevention*	3,427,803
15.	*People Weekly*	3,424,858
16.	*Redbook*	3,401,775
17.	*Playboy*	3,401,264

18.	*Sports Illustrated*	3,252,641
19.	*Newsweek*	3,158,617
20.	*Cosmopolitan*	2,527,928
21.	*Southern Living*	2,472,649
22.	*U.S. News*	2,240,710
23.	*Smithsonian*	2,214,509
24.	*Glamour*	2,181,316
25.	*Field & Stream*	2,004,087
26.	*Money*	1,982,123
27.	*Seventeen*	1,978,155
28.	*Ebony*	1,937,095
29.	*YM*	1,933,775
30.	*Country Living*	1,932,840

SOURCE: *Adweek*, Feb. 27, 1995

The Most Fantasies

LOOKING for a good read, a classic even? Then consider one of the great fantasy books. You may recognize some of the titles, or perhaps you've even read one or two or all of them! You know already then that **most** would agree, these are some of the **most** fantastic of all books ever!

	Title	Writer	Year First Published
1.	*Gulliver's Travels*	Jonathan Swift	1726
2.	*Frankenstein*	Mary Shelley	1818
3.	*The Narrative of Arthur Gordon Pym*	Edgar Allan Poe	1838
4.	*A Christmas Carol*	Charles Dickens	1843
5.	*Wuthering Heights*	Emily Brontë	1847
6.	*Moby-Dick*	Herman Melville	1851
7.	*Dr. Jekyll and Mr. Hyde*	Robert Louis Stevenson	1886
8.	*Dracula*	Bram Stoker	1897
9.	*Tarzan of the Apes*	Edgar Rice Burroughs	1912
10.	*Conan the Conqueror*	Robert E. Howard	1936

SOURCE: James Cawthorn and Michael Moorcock, *Fantasy: The 100 Best Books, Carroll and Graf, 1991*

Plays with the Most Legs

THE Broadway plays with the **most** performances of all time (not including previews) as of July 21, 1996, are:

Play	Performances
1. *A Chorus Line*	6,137
2. *Oh! Calcutta* (revival)	5,959
3. *Cats*	5,748
4. *Les Misérables*	3,845
5. *Phantom of the Opera*	3,542
6. *42nd Street*	3,486
7. *Grease*	3,388
8. *Fiddler on the Roof*	3,242
9. *Life with Father*	3,224
10. *Tobacco Road*	3,182

You might have been thinking that *The Fantastiks* would get the number one nod. But remember, the theater in Greenwich Village where *The Fantastiks* is playing is designated as "off-Broadway," thus the 15,000 performances of this marvel do not qualify here.

SOURCE: *Variety*

Dicing Up the Tonys the Most

IN 1948, Judith Anderson was awarded a Best Actress Tony Award for her performance in *Medea*. Also receiving the same award were Katherine Cornell for *Anthony and Cleopatra* and Jessica Tandy for *A Streetcar Named Desire*. This three-way tie represented the **most** actresses ever to tie for a Best Actress Tony in Broadway history. But this wasn't the only three-way tie that year. Tonys for the Best Performance by a Male Actor in Drama were awarded to Henry Fonda for *Mr. Roberts*, Paul Kelly for *Command Decision*, and Basil Rathbone for *The Heiress*, the **most** actors ever to tie for that award.

SOURCES: American Theatre Wing;
League of American Theatres and Producers

The Most Thrills

THE amusement park with the **most** roller coasters is Cedar Point in Sandusky, Ohio, with 12. Also at Cedar Point is the Gemini, the roller coaster that annually is ridden the most with over 56.8 million rides given to date. The park with the **most** wooden roller coasters, a total of 4, is Paramount Kings Dominion in Doswell, Virginia. The **most**-ridden roller coaster of all time is the seventy-year-old Cony Island Cyclone.

SOURCES: Cedar Point, Paramount's Kings Dominion, and Cony Island

The Most Take the Plunge

ON October 12, 1994, members of the skydiving team Diamond Quest '94 joined in the skies over Davis, California, in the largest open-canopy diamond formation ever. The forty-six parachutists were the **most** ever to jump in a canopy formation. The team members were Luke Aikins, Lon Baillargeon, David Bassinger, Nasser Basir, Schantz Basir, Francis Bender, Teresa Bizzell, Ian Bobo, Alex Borsutzky, Chas Bunch, John Carlisle, Ted Cheung, John Coldren, Scott Fiore, Scott Franklin, Andy Gamache, Chris Gay, Lillian Goodin, Al Gutshall, Rich Hall, Jackson Hoffman, Kevin Ingley, Tommy Lentz, Pat Linder, R.G. Long, Frank Matrone, Terrina McMichael, Bill Merson, Joe O'Leary, Red Payne, Pasi Pirttikoski, Mark Puckett, Kevin Resnick, David Richardson, Bruck Robertson, Peter Schaller, Ray Sermet, Jon Sikorsky, Scott Smith, Ken Smith, Terry Sparrow, Bill Thomasson, Kirk Van Zandt, Levom Better, Sjaim Vineyard, and Robert Williamson.

SOURCE: *Ten Most Memorable Record Flights of 1994,* March 13, 1995, National Aeronautical Association

The Most Precious

WANT to win over that special person that's **most** precious to you? May we suggest a little romantic music, and a nice, expensive gemstone? You're probably on your way to the local jeweler's right now, aren't you?

First, though, you'll need to know which are the **most** precious of the **most** popular gems. Below is a list.

	Gemstone	Average Cost of a 1-carat stone
1.	Ruby	$6,000
2.	Emerald	3,500
3.	Sapphire	1,600
4.	Tanzanite	230
5.	Aquamarine	150
6.	Pink Tourmaline	100
7.	Green Tourmaline	80
8.	Peridot	50
9.	Rhodolite Garnet	40
10.	Amethyst	16

Prices are based on averages through April 1995 and are for fine grade stones only. (Four grades of gemstones exist: commercial, good, fine, and extra fine. Prices increase dramatically with the increase in grade).

As the quality of a diamond is measured differently, diamonds are not included in the above.

SOURCE: Richard Drucker, publisher, *The Guide*

The Most Valuable Toys

PLAN on cleaning out your basement or the attic or any of your closets anytime soon? If you do, and if you've had kids or are a kid yourself, watch out for the following toys. They've appreciated the **most** over the years and are worth small fortunes now.

So please, if you find one of the below toys, resist the temptation to play with it. Either run for the nearest collector or build a glass case and seal it up inside.

	Toy	Minimum Value	Maximum Value
1.	1959 Barbie	$3,000	$5,000
2.	Battery-operated Robbie the Robot	3,000	5,000
3.	1967 GI Joe Nurse	N/A	3,000
4.	Beatles Ceramic Figurines	500	600
5.	Japanese Toy Cars (tin)	300	600
6.	Howdy Doody Puppets (tin, wind-up)	300	500
7.	PEZ Candy Dispensers (Santa Claus, etc.)	200	300
8.	Star Trek Memorabilia	100	300

What do experts say will appreciate the **most** in the future? Not Elvis memorabilia. That market peaked in the eighties with personal items of the King's going for tens of thousands of dollars. The next wave might be anything to do with the rock bands, U2, Pearl Jam, and Nirvana. Dolly Parton, Liberace, and Madonna memorabilia may also become hot.

N/A=not available

SOURCE: *Family Life* magazine;
The Practical Guide to Practically Everything, Peter Bernstein and Christopher Ma, editors, Random House, 1995

The Most Popular Credit Cards

WHAT companies have issued the **most** credit cards? If you have good credit, if you have bad credit, or even if you have no credit, you've probably received something in the mail from at least one of the following:

	Company	Number of Accounts
1.	Discover	29,300,000
2.	Citicorp	23,600,000
3.	MBNA America	12,000,000
4.	AT&T Universal	11,700,000
5.	First Chicago Corporation	10,275,137
6.	Household	10,064,811
7.	Chase Manhattan	8,000,000
	First USA	8,000,000
9.	Chemical Bank	5,200,000
10.	Signet Bank	3,406,691

You may have noticed the absence of American Express and Diner's Club. Cards issued by them are not included, as they are charge cards that require full payment each month, whereas the above are credit cards with which repayment can be drawn out.

SOURCE: *The Practical Guide to Practically Everything,* Peter Bernstein and Christopher Ma, editors, Random House, 1995

What a Gas!

WHO's paying the **most** taxes on their gas? Maybe you are. Glance down to see if you live in or are planning a trip to one of the states listed. They're notorious for making you pay the **most** in gasoline taxes. As if income taxes aren't enough!

	State	Gasoline Tax (cents per gallon)
1.	Connecticut	29.0
2.	Rhode Island	28.0
3.	Nebraska	26.0
4.	Montana	24.0
	Oregon	24.0
6.	Maryland	23.5
7.	Wisconsin	23.2
8.	Nevada	23.0
	Washington	23.0
10.	Tennessee	22.4

Think of it this way: if you purchase ten gallons of gas in Connecticut, you pay nearly three dollars in taxes.

SOURCE: Tax Foundation, *Special Report,* January 1994

Most of Your Money: Where Does it Go?

WONDERING what happened to your paycheck? Wasn't there supposed to be enough money left for you to go out over the weekend? Well, we can tell you where all that money went. Following is a list of the items the typical American family spends the **most** money on.

	Expenditure
1.	Federal taxes
2.	Housing and household expenses
3.	State and local taxes
4.	Medical care
5.	Food
6.	All other
7.	Transportation, including cars

8. Recreation
9. Clothing

SOURCE: Tax Foundation, *Special Report,* Nov. 1994, No. 43

The Most Traditional Wedding Gifts

Most agree, the following are among the **most** traditional gifts you can give on wedding anniversaries from times gone by and for the more modern era.

Anniversary	Traditional Gift	Contemporary Gift
1st	Paper	Clocks
2nd	Cotton	China
3rd	Leather	Crystal, glass
4th	Linen, silk	Appliances
5th	Wood	Silverware
6th	Iron	Wood
7th	Wood, copper	Desk sets
8th	Bronze	Linens, lace
9th	Pottery, china	Leather
10th	Tin, aluminum	Diamonds
11th	Steel	Fashion jewelry
12th	Silk	Pearls, colored gems
13th	Lace	Textiles, furs
14th	Ivory	Gold jewelry
15th	Crystal	Watches
20th	China	Platinum
25th	Silver	Sterling silver
30th	Pearls	Diamonds
35th	Coral, jade	Jade
40th	Rubies	Rubies
45th	Sapphires	Sapphires
50th	Gold	Gold
55th	Emeralds	Emeralds
60th	Diamonds	Diamonds

When only a resource is listed, it is customary to give a couple something made out of that resource, rather than just a hunk or bolt of it.

SOURCE: *The 1996 World Almanac and Book of Facts,* St. Martin's Press, 1996

The U.S. Has the Most Computers

THE U.S. has the **most** computers of any country in the world, with over six times as many as Japan and over eight times more than Germany. In fact, the U.S. has nearly twice as many computers as all of Europe combined. The U.S. also has the **most** per capita computers of any country, with just under ten times the worldwide average.

Zeroing In on the Most Zones

THE Book of Mosts is basically all about numeric comparisons of one kind or another. Even questions of popularity or opinion are answered by market surveys or sales analysis. But not every society has the same urgent need to know "how much" or "how many." In fact, the Nambiquara, an Indian people who live on the fringes of the Amazon forest in Brazil, have no system of numbers at all. Their nearest equivalent is a verb which means "to be two alike." However, if you wanted to count, say, to a million, and you counted at a rate of 100 per minute for 8 hours a day, 5 days a week, it would take you a little over 4 weeks. If you were really obsessed with numbers and wanted to try to count to a billion, at that rate it would take you over 80 years. (But before you start, consider the fact that only one country—Japan—has citizens whose average life expectancy even approaches that time span.) And what is the largest number possible? British astronomer Sir Arthur Eddington (1882–1944) once estimated that the total number of fundamental particles in the universe was 10^{89}, or the number 1 followed by 89 zeroes. Around 1935, American mathematician Edward Kasner (1879–1955) introduced a name for an even larger number. At the suggestion of his nine-year-old nephew, Kasner called the number 10^{100} a googol. The named number with the **most** zeroes, known as a googolplex, is 10^{googol}, or the number 1 followed by 10^{100} zeroes. Unfortunately, since there aren't enough particles in the universe to carry that many zeroes, this number can never be written out.

SOURCE: The Math Forum, Swarthmore College

Inventing the Most

THOMAS Edison holds the **most** patents of any inventor, either individually or jointly. His 1,093 inventions include the microphone, the motion-picture projector, and the incandescent electric light.

SOURCE: *Encyclopedia Americana Grollier,* 1996

Nobel Prize Mosts

MARIE Curie has won the **most** Nobel Prizes of any woman. In 1903, she and her husband, Pierre, were both honored with the Nobel Prize in physics. Then, in 1911, she was awarded a second Nobel Prize, this time in chemistry for her discovery of radium. Sharing the distinction of being a two-time winner is Dr. Linus Pauling. In 1954, he was awarded the Nobel Prize in chemistry, and in 1962 he received the Nobel Peace Prize.

SOURCE: *The World Almanac and Book of Facts 1997,* World Almanac Books, 1996

The Most Commonly Misspelled English Words

THE **most** commonly misspelled words? Or is that mispelled? Nope, it's definitely *misspelled.* Did we spell definitely right?

Read on to see which words many of us are misspelling **most** of the time.

accidentally	despair	lightning
accommodate	desperate	liquefy
acquainted	eliminate	maintenance
all right	fascinating	marriage
already	finally	miniature
amateur	fluorine	misspelled
appearance	foreign	mysterious
appropriate	forty	necessary
bureau	government	opportunity
character	grammar	optimistic
commitment	harass	performance
conscientious	humorous	permanent
conscious	hurrying	rhythm
convenience	incidentally	ridiculous
deceive	independent	similar
describe	inoculate	sincerely
description	irresistible	transferred
desirable	laboratory	

SOURCE: *The 1996 World Almanac and Book of Facts,* World Almanac Books, 1995

The Most Hang Time

WHAT bridges have the **most** span in the U.S. and Canada? That is, which of these countries' great bridges cover the **most** distance without support? The following do:

	Bridge	Location	Span (feet)
1.	Verrazano-Narrows	New York, NY	4,260
2.	Golden Gate	San Francisco Bay, CA	4,200
3.	Mackinac	Straits of Mackinac, MI	3,800
4.	George Washington	Hudson River, NY to NJ	3,500
5.	Tacoma Narrows	Washington State	2,800
6.	Transbay	San Francisco Bay, CA	2,310
7.	Bronx-Whitestone	East River, New York, NY	2,300
8.	Pierre Laporte	Quebec	2,190
9.	Delaware Memorial	Wilmington, Delaware	2,150
10.	Del. Memorial (new)	Wilmington, Delaware	2,150
11.	Walt Whitman	Philadelphia, PA	2,000
12.	Ambassador	Detroit-Canada	1,850
13.	Throgs Neck	Long Island Sound, NY	1,800
14.	Benjamin Franklin	Philadelphia, PA	1,750
15.	Bear Mountain	Hudson River, NY	1,632

SOURCE: 1995 Survey of State Highway Engineers